RUSSIAN POETRY: THE MODERN PERIOD

IOWA TRANSLATIONS

Contemporary Korean Poetry
Modern Chinese Poetry
Mihail Eminescu
The Poetry of Postwar Japan
Contemporary Yugoslav Poetry
Russian Poetry: The Modern Period

GENERAL EDITORS

Paul Engle
Hualing Nieh Engle

RUSSIAN POETRY: THE MODERN PERIOD

Edited by
JOHN GLAD and DANIEL WEISSBORT

University of Iowa Press
Iowa City

Grateful acknowledgment is made for permission to reproduce translations that have previously appeared in the following publications:

Boundary 2; Index on Censorship; The London Magazine; The Massachusetts Review; Modern Poetry in Translation; New Measure; Nikolay Kliuev: Poems (Ardis); *Paintbrush; Poet & Man: In Memory of Yury Galanskov* (A. S. Forlag, Oslo); *Poetry Wales; Post-War Russian Poetry* (Penguin Books); *Russian Literature Tri-Quarterly; Shantih; Stand; Triquarterly; The War is Over: Selected Poems of Evgeny Vinokurov* (Carcanet Press).

The following poems first appeared in *Poetry* and are reprinted by permission of its editors: "My insatiable memory . . ." by Olga Berggolts; "When the Parachute Does not Open" by Yevgeny Vinokurov; "Do you envy, my comrades-in-arms, . . ." by Viktor Sosnora. © 1974 The Modern Poetry Association.

Special thanks are also due to Alexander Petrov for his assistance in the preparation of this anthology.

Library of Congress Cataloging in Publication Data
Main entry under title:

Russian poetry, the modern period.

(Iowa translations)
1. Russian poetry—20th century—Translations into English. 2. Russian poetry in foreign countries—Translations into English. 3. English poetry—Translations from Russian. I. Glad, John. II. Weissbort, Daniel. III. Series.
PG3237.E5R8   891.7'1'408   78–8650
ISBN 0–87745–083–8
ISBN 0–87745–084–6 pbk.

University of Iowa Press, Iowa City 52242
© 1978 by The University of Iowa
Printed in the United States of America

. . . in my cruel age I extolled Freedom.

— Aleksandr Pushkin, 1836

. . . iniquitous courts have banished
the moonlight into distant exile.

— Natalya Gorbanevskaya, 1965

CONTENTS

III POST-WORLD WAR II POETRY IN RUSSIA

IV POST-WORLD WAR II ÉMIGRÉ POETRY

V THE NEW WAVE IN RUSSIA

VI THE NEWEST ÉMIGRÉ WAVE

FOREWORD

Theology once believed that "translation" could mean direct removal of the body to heaven without intervening death. All too often in being translated, a poem does lose its life.

Literal translation of a poem into bare prose may help understanding, but the plain verbal text of a translation may actually not be true to the poem. What a poet writes is not merely language, not a literal account of his life, but an imaginative vision of it. No matter how direct and simple the language he uses may seem, it must have its words put together in such new ways that a word-by-word version is a lie. Only a translator with imagination can truly translate the imaginative language of the poem.

The Iowa Translations series brings together people with creative talent (who, in some instances, may not even know the language being translated) with a poet native to the language. Together they attempt a version in English which tries to be partly as imaginative as the original.

We believe that in the dangerous twentieth century people of good mind and good will must translate or die. People talking to each other (poetry is the highest form of talk) are not fighting each other. We believe that translating poetry, that insight into the emotionalized ideas of men and women, is an honor, a privilege, and one of the toughest jobs offered to the human race.

This is an anthology of twentieth-century poetry in the Russian language, chosen without regard to the place where the poets wrote. Of the living poets, some are outside the Soviet Union, either because they were forced out under threat, or left voluntarily. Most still live within its borders. To us, they are all Russian poets, who learned that rich and resonant language from the mouth of their mother, not from books and foreign voices.

One of the most curious aspects of this century has been the way in which powerful heads of state, with armies, secret police and the press at their disposal, have been frightened by helpless poets, whose only resource was the powerful and beautiful words of the language. Yet for writing a satirical poem, Mandelshtam was condemned to wander from city to city, to have his work banned, and finally was sent to a camp in eastern Siberia, dying miserably on the way. He once said, "Do you know what happens after you write a poem like this? Three men come for you . . . in uniform." His poems survived because his wife Nadia hid them in saucepans, cushions, and shoes. Later, there were no cushions.

Galanskov: "an intellectual with a pen in his fist finds that his cuffs hang on his wrists heavy as chains." Novikov: "prison is the morality of our world." Akhmatova: "the words of a prison sentence struck her in the breast like a stone." Gorbanevskaya: "I shall scald myself with a handful of snow." Life turns against its own self, one lives in opposites. Yet the poet, when not actually killed, survived for Pasternak's reason:

Life like autumn stillness lives in its details.
The fever of genius is stronger and whiter than cement.

Poets have lived in exile before, but never on the scale of the twentieth century, which has sent them out from many countries and many languages, or forced them into exile within the boundaries of the state. Yet one astonishing fact is that they go on cherishing that same country. Out of his hard darkness Mandelshtam's lines about return shine like light:

In Petersburg we shall meet again
As if we had buried the sun there.

It is possible to be homesick for your own land while still living in it. Mayakovsky said it; he spoke of carrying his broken heart as a dog carries to the kennel his paw crushed by a train.

Russian poets have lived close to the bone of all the tragedies and deaths of this doomed century. As Nadezhda Mandelshtam said, they lived for almost thirty years "with clenched teeth." They had to scurry back and forth between Stalin and Hitler. They were attacked by the internal and the external enemy. In "The Morning of Acmeism," Mandelshtam wrote that "An artist's feeling for the world is a tool, like a mason's mallet, and his only tangible product is the work itself." This anthology's poems are the product of that shattered and shattering world in which these poets stumbled through their lives. Think of our indulged American poets; no bullet, camp, censorship, or beating waits for them. They need not wrestle with rending tragedy, only with mortal ills and the pathos of industrial society, sheltered, often, within the flexible and mothering walls of universities.

Vinokurov picks up the body of a fellow soldier whose eyes had been shot out in battle. Later he remembers that the eyes were light blue. Later he comments that Adam saw in his dreams Auschwitz and ditches of corpses, but he slept well because he did not yet know the difference between good and evil. These Russian poets know good and evil as if they were household pets living in their rooms and sleeping on their beds.

Translation is often clearly described by the old saying that to translate is to betray, a pun in its original. Of course it is never the original, save for a few brilliant examples (Rilke of Valéry and Elizabeth Barrett Browning, the latter perhaps even better), yet often poetry is not what is killed in translation, but what is so profoundly strong that it is what survives translation. Mandelshtam lived by translating. This from Nikolay Klyuev, a poet little known:

The angel of simple human affairs
Flits into my hut like a lark.
The stove and bench smiled,
The rain barrel honked,
And a fly mumbled in darkness at the cat.

Anna Akhmatova wrote, "You will pick up a stick and trace on the trodden snow (the) houses where we shall be together always." It moves the reader in English.

Perhaps Novella Matveyeva wrote down the ultimate comment on all translated poems.

"I have made silken verses
from stone,"
the great Rudaki once said.
Aye, but he did not know
the translator would
re-convert them.

Yet in this book there are poems which were not re-converted, but converted from texts in Russian to texts in English, keeping their life and their force and their newness. Voznesensky called time, "Enigmatic as the woman-breasted/Bird with a duralumin chassis."

Poets of the New Wave, whether in the Soviet Union or outside, seem far more lyrical, much less political (save for certain exiles) and more concerned with the individual's responsibility for his own nature. They make what might be called an existentialist assertion of the right to personal freedom and decision-making, in contrast to the authority of the state.

These poets are also children of their new environment, immersed in planes, science, cities. As Brodsky wrote in his poem about Venice and its many lights and colors:

In the age of friction
light speed is the speed of sight, even
when no light exists.

Lev Mak similarly uses a contemporary language:

In the system of unities, the pain of freedom
Is isometric with love. The distance
Of one from the other is equal to the sum
Of chasms. Hell and Paradise are metaphors of freedom.

They rely on irony as a glass wall protecting them from the rigors of suppressing society. After describing how even a deep sea diver in his grotesque suit of rubber and metal will find somewhere a woman who likes a man who looks just that way, Vladimir Uflyand writes:

And now
although not rubbery,
you stand,
another slimy fellow and
quite repulsive,
especially when nude.

But since this is precisely what she wants,
there is a woman waiting just
for you.

One of the lines in a Lev Mak poem is, YOU GET USED TO ANGUISH, LIKE THE SMELL OF FISH THE NEIGHBORS ARE FRYING. That is the new, late twentieth-century, completely candid look at the world. Words which have taken off their clothes. Nerves which have taken off their skin. As Mak also wrote:

To destroy a man
Is much easier than to cure a toothache. It is simpler
To stifle our souls than to know them.

Poetry defies history, as the individual defies the mass. Sergey Chudakov writes about the extraordinary fact that a great ocean liner will stop when a man goes overboard, but that when one person is choking with fear and despair, "Then even his own house/Doesn't stop for him but continues on its way."

This is a new tone in Russian poetry, skeptical, laconic, ironic. Is there any earlier voice speaking precisely these lines by Brodsky?

I submit to your judgment, for condemnation or pardon
Whether (i) he was a serious student, on reflection
Or (ii) for the Russian public it was something new,
Or (iii) it was his weakness for case-endings and
                                    for flexion.

The same attitude occurs in Vladimir Burich, who reports that he brushes his teeth, drinks natural juices, and "In this way I have reached the age of twenty-six./And what for?/To keep my money in a savings bank."

The New Wave poetry is accurately imaginative. Writing of Venice, Brodsky said that "the rays of a star out at sea stir the blinds." No "socialist realism" there, only the absolute fantasy of the human mind.

There are of course horrors in the poetry of the young poets. Sergey Chudakov quietly comments that "The butchers will cut up hatred,/Like a liver, with their clanking knives." That is the way the sharp-honed twentieth century cuts up its poets. Who die. Who write. Who survive.

These are poems written with suffering hands. They are to be read with suffering eyes.

Hualing Nieh Engle, Director
Paul Engle, Consultant
International Writing Program
School of Letters
The University of Iowa

GENERAL EDITORS' ACKNOWLEDGMENTS

Special acknowledgment is made to the Northwest Area Foundation of Saint Paul (A. A. Heckman, former executive director, and John D. Taylor, present executive director) for a grant in translation made to the International Writing Program. This anthology is one of the many books of translated poetry made possible by that grant. Many other foundations, corporations and private individuals have contributed to the Program's efforts to bring the writers of the world to The University of Iowa and to help them bring their work over into English.

The University of Iowa was the first in the U.S.A. (in the world?) to state in its general catalog that a thesis for an advanced degree could be not only a contribution to knowledge, but also a creative work in poetry, fiction, playwriting, painting, sculpture, musical composition. Hence the extraordinary amount of all the arts on its campus. Such hospitality to the arts when they were generally regarded with suspicion not only by the general public but perhaps even more so by scholars made it natural for the University to permit us to establish the first "Translation Workshop" anywhere. To support imaginative work is itself an act of the imagination.

RUSSIAN POETRY SINCE THE REVOLUTION

Poetry has traditionally been much more popular in Russia than in the English-speaking world. It is common for editions of poetry to be published in the hundreds of thousands in the Soviet Union, and poetry readings attract large crowds. When one thinks of Eliot afraid to leave the financial security of a position at a bank, the contrast between our countries' respective reading tastes becomes particularly striking. To an extent, this is part of the general tendency of Russians to read more — both of prose and of poetry.

At the same time, the interest in poetry in Russia has varied radically in different periods. Aside from the folk tradition, poetry was not widely written in Russian until the second half of the eighteenth century. In the eighteenth century Lomonosov and Tredyakovsky traveled to Europe and brought back with them ideas for the creation of a system of Russian versification. With this theoretical foundation already laid and with the inspiring example of Derzhavin's and Lomonosov's actual verse, the "Golden Age" of Russian poetry blossomed in the early nineteenth century. Considering the brief period of preparation, the poetic achievement of the age was impressive: Zhukovsky, Batyushkov, Pushkin, Delvig, Baratynsky, Yazykov, Lermontov. Abrupt, however, as the development of Russian poetry was, its decline was even more rapid. The middle of the nineteenth century was marked by a shift of interest to prose. Even Pushkin and Lermontov began to write prose, and Fet was silent for a number of years. The poetry that was written, such as that of Nekrasov, was often intentionally lowered in style — prosified as it were.

The shift from poetry to prose was related to the rise of what would today be termed "relevance." Poetry, particularly the romantic variety of the early part of the century, was felt to be out of place. One critic, Dmitry Pisarev, even declared a pair of boots to be more valuable than Shakespeare and attacked Pushkin for insufficient social conscience. The great age of Russian prose ensued: Turgenev, Tolstoy, Dostoyevsky.

The cyclical struggle between prose and poetry entered a new phase in the 1890s when Symbolism made its appearance — later than in Western Europe, as is true for so many movements in Russian literature.

As the Russian formalist critic, Yury Tynyanov, has pointed out, artistic evolution is characterized by change, in which the innovators react against the parent generation only to return in the end to the traditions of their grandparents. Thus the era of prose, positivism and social consciousness engendered a reaction in the form of a new-romantic literary movement: Symbolism.

As in Western Europe, Symbolism was fundamentally an art-for-art's-sake movement. Underlying the philosophy of Symbolism was the Neo-platonic idea of a "higher reality" and Schopenhauer's concept of an ideal inaccessible to the rational faculty. Creativity was viewed as a spiritual act which did not so much communicate as suggest. One line of Tyutchev's became an important slogan for the Russian Symbolists: "A thought expressed is a lie." The mysterious and the exotic were almost prescriptive elements, and social mindedness — at least at first — was rejected in favor of a highly personal, individualistic view. Synaesthesia in art caught the imagination of many, and there were numerous attempts to duplicate the effect of music in poetry. Decadence played a strong role in the development of Russian Symbolism (Merezhkovsky [1865–1941], Zinaida Gippius [1869–1945], Sologub [1863–1927]), but many Symbolists — particularly members of the so-called "younger generation of Russian Symbolists" — saw in poetry an instrument for mystic prophecy (Blok, [1880–1921] — see his "On the Field of Kulikovo," Bely [1880–1934], and Vyacheslav Ivanov [1866–1949]). Balmont (1867–1942) seemed comfortable combining the eschatological and the decadent, and Briusov (1873–1924) advanced the view that poetry should limit itself to aesthetic considerations.

Symbolism is essentially a prerevolutionary phenomenon in Russia. Blok died in 1921, Bryusov in 1924. Minsky (Vilenkin), (1855–1937), emigrated before the revolution, Balmont in 1918, Merezhkovsky in 1919, and Vyacheslav Ivanov in 1924. Bely (Bugayev) and Merezhkovsky were known primarily as prose writers.

Symbolism is the immediate prehistory, the legacy which had to be assimilated and surmounted by the new poetic movements, one of the more important of which was Acmeism. This term was coined from the Greek *akme:* meaning "peak" or "summit." The movement was also called "clarism" from the Latin "clarus" (clear), pointing to its rejection of the vague mysticism of the Symbolists, and "Adamism" — after the first namer of things, this latter term emphasizing its heroic, virile side (particularly evident in the poetry of Gumilyov) as opposed to what was felt to be the overly refined, feminine nature of Symbolism.

Founded in 1912 by the poets Gumilyov (1886–1921) and Gorodetsky (b. 1884), who were later joined by Mandelshtam (1891–1938), Akhmatova (1889–1966), Kuzmin (1875–1936), Zenkevich (b. 1891), Narbut (1888–1944), Sadovskoy (b. 1881), and others, Acmeism set out to make specific what the Symbolists had hinted at; it represented, in this sense, a return to the classicism of an earlier tradition. While the Symbolists often viewed the poet as a prophet and creator of myths, the Acmeists regarded him as a verbal artisan and adopted a collective name: "The Guild of Poets" (Tsekh poetov). Emphasis was placed on the intrinsic value of the concrete world in opposition to the Symbolists' framework of unseen metaphysical referents. The Acmeists thus expressly rejected any philosophical or metaphysical superstructure.

Mandelshtam is now recognized as one of the major poets of the twentieth century. His early poetry came under the banner of clarism and was heavily dependent on such words as crystal, transparency, ice, diamonds, brightness, glass, etc. This lexical range was later extended, lightness being contrasted with darkness, when, in the most literal sense, his world, like "yesterday's sun, was borne away on black stretchers."

In 1930–31 a surrealistic note appeared in the work of the former "clarist": see, for example, such poems as "Impressionism" and "Lamarck." The latter refers to the French scientist (1744–1829) who believed that environment influenced genetic development. If this were true, implied Mandelshtam, then what must be happening to people living through the Stalinist terror? It is as though the images of Hieronymus Bosch had come alive in Russian poetry. Mandelshtam, who had always felt that Russian poetry should renew itself by returning to the classical tradition, wrote in 1933, "What if Ariosto and Tasso who so charmed you are monsters with a lilac brain and scales of moist eyes?" The "Age," with all its political terror, material deprivation, and other horrors, was taking its toll. On the other hand, these poems clearly represent a search for a new poetic strategy though Mandelshtam did not himself continue this experimentation in his late work, written in exile in Voronezh, but instead preferred to reintroduce earlier images and themes.

The Acmeistic emphasis on concrete reality, the "thing in itself," makes Mandelshtam's poetry singularly static, emblematic, imagistic. There is virtually no development, physical or psychological. The poems are very brief descriptions of objects, persons, situations, at a given point. Mandelshtam is more a poet of sensations than emotions. Love, for example, plays a minor role in his work. In *The Noise of Time*, a prose work, he writes about childhood street impressions: "Of what concern was all this to me? I don't know. But these were strong and bright impressions, and I treasure them to this day." This statement is characteristic of his work as a whole.

Akhmatova, unlike Mandelshtam, devoted a great deal of attention to romantic themes in her verse, which also contains a strong if subtly underplayed sensual element. The prevailing mood of her poetry is one of sadness. Whereas Mandelshtam was driven by external circumstance to poems of despair, there is an intrinsic tendency in Akhmatova's work toward melancholy and grief.

The Soviet *Brief Literary Encyclopedia* states laconically that "after the October Revolution Acmeism ceased to exist as a literary school." In fact, Gumilyov was shot in 1921 for supposed complicity in an anti-Soviet conspiracy; Gorodetsky publicly recanted and attacked his former colleague; Mandelshtam died in 1938 in a "Corrective Labor Camp" outside of Vladivostok, sentenced for such works as "Within the Mountain dwells an Idol" and "We don't know the land we live on," with their grotesque characterizations of an unnamed Stalin.

Akhmatova somehow survived the holocaust — to her own bewilderment. Not only was her former husband Gumilyov executed but their son was arrested and sentenced to hard labor in a concentration camp for many years; her long poem or sequence of poems, "Requiem," is dedicated to him. As a preface to the work she wrote the following: "In the terrible years of the Yezhov period I spent seventeen months waiting in line outside Leningrad's prisons. On one occasion, someone 'recognized' me. Then the woman behind me, her lips blue with cold, who, of course, had never heard of me, emerged from the stupor which held us all and whispered (we all whispered then) this question into my ear:

'Could you describe it?'

And I said: 'I could.'

Then something like a smile passed over what had once been her face."

"Requiem" was written between 1935 and 1940 and is one of the few pieces dating from this period. Essentially a poet of personal themes, Akhmatova was impelled by circumstances to seek larger, more expansive forms. Nevertheless, "Requiem" is perhaps more an impressionistic collection of lyrics than a single, comprehensively conceived piece. In it, however, and even more so in her other major long work, "Poem without a

Hero," we can see the poet struggling to express the historical experience of her time.

Another movement that conceptualized itself as a reaction against the heritage of Symbolism was Futurism. Futurism had its origins in Italy between 1910 and 1915, having been founded by the writer, Filippo Marinetti. The 1912 Italian *Initial Manifesto* sets forth in typically polemical fashion the fundamental principles of the school:

> Literature has hitherto glorified thoughtful immobility, ecstasy, sleep; we shall extol agressive movement, feverish insomnia, the double quick step, the somersault, the box on the ear, the fisticuff.
> We wish to glorify War — the only health-giver of the world — militarism, patriotism, the destructive arm of the anarchist, the beautiful ideas that kill, contempt for woman.
> We wish to destroy the museums, the libraries; we fight against moralism, feminism and all opportunistic and utilitarian meanness.
> Set fire to the shelves of the libraries! Divert the courses of the canals to flood the cellars of the museums! Oh, may the glorious canvases drift helplessly! Seize pickaxes and hammers! Sap the foundations of the venerable cities!
> We stand upon the summit of the world and once more cast our challenge to the stars!

While Russian Futurism had none of these patently Fascist overtones, its own manifesto, "A Slap in the Face of Public Opinion" (Moscow, 1912), reads in much the same way. It was signed by the poets, Aleksey Kruchenykh (1886–1968), Vladimir Mayakovsky (1893–1930), Velemir Khlebnikov (1885–1922), and the painter, David Burlyuk (1882–1967):

> To Those who read our first new startling (statement):
> Only *we* are the *face* of *our* Time. The trumpet of time sounds through us in the verbal art.
> The past is crowded. The Academy and Pushkin are less comprehensible than hieroglyphics.
> Pushkin, Dostoyevsky, Tolstoy, etc., etc., are to be thrown overboard from the Ship of Contemporaneity.
> He who does not forget his *first* love shall never know his last.
> What gullible person would turn his last love to the perfumed lechery of Balmont: Is there in it any reflection of today's masculine soul?
> What coward would fear to tear the paper chain mail from Bryusov's tuxedo? Is it that he might find there the dawns of unknown beauty?

Wash your hands, sticky with the dirty slime of books written by these endless Leonid Andreyevs.

All these Maksim Gorkys, Kuprins, Bloks, Sologubs, Remizovs, Averchenkos, Chernys, Kuzmins, Bunins, etc., etc., need only a cottage by the river. That's a reward for tailors.

We view their worthlessness from the height of our skyscrapers! . . .

We *command* that the *rights* of poets be honored:

1) That the lexicon be quantitatively supplemented with arbitrary and derivative items (The word is novelty).

2) We call for hatred of the language that existed earlier.

3) May the crown of twigs from a bathhouse and its cheap glory be cast with horror from the proud brow.

4) We shall stand on the rock of the word 'we' in the midst of a sea of catcalls and indignation.

And *if for the time being* there remain in our lines the dirty brands of your 'Common Sense' and 'good taste,' nevertheless there tremble within them the Dawns of a New Coming Beauty of the Self-Valuable Word."

Futurism became popular on ideological and artistic grounds. The early twentieth century was far less apocalyptic in its vision of technology than was the case later on. There was no atomic or hydrogen bomb, and while the dehumanizing effect of modern urban life was already evident, the mood was one of optimism and belief in progress and the triumph of science. In this context, the idyllic nature of much of the earlier poetry seemed irrelevant. Artistically the "Age" also called for a renovation of poetic technique and language. The imagery of Symbolism was no longer perceived as fresh by the contemporary ear, and the Futurists radically "lowered" the manner of poetry, introducing into it the vocabulary of the street. In his long poem, "A Cloud in Trousers," Mayakovsky wrote: "in its (the city's) mouth/dead words rot,/only two grow fat:/'bastard'/and I think the other/is 'borsch.'/Poets,/sopped with lamentation,/rush from the street, their long hair matted,/'how can those two words sing/of maidens/ and love/and tiny flowers in the dew?'"

At the same time, Futurist poetry often revealed striking affinities with the odic declamatory manner of the eighteenth-century classicists. The majestic ode which was so popular and so successfully practiced by Lomonosov (1711–65) and Derzhavin (1743–1816) had disappeared for a century, replaced by such "chamber" genres as the lyric and the elegy. These genres were naturally preferred by the Symbolists. The entire atmosphere of their literary soirées was one of exclusivity; poetry readings were conducted for small groups of highly educated aesthetes; Vyacheslav Ivanov's apartment was even called the "tower." Here delicate nuances could be appreciated in an atmosphere of quiet dignity. It is against this restrained background of tuxedos and tea, of subtle hints and symbols, that there resounds the powerful shout of Vladimir Mayakovsky who mocked the older style of reading and wore a carrot in his lapel instead of a chrysanthemum. It is his style, hearkening back to the stentorian manner of the eighteenth-century ode, that prevails in Russia today and that Western audiences find so exciting.

The principal figures in the Futurist movement were Khlebnikov, Kruchonykh and — especially — Mayakovsky, whose poetic career spanned the period 1912 to 1930. Mayakovsky's striking metaphors, aggressive urbanism, startling hyperbole, and rejection of the traditional Russian meters amounted to a revolution in verse. Just as he identified totally with the Bolshevik Revolution, he strove consciously to reflect in his work the language and aspirations of the "new world" which had arisen virtually overnight. To advance the cause that he had accepted since childhood, he felt it necessary, in his own words, to "step on the throat of his own song," composing political slogans, drawing posters and creating a great deal of poetry that was deliberately geared to a popular level of aesthetic appreciation. Even so, he was viewed by many as simply a "fellow traveller" and was by no means universally trusted by the proponents of the revolutionary cause.

Mayakovsky took his own life in 1930. His suicide is often explained away in terms of personal tragedy or mental aberration. On the other hand, his aspirations for the Revolution were so far-reaching that they were bound to be disappointed. Furthermore, the sacrifice of his own lyrical talents inflicted a great deal of psychological damage.

Mayakovsky was not just an "interesting" figure; his innovations were so startling, so original, that almost a half century after his death, his influence is still a major force in contemporary Russian poetry. Nearly sixty million copies of his books have been sold in the USSR, and his works have been translated into thirty-nine foreign languages.

Khlebnikov was another major figure in the Futurist movement. He combined Futurism with his own personal brand of Slavophilism, developing a so-called "trans-sense" language (zaum'), which consisted of neologisms created from original Slavic roots. Together with Kruchonych, another Futurist poet, he formulated predications as to a universal language of the future which was ultimately to arise from *zaum*. In one famous example, Khlebnikov wrote an entire poem consisting of nothing but derivatives of the word *smekh* (laughter): "O, rassmeites', smekhachi!/O, zasmeites', smekhachi!/Chto smeyutsa smekhami, chto smeyanstuvuyut smeyal'no," etc. His later work is less concerned with etymology and Slavic folklore and mythology, and was cut short by his premature death, at the age of thirty-seven, after a life of vagabondism, in a country hospital during his wanderings.

Pasternak (1890–1960) as a young man was associated with the Futurist organization "Centrifuge"; it became rapidly evident, however, that his poetic manner was radically different from theirs. Under the general influence of modernism, the young Pasternak developed a relatively complex manner which requires careful reading. He later rejected complexity and in 1956 made the famous comment that he did not like his own poetry written before 1940.

Although Pasternak did write some long poems (what the Russians call *poemy*), his work is essentially lyric. Most commonly he involves himself in metonymic descriptions of nature with which he so intimately identified that their details appear almost as extensions of his own personality. A kind of ecstasy of living illuminates much of his work.

Pasternak the poet was basically non-political. In one of his poems he asks with wonder, "what millenium it is outside." Most of his themes are quite divorced from the political life of the country. It is difficult to understand how he could have become such an object of political controversy, except that in a totalitarian system neutrality is as suspect as opposition.

Like Mandelshtam and Akhmatova, Pasternak had his period of silence; he wrote virtually no poetry in the thirties, a period of political terror when people literally disappeared by the millions. Denounced as "idealistic," "bourgeois," "class-oriented," "intellectual," he was not published and supported himself through translation. His renderings of Shakespeare are excellent, albeit over-praised. In 1940 he again took up writing.

Whereas Pasternak gradually dissociated himself from the Futurists by virtue of his very different poetic manner, the "peasant poets" were from the very beginning absolutely opposed to everything the Futurists stood for. Their Utopia was the *mir* — a semimythical, prefeudal, prearistocratic peasant commune.

The written tradition in Russian literature extends back to the ninth and tenth centuries — the beginning of Christianization of the East Slavs by Byzantium. With the new religion came an alphabet and a literary tradition: the canonical texts, paterica, hagiographic genres, etc. There also existed a rich, indigenous folklore; but the church, the exclusive bearer of literacy, was not eager to preserve what it considered to be a "heathen" tradition. The seventeenth and eighteenth centuries accomplished a secularization of literature, but only in the nineteenth century was there evidenced any real interest in Russian folklore such as heroic ballads, tales, ritualistic songs, incantations, proverbs, sayings, historics, etc. Some of the folklore was written down and certain writers, such as Pushkin and Nekrasov, even imitated folk forms on occasion. Nevertheless, it was only in the early twentieth century that poets of the "people" whose roots were in the oral tradition began really to participate in the larger literary scene.

Undoubtedly, the most talented of the so-called "peasant poets" was Nikolay Klyuev (1887–1937). The world that Klyuev came from was a rural one. The closest port was Vytegra (population 3,625 according to the census of 1890) situated on the edge of an endless forest; it was 500 kilometers even to the railroad. The sparse and illiterate peasantry lived virtually as it had a thousand years before. Civilization had touched it through religion, but even the Orthodox Church found itself on shaky ground. Klyuev's mother and Klyuev himself were involved with the Khlysts — an ascetic sect that condemned most joys of the flesh, but which conducted ecstatic prayer meetings in which members would be "possessed" by the spirit. Such meetings were often followed by wild orgies. Aside from the Khlysts, the pagan religion had not yet totally disappeared in the region. The resulting confusion of world view was beautifully described in Klyuev's "A Conversational Melody, A Good Verse": "There was born the iron Kingdom/ Of Wilhelm, the heathen tsar./ He is strong — this heathen./ His people believe in the Luther-god./ They make no cross on themselves,/ Observe not the Great Fast,/ Decorate no branch on Semik-Day,/ Do not steam themselves in the bath hut,/ Washing off the unseen spirit./ And afterwards they do not cry out to the goddess Udilyona:/ 'Udilyona, mother of the rye,/ Comb out your gold hair from the straw/ And plunge each ear in mead and molasses. . . .'" Pantheistic imagery and pagan gods coexist in the peasant mind with Christian holidays and rites. The poem is composed in the manner of the oral folk epics. The entire work, which displays a magnificent command of Northern dialect, is based on the tradition of the folk epic: negative parallelisms, hyperbolic animistic imagery, a pantheistic world view.

"Mother Sabbath" is an important piece for Klyuev. In it he composes a hymn to the traditions of rural Russia. Klyuev referred to his "poemy" as *pestryad'* — a complex quilt of imagery in which each piece and stitch played an important role. The idyllic, even mythical life he describes contrasts strikingly with the manifestos of the Futurists and such works as Mayakovsky's "Cloud in Trousers." In the smaller poems, "You twist your death in nooses" and "The sky lies blue — like a sea," Klyuev is involved in polemical dispute with the new iron age which threatens to engulf old Russia.

This is not to say that the peasant image projected by Klyuev should be taken strictly at face value. Even though he had no formal education, he was well read in contemporary literature, and there was undoubtedly an element of exaggeration and publicity-seeking in his peasant pose. Klyuev's powerful imagination, in fact, transcended the folk tradition. Composed and transmitted orally, Russian folklore generally gravitates away from ornate style and lays heavy emphasis on plot. The stylistic ornamentation that does exist often takes the form of ready-made formulas which are repeated from work to work. Klyuev's poems, however, do not make use of such prescriptions. Not only are the dense similes utterly unexpected, unpredictable, but the syntax maintains maximum tension so that the poems have to be literally dissected before they can be fully comprehended. Thus Klyuev's poetry belongs to a written rather than an oral tradition. The absence of plot and cryptic nature of his more or less static descriptions (most of his predicates are verbs of being) are foreign to the Russian epos. Although he originally wrote poetry that was read primarily by his local peasant neighbors, his later works lean more heavily on dialect than the earlier ones. This is remarkable, in that he had been "discovered" by Aleksandr Blok and was writing for an extremely select, sophisticated, urban audience which was obliged to read him with a dialectal dictionary in hand.

The entire mood and message of Klyuev's verse was essentially opposed to the forced march of industrialization planned out by the government for the people. Written in praise of the natural life, it represented virtually a return to the Slavophilism of the nineteenth century. And when he exclaimed of "Russia-mother-in-law smearing her bread with blood," he was accused of being a *kulak* [1] ideologue. Klyuev was arrested in 1933 for "kulak agitation." Even the poems he had written praising Lenin did not help him, and he was exiled to the Narym area in Northwestern Siberia. Later he was transferred to Tomsk, thanks to Gorky's intercession. In 1935 he was arrested again. According to one version he was allowed to return in August 1937 but died from a heart attack on the Trans-Siberian Railroad. According to another version he was executed.

Klyuev was supposedly returning with a suitcase full of unpublished manuscripts — the product of exile. At some unknown way station along the Trans-Siberian Railroad, a ragged, bearded man became an anonymous corpse — buried at the expense of the state. One may muse as to the fate of some scribbled-over papers when any sort of paper was scarce (Siberia, 1937!), but it is almost certain that they were lost to the world. One of the few writings of Klyuev that got through from Siberia was a petition for clemency. It began: "I, who have been condemned for my poem 'Detractors of Poetry' and insane lines of my rough drafts . . . ." As was the case with so many others, no official account of Klyuev's fate has ever been offered. His poetry has not been published in the Soviet Union for over forty years.

Sergey Yesenin (1895–1925) was a peasant poet who achieved enormous popularity — a popularity that has continued to this day, despite the highly ambivalent attitude of the authorities. Yesenin came from an Old Believer background and was greatly influenced by Klyuev, whom he recognized as his teacher.

Like Klyuev, Yesenin wrote much of his poetry in praise of "wooden Russia," that archetypal world of his childhood that existed as much in his imagination as in reality. His early poetry is devoted to country landscapes, the joys of village life, and is dominated by a mood of nostalgia. His simple, intensely melodious lyrics, while less sophisticated and complex than the work of Klyuev, won immediate acclaim. He was praised by Blok

1 "Kulak" was the term the government used to signify those members of the peasantry who had been successful enough to create modest but comfortable farms, thus avoiding the constant threat of dire poverty and starvation. They resisted collectivization and were obliterated as a class in a blood bath of millions.

and Gorodetsky and was even received in the literary salon of Dmitry Merezhkovsky and Zinaida Gippius. For a brief period he was married to Isadora Duncan — a strange marriage, considering neither could really speak the other's language.

Even Yesenin's early nature idylls were touched with a note of anxiety, but he accepted the Revolution, believing that it heralded the coming of the peasant Utopia. As these populist, messianic expectations were disappointed by all-out Bolshevik industrialization and proletarianization, Yesenin turned more and more to drink and a life of dissipation. The desperate, scandalous, Bohemian life of the so-called tavern holligan was a kind of protest, though a more or less inchoate one. While he had been denounced earlier as a *kulak* poet, he was now criticized for popularizing "hooliganism"; and the word "Yeseninism" became a common pejorative on the sheets of the Soviet press.

During this Bohemian period, he became involved with the "Imaginists" — a group that borrowed its name from the Anglo-American Imagists. The group existed from 1919 to 1927 and included a number of minor poets: Anatoly Marienhof (1897–1962), Ryurik Ivnev (b. 1891), Vadim Shershenevich (1893–1942), and others. The Imaginists proclaimed "the victory of the image over meaning" and its "emancipation from content." Shershenevich declared that his poems were catalogs of images and denied the necessity for logic in poetry; one of his books was even titled $2 \times 2 = 5$.

Driven to despair by the destruction of his revolutionary hopes, alcohol, personal problems, and attacks in the press, Yesenin committed suicide, the act precipitated apparently by a quarrel with Klyuev. For many years Yesenin's verse was not reprinted in the Soviet Union. His influence was regarded as undesirable by the Party; however, his immense popularity remained undiminished.

Of the other peasant poets, one might mention Pyotr Oreshin (1897–1938) and Sergey Klychkov (1889–1940). Oreshin and Klychkov were victims of the purges and "posthumously rehabilitated" in the Khruschev era. Pavel Vasilev (1910–37) and Boris Kornilov (1907–39) had certain affinities with the peasant poets, although they were not peasants themselves. Both died in the purges and were also subsequently "rehabilitated."

The "peasant poets" were, however, pretty much an exception to the general scene. Art in prerevolutionary Russia was confined mainly to a small group of aristocrats who possessed the wealth necessary to acquire an education and the leisure to devote themselves to literature. In poetry especially, the aristocratic class which produced Pushkin and Lermontov was far more productive than the class that produced Lomonosov. It is the former which was largely responsible for the "Golden Age" in the early eighteen hundreds and the "Silver Age" again at the end of the century. The new socialist political order was established during a general artistic flowering, largely brought about by a small and privileged elite. The early Soviet period in Russian literature was relatively pluralistic, reflecting the ferment that both preceded and followed the Revolution. Among the most vocal of the literary groups, many of which published their own manifestos, were those that aimed to create a new, "proletarian" art: "The Association of Proletarian Writers," "October," "The Smithy," etc. In 1932, however, the Central Committee of the Communist Party issued a directive received with "great satisfaction," according to the *Brief Soviet Literary Encyclopedia*, disbanding all literary groups and creating a single Writers' Union which could be more easily controlled by the Party. In 1934 the First Writers' Congress was held, chaired by Gorky. It was made quite clear that not only would no anti-establishment writing be tolerated, but also that all writers would be expected to propagandize actively the policies of the government. The writers capitulated totally and concluded the Congress with a telegram to Stalin proclaiming: "Long live the Class that bore you and the Party that raised you!"

The insane terror of the great purges physically destroyed both poets and their poems. How many manuscripts were burned in the furnaces of the secret police will never be known. The figures that survived, such as Akhmatova and Pasternak, wondered to the end of their days how they had escaped. Much of what appears in this anthology, such as the poems of Mandelshtam, was saved only through the tremendous dedication of readers, relatives, and by luck. How many were not lucky? We will never know. In Pasternak's words, "literature ceased to exist." This could be termed the second decline of Russian poetry; but "decline" is hardly an apt description of what was in fact, a cataclysmic collapse on an unprecedented scale, brought about solely by external circumstances, and not, as in the nineteenth century, through any internal, gradual dynamic.

Among the major victims (though he survived) of the late thirties was Nikolay Zabolotsky (1903–58). He is one of the most respected poets in the USSR, although his works are not nearly so widely published as they deserve. Zabolotsky's poems have a strong pantheistic note running through them — particularly in his early period when he was strongly influenced by his contemporary Khlebnikov, and also by the great nineteenth century poet, Tyutchev. A poet with Utopian illusions somewhat similar to those of Yesenin, Zabolotsky nevertheless devoted his early energies, in his remarkable first book *Stolbtsy/Scrolls* (1929), to a grotesque, expressionistic description of urban life (Leningrad) of the NEP[2] period. At the heart of this poet's work, however, is a philosophy of nature based on a kind of literal, materialistic belief in immortality. Among the Zabolotsky poems in this anthology, one encounters such protagonists as snakes, horses, trees, birds, wolves, dogs, stones, flowers, and a grasshopper against the background of a mythicized nature. Man, too, is woven into this living tapestry: "And Pushkin's voice was heard above the foliage,/ The birds of Khlebnikov sang by the water's side./ I met a stone; the stone was motionless;/ And in it Skovoroda's[3] face appeared." The mood of Zabolotsky's poetry is strikingly reminiscent of that created by the primitivist painter, Rousseau. In "Metamorphoses," perhaps the most succinct statement of his philosophical position, Zabolotsky engages that most taxing of all questions: individual identity. In his later work Zabolotsky's manner changed somewhat in the direction of classical simplicity, as with Pasternak, but his essential vision remained unchanged. Aside from original poetry, he also translated extensively. His rendering into modern Russian of the medieval epic "The Lay of the Host of Igor" is particularly well regarded.

An interesting footnote to Zabolotsky's work is his affiliation with the OBERIU — an acronym for a group calling itself "The Union of Real Art" (Ob'edinenie real'nogo iskusstva). Its manifesto, reportedly largely written by Zabolotsky, declared its own absurdist black humor to be the art of the future. While the members of the group had ties with avant-garde artists such as Malevich, they attempted to set themselves off from other modernists like the Futurists and pointedly denounced the latter's use of "trans-sense language." The other poets in the group were Nikolay Oleynikov (1898–1942), A. Vvedensky (d. 1942), and Daniil Kharms (1905–42).

2 NEP: New Economic Policy; when Lenin permitted a limited return to private enterprise, in the face of the post-Revolutionary economic collapse.

3 Skovoroda (1722–94) was a poet, theologist, and pantheistic philosopher.

The group's fate was a tragic one: Zabolotsky spent from 1938 to 1946 in forced labor camps in Siberia; Kharms, Vvedensky, and Oleynikov all died in 1942 while under arrest. It is unknown if they were executed.

A very large and significant chapter in the history of modern Russian literature has been written abroad. Russian emigration has been concentrated in two main "waves," the first occurring immediately after the Revolution and the second during and immediately following World War II. Emigration between these periods and in the later postwar period has not been significant, except for the recent Jewish emigration.

With the Revolution there occurred a massive exodus of the intellectual community. In 1920 the White armies suffered defeat on all fronts. In that year Denikin evacuated his army from Novorossisk on the Black Sea, and Wrangel evacuated his army from the Crimea to Constantinople. In the Far Eastern territories of the Russian Empire, Admiral Kolchak retreated; and there occurred a vast dispersion of Russians into China, adding to the appreciable Russian community already there (partially in connection with the Trans-Siberian Railroad).

In the Far East the major émigré centers were Shanghai and Harbin; in Western Europe, Paris and Berlin became even more important. Conditions in Berlin were particularly advantageous for Russian writers because the German government early established friendly relations with the new Soviet state, and Russian publishing houses were able to service simultaneously both the Soviet and the émigré community. There were at least eight Russian publishing houses in Berlin in the early postwar years, some of them with joint offices in Berlin and Petrograd.

It was Paris, however, that was destined to become the main center of émigré cultural life. There the Merezhkovskys established their philosophical literary society, "The Green Lamp." Among the writers were Bunin (1870–1953), Teffi (1875–1952), Don Aminado (1888–1957), Remizov (1887–1957), Kuprin (1870–1938), Balmont, Adamovich, Berberova (b. 1900), Weidle (b. 1895), Knut (1900–55), Terapiano (b. 1892), Tsvetayeva (1892–1941), and many, many others.

The vast scope of Russian émigré life was not limited, however, to these few centers. Many Russians found themselves in Czechoslovakia, Bulgaria, Yugoslavia, and the Baltic states. In 1920 alone, no less than 138 new Russian newspapers were founded, and another 112 saw the light of day in

1921. Most of them proved unsuccessful; by 1923 180 of them had collapsed, but even so 100 continued to exist! Fifty-eight Russian magazines and papers were founded in Berlin alone, and Harbin had at least that many itself.

Although three important Symbolist poets — Konstantin Balmont (1867–1943), Vyacheslav Ivanov (1866–1949), and Zinaida Gippius (1867–1945) — emigrated to the West, the impact of Symbolism on émigré poetry was not as significant as one might have expected. Balmont continued to publish, but, rightly or wrongly, he was considered to have "written himself out." He settled in France where he lived a life of relative poverty and spent some time in a psychiatric institution. Zinaida Gippius (occasional pseudonym as a critic: Anton Krayny — Anton the Extreme) continued to publish her verse abroad, but she is primarily remembered for the literary salon which she kept with her husband, Dmitry Merezhkovsky. Vyacheslav Ivanov settled in Italy where he taught classics. He largely dissociated himself from émigré circles and published relatively little in émigré journals.

In the cyclical history of literary fashions, the hour of Symbolism had passed. Acmeism rather than Symbolism dominated the émigré scene; its main prophet abroad was Georgy Adamovich (1884–1972). Adamovich is generally credited with being the most decisive influence behind the so-called "Parisian Note" in émigré poetry between the two wars. Literature, it was asserted, should serve as a medium for the exchange of thoughts on the "eternal themes" of the human condition, such as life, death, love, loneliness, etc. If the artist was to achieve anything of lasting value, he had to search out those themes which had concerned all men at all times. To be avoided were exaggerated use of metaphor, eloquence for its own sake, picturesque or ornamental imagery, or "modernism" in general. The goal was simplicity and the minimal use of poetic means.

Perhaps one of the more remarkable representatives of the Parisian Note was Anatoly Steiger who created some exquisite miniatures. He is also unusual in that he wrote homosexual verse in the largely puritanical context of Russian literary life at home and abroad.

Georgy Ivanov (1894–1958) was the leading Russian émigré poet. He began his literary career as a member of the Acmeist group in Petersburg. His style, however, evolved (particularly after his prose work of 1938, *Raspad atoma/ The Splitting of the Atom*), and in the last ten years of his life he was able to shuffle off all the aestheticism and refinement of his Petersburg period while retaining the technical mastery he had acquired so early on. The "abstractness" of much of Ivanov's later work led to his being accused of "trans-sensism" by some of his more conservative associates. However, it is probably true to say that Ivanov, of all the older émigrés, was one of the more successful poets to go beyond the "beautiful clarity" of Acmeism. His philosophical neutrality, his existentialism, remained consistent with Gumilyov's original requirement, "Not to amend life," but lexically and from the deeper point of view of poetic strategy, Ivanov's work constitutes something of a revolution in its own right.

Although radical innovation was not a prominent feature of the Parisian Note, the picture was by no means a homogeneous one. Alongside the classical simplicity of an Anatoly Steiger, one encounters the phantasmagoric visions of Boris Poplavsky; besides Adamovich's seriousness, there is also charming, humorous verse on the ups and downs of émigré life by Don Aminado (pseudonym of Aminad Shpolyansky). Others only occasionally adhered to the prevailing mode, while Marina Tsvetayeva presented a total contrast to her compatriots. In this period, there was not much interaction between the Russian literary émigrés and Western European writers. In view of the fact that Paris was the center of Russian émigré literature and that Russian writers had lived in close contact with French literature for over two decades, this is rather surprising. Vladimir Nabokov commented on the phenomenon thus: "As I look back at those years of exile, I see myself, and thousands of other Russians, leading an odd but by no means unpleasant existence, in material indigence and intellectual luxury, among perfectly unimportant strangers, spectral Germans and Frenchmen in whose more or less illusory cities we, émigrés, happened to dwell. These aborigines were to the mind's eye as flat and transparent as figures cut out of cellophane, and although we used their gadgets, applauded their clowns, picked their roadside plums and apples, no real communication, of the rich human sort so widespread in our own midst, existed between us and them."

At the present time, the same is fundamentally true of Russian émigré poetry in America. There does not appear to be any significant crosspollination between it and Anglo-American poetry. That American poets are largely unaware of the presence of Russian poets in their midst is hardly surprising. In a country where even small poetry journals are besieged by hopeful contributors but where the poetry readership is hopelessly small, Russian poets are simply lost in the crowd. Furthermore, who, except momentarily, has time for the émigré when attention is focused on the country whence he emigrated? Nevertheless, one cannot but be struck by the extent to which most of Russian émigré poetry is developing along lines quite independent from the Anglo-American tradition, which surrounds it on all sides.

Perhaps the reason for the émigré poet's apparent isolation from his environment lies in his shocked dismay at this unexpected and undesired separation from his roots. Russian émigré poetry, throughout its history, has exhibited a strong mood of nostalgia, a sense of anguish, a longing for return. The poet clutches desperately at those traditions with which he is most familiar, hoping to preserve the sense of belonging they give him, and ignoring the rich but alien tradition of the host country.

Marina Tsvetayeva (1892–1941) took a resolutely anti-Bolshevik stand and spent seventeen years in emigration — from 1922 to 1939. Although she had published some poetry before emigration, the bulk of her writing was done abroad. Tsvetayeva was a highly individualistic poet who did not fit at all into the "Parisian Note." She has been compared with Pasternak in her ecstatic identification with the forces of life; the powerful driving rhythm of her lines frequently recalls Mayakovsky; in addition much of her output draws on the tradition of folk poetry, but she was quite unique in the comprehensiveness and intensity of her themes and manner.

Tsvetayeva's telegraphic style is hard to render in translation, but something of her compressed lyricism may be conveyed in these lines from her poem, "An Attempt at Jealousy": ". . . How is it/ With a commodity?/ Expensive, eh? Plaster of Paris/ Isn't as good as marble/ Of Carrara? (God was hewn/ From it but he's smashed/ To dust!) How is it with one/ of a hundred thousands/ You who have known Lilith . . . ."

Tsvetayeva felt that she was not sufficiently appreciated in émigré circles, although there is reason to question the validity of her resentment. She was, for example, published in 36 of 70 issues of the leading émigré journal of the day, Contemporary Notes (*Sovremennye zapiski*). Nevertheless, she clearly felt out of sympathy with the more decorous manner of her compatriots. In any case, her material situation was desperate, and nostalgia and the longing to return finally prevailed. In 1939 Tsvetayeva did return to the USSR. She was received coldly, and all avenues of publication were closed to her. Two years later she hanged herself.

Life abroad was hard — especially for the poets who not only suffered all the usual material deprivations but who were particularly dependent on language. Editions were tiny and often published at the author's own expense — a practice that continues even to this day. With the occupation of France by the Germans in 1940, a heavy blow was dealt to Russian literature abroad. Virtually all publication ceased immediately. Weakened by death, further emigration, and the general chaos of the time, Russian cultural life in Paris never recovered — even after the war.

In other areas, such as the Baltic states, Czechoslovakia, and Bulgaria, Russian writers found themselves overtaken by advancing borders. Many Russian writers in Prague who had not managed to escape to the West were forcibly repatriated to the USSR. The large émigré community in Yugoslavia was deported en masse to DP camps in Trieste after Tito's break with Moscow. The same fate was suffered by the Far East community. Russians who had lived in China for generations were relieved to be allowed to leave the country with only the clothes on their backs. From Europe many émigrés left for South America, Canada, and especially the United States. The Far East community was dispersed over Australia, South and North America.

In the USSR the Germans had advanced with astounding rapidity; the Red army leadership had been decimated in the purges; the peasantry in the Ukraine was greeting the Germans as liberators; and so many dissatisfied Soviet soldiers were surrendering to the enemy that Hitler was able to form an entire army under General Vlasov that fought against its former countrymen. Western Europe had been largely conquered, and the ultimate defeat of the Soviet Union appeared close at hand. In her powerful poem "To Shakespeare," Nina Berberova, an émigré poet now living in the U.S., and widow of the late doyen of the émigré scene, Vladislav Khodasevich, wrote of the terror that Stalin himself must have felt at this time: ". . . Music is silent,/ Love does not burn and thought shrivels away./ Only blood still flows. There is/ Blood. We are all in blood,/ Water in blood, land in blood, air/ In blood. He who has not eaten dead flesh/ Throughout his life — as we —/ He too stands chest-deep in blood."

To gain the support of an alienated population, the war was characterized as a struggle, not for communism, but for Mother Russia; church officials were promised an end to religious persecution in return for their support (a promise broken as soon as the danger was past). Russian, Slavic patriotism became the order of the day, and the government called upon writers to come to the support of their fatherland in its hour of need. Many, as might have been expected, did.

Olga Berggolts was one such writer. Although her former husband, Boris Kornilov (himself a poet), had died in the purges and although she herself had spent two years in prison, she devoted herself to the war effort and lived through the terrible days of the Leningrad blockade, working on the radio. She describes how once, walking to work on a cold winter night, weak from hunger, she heard people coming up behind her though she did not have the strength to turn around. When they drew level, she saw it was a man and woman and realized from their full faces that they must be cannibals. There was no one near to help her. "I felt that I was about to lose consciousness, and through a sort of gray haze I saw a man on a bicycle. I shouted 'cannibals!' and fell unconscious into a snow drift. When I came to, I was told they had been shot by a militiaman who had driven up." An hour later she was reading her poems over the radio.

Berggolts survived the blockade, although over a million Leningraders perished in it. Among them was her second husband, who died from hunger. It is against such a background of universal and unexampled suffering that one must read not only her poetry, but also the fragment from "Son" by Pavel Antokolsky, "In Those Years" by Sergey Narovchatov, "I don't Remember Him," "Eyes," and "Objects" by Yevgeny Vinokurov, and "I Saw It" by Ilya Selvinsky. The war itself became the theme of much of the best literature of the war years, and even today, thirty years after, remains a preoccupation with many writers of that period, like Berggolts herself, or Yevgeny Vinokurov. It should be added that this, in many cases genuine obsession with a traumatic experience, suits the regime's propagandistic purposes by stimulating patriotism, if not directly then through association, and acting as a convenient channel for powerful emotion, while not touching upon the status quo.

With the conclusion of the war, many expected a certain political liberalization. The government, however, reasserted its control over all facets of social life, which had been relatively relaxed in the war years. It was felt, furthermore, that postwar reconstruction required a vast propaganda effort, necessarily including poetry (what Mandelshtam once referred to as harnessing the swallows into legions). The official policy was formulated by Andrey Zhdanov in 1946 in a Central Committee resolution, which amounted to a multipronged attack on the independence of all the arts and was particularly devastating to poetry.

Akhmatova was singled out for particular attention. She had emerged from a long period of silence and had published some verse, much of it on patriotic themes. However, in 1946, Zhdanov wrote: "Akhmatova is a typical representative of nonideological poetry which is alien to our people. Her poems are filled with a spirit of pessimism and decadence, and express the tastes of the older Salon poetry based on aestheticism and decadence. Such "art-for-art's-sake" which does not wish to keep in step with the people is harmful to the education of our youth and cannot be tolerated in Soviet literature." For Akhmatova a new silence ensued.

Again, in 1948, a campaign was initiated in the Writers' Union against "formalism, aestheticism and rootless cosmopolitanism"; — "rootless cosmopolitans" is a rather transparent reference to the Jews. In 1952 a number of Jewish writers and intellectuals were indeed tortured and executed Nazi-style, and many now believe that Stalin was preparing a new series of purges in which the Jews would have served as a prime scapegoat. It is hardly surprising that in this atmosphere of almost total terror *poetry* did not flourish, though there was an abundance of so-called "poems" with titles such as "Thank you, Comrade Stalin!"

Stalin's death in 1953, however, reshuffled all the cards. The execution of Beria, the deposition of Malenkov, and the Byzantine power struggles, thinly veiled under the claims of "collective leadership," culminated in Khrushchev's rise to power and his famous de-Stalinization speech at the Twentieth Party Congress in 1956. The process of re-evaluation that was somewhat unwittingly initiated amounted, in the frozen conditions that prevailed, to a "thaw," as Ehrenburg put it; and many again, as just after the war, hoped for a far-reaching liberalization.

At the same time, it was unclear just how far the movement of de-Stalinization would go. Thus, when Pasternak was awarded the Nobel Prize in 1958, he was vilified by *Pravda* and compared to a serpent breathing the high mountain air of the Revolution and surrounded by eagles: "He writhes at our feet and is irresistibly drawn to his native swamp with its odors of putrefaction and decomposition — where he can feel at ease among its poetic sewers and lyric dung." The General Secretary of the Young Communist League, Semichastny, declared him to be "worse than a pig because even a pig will not dirty the place where it eats and sleeps." TASS announced that the Soviet government would not oppose Pasternak's departure to his "capitalist paradise." Expelled from the Writers' Union and sixty-seven years old, Pasternak wrote a letter to Khrushchev, published in *Pravda*:

"I (have) never had the intention of harming my country or my people. . . . I seem to have affirmed that no revolution can be historically justified and that the October Revolution constitutes an illegitimate phenomenon, that it was a calamity for Russia and that it destroyed the old Russian intelligentsia. It is evident to me that I cannot subscribe to such affirmations carried to the absurd. Now my work, rewarded with the Nobel Prize, has lent credit to this false interpretation; it is for this reason that I have finally renounced the prize."

He begged not to be exiled from his country and was allowed to remain in Russia. He died three years later. Today his poetry is published in limited editions and is difficult to obtain in the Soviet Union — just as is Mandelshtam's, Akhmatova's, Khlebnikov's, Tsvetayeva's, and that of many others of Russia's finest poets.

As for more recent poetry, the situation is, in many respects, quite dismal. The systematic use of poetry created by party hacks as political propaganda is still very much a fact of Soviet literary life. And although the War or themes of labor have genuinely inspired poets, the plodding army of official poetasters is depressing in its ubiquity and self-complacence — particularly in view of the inability of many talented poets to break into the government monopoly of print.

A fairly typical example of an officially approved poet was Mikhail Lukonin, who enjoyed enormous printings although his dreary, patriotic work was quite uninteresting. In a speech he delivered during a visit to the U.S. in 1973, Lukonin noted that he had found a large number of his books in the Library of Congress and expressed great satisfaction at this. Afterwards he was asked why the first edition of Mandelshtam in nearly forty years was being delayed; his response was that Soviet publishers could not be bothered with "third-rate writers." Such a statement might be regarded as simply ludicrous were it not for the fact that Lukonin was a force in Soviet literary affairs. He was even, for a while, a member of the editorial board of the important journal *Novy mir*.

In spite of the fact that modern Russian poetry is still convalescing after the ultra-repressive years of the immediate postwar era, there are individual talents that merit at least the attention of the outside world. It is true that the brilliance of the twenties has yet to be matched, but to gain a truer perspective on this, one might ask who in contemporary Anglo-American poetry stands comparison with Yeats, Eliot, or Pound?

Special mention should be made of Russia's bards. Aleksandr Vertinsky performed his lyric, exotic songs to music all over the globe before eventually returning to the USSR after a quarter century of emigration.

Bulat Okudzhava (b. 1924) continues in the same lyric tradition as Vertinsky, but with more close-to-home imagery. Aleksandr Galich (1924–77) writes songs in an intentionally lowered manner with the emphasis on political satire. In 1976 he was forced to emigrate.

Boris Slutsky was born in the Ukraine in 1919. Between 1941–45 he served in the Red Army, his war experiences coloring much of his poetry. In 1956 Ehrenburg created a sensation with an article quoting a number of hitherto unpublished poems by Slutsky, and in 1957 his first book of poetry, *Memory,* was published. Slutsky is one of the most important representatives of the war generation of poets and a crucial figure in the post-Stalin literary revival. His poetry is deliberately prosaic and conversational, often devoted to everyday objects or themes, and intimate in tone; many of his poems could best be termed musings. There is a dry, polemical quality about them that reflects, perhaps, the poet's early training as a lawyer. Slutsky's search has been for a language stripped of poeticisms and ornamentation, far removed from the hollow rhetoric of establishment apologists.

Yevgeny Vinokurov (b. 1925), together with Konstantin Vanshenkin (b. 1925), was one of the first postwar poets to free poetry from the officially favoured declamatory mode. As a poetry editor of the influential magazine, *Oktyabr* (October), he helped to confirm the reputations of Zabolotsky and Slutsky, among others, and to establish that of Akhmadulina. Much of his early and even later poetry, as for instance, "I don't Remember Him" and "Eyes," is concerned with his wartime experiences and has a starkness, an edge to it, that at times almost recalls the World War I poetry of Siegfried Sassoon. Vinokurov's later work has become more psychological and philosophical. He explores "characters," exploits the potential of allegory, and continues to develop a more discursive and relaxed manner. Though his rhythms are smoother, more comfortable than Slutsky's, Vinokurov too seems to have deliberately chosen the path of prosaicism, of understatement. It is no mean achievement, under the circumstances, to have been able to espouse, as convincingly as he has done, the cause of the "little man," i.e., the "individual."

Vanshenkin's first collection of poetry, *Song about the Guards,* was published in 1951. Many of his poems have been set to music and become very popular; in 1965 a collection of these songs, with music, was published. A more lyrical poet than Vinokurov, he seems less intent to generalize than simply to record. Vanshenkin has mapped out a restricted but authentic area for himself in which he is able to avoid the prescriptive optimism of official literary theory. The note he sounds is a wistful rather than a tragic one.

The poetry of Yevgeny Yevtushenko (b. 1933) is quite different from that of Slutsky, Vinokurov, or Vanshenkin. His is primarily a declamatory style; in his pace, journalistic verve, and comprehensiveness, he hearkens back to Mayakovsky. Like Andrey Voznesensky (b. 1933), Yevtushenko reads very dramatically and has even been known to use music and light effects. While he has enjoyed great popular success, the small intellectual community has frequently held him in lower regard; Anna Akhmatova, for example, is said to have called both him and Voznesensky *estradnye poety* (platform or stage poets).

Yevtushenko owes his initial popularity to the political "protest" poems he published during the period of "thaw," pleading against the resuscitation of Stalinism and even touching upon the taboo subject of anti-Semitism in the Soviet Union. In 1963 he committed a cardinal sin in circumventing the Soviet censorship to publish his *Precocious Autobiography* in France, without receiving official authorization.

At one time the subject of attacks in the Soviet press, Yevtushenko now travels abroad fairly freely. In addition his poetry is published in large editions. Increasingly, his verse has ceased to reflect anything but the most conformist patriotic sentiments, although he can still surprise from time to time with an original and insightful piece. Understandably perhaps, most Soviet dissidents, and many Western liberals too, regard him as a token rebel who has, in effect, sold out to a regime that he is also trying to modify.

Although much of Yevtushenko's popularity derives from the political nature of his subject matter, Voznesensky has largely abjured this type of material — aside from the almost obligatory praises of Lenin and some facile criticism of things foreign. He was severely criticized in the Soviet press in 1963 for pandering to Western tastes and for "formalism," and he has preferred to keep a low profile politically, retaining the material of handouts of the regime.

Although Voznesensky maintains that Pasternak was his "only master," Mayakovsky would appear to have exercised a stronger influence on him.

He specializes in the short, staccato line, which he declaims in a manner similar to that of Yevtushenko. Many of his experiments in sound are novel; but, unrelieved, they can create a sterile, mechanical impression. At his worst, he has a tendency to cater rather tastelessly to the prejudices of his audience. He can also be sentimental to the point of mawkishness. Nevertheless, he is an inventive poet whose work points back to the radical experimentation of Soviet Russia's lost youth. In the Soviet Union, Voznesensky enjoys a great deal of popularity; and he has been overly acclaimed in the West as well, although the stentorian sound effects of his verse are best perceived in oral presentation.

Victor Sosnora published his first work in 1962. His early verse, with its emphasis on musicality and its use of industrial imagery, was often compared to Voznesensky's; and indeed, like Voznesensky, he has been much influenced by the early Futurists. His Slavic roots, in word play, particularly recall the experiments of Khlebnikov. Some of Sosnora's early work related starkly to the traumatic experiences of childhood — tuberculosis, the Leningrad blockade, and evacuation to the Kuban (where he narrowly escaped being shot by the Gestapo as a Jew). In his more recent poetry, however, he seems to be discovering and assembling what may become a modern mythology, drawing mainly on the legendary and historical chronicles of Kievan Russia and on Russian fairy tales. Anchoring himself in legend, history, or the life of nature and the animals (for which, like Zabolotsky, he has great feeling), he is capable of evoking an archetypal world underlying contemporary existence. A very different but fascinating side of his poetry is evident in the surrealistic fable *The Owl and The Mouse*, with its obvious political overtones.

Bella Akhmadulina's (b. 1937) first collection, *String,* was published in 1962 and criticized by the Party as "superfluous," overly intimate, etc. It was composed mainly of short lyrics, witty, whimsical, well-turned, and strongly influenced by Akhmatova in their sobriety of form and preoccupation with individual emotions. Although Akhmadulina's work appeared thereafter in magazines and almanacs from time to time, it was not until 1969 that her second collection, *Music Lessons,* was published. In 1963 a fragment of her long poem, "A Fairy Tale About the Rain," was published in *Literary Georgia*. Since then she appears to have done more translating, especially from Georgian, than original writing, although the indications are that she has again entered a more creative period. Akhmadulina has considerable potential and is generally highly regarded. Her work became rapidly more complex after the early short lyrics, on occasions employing a symbolic technique of considerable subtlety. Her first marriage was to Yevtushenko, who has claimed that she is the foremost woman poet in Russia since Akhmatova. In the public mind she is associated with Yevtushenko, Voznesensky, Okudzhava — in short, with those poets who came to the forefront initially during the "thaw" period — although in fact, her work is very different from theirs, more meditative and lyrical and far less forceful.

Vladimir Soloukhin (b. 1924) began to publish seriously in the early fifties and soon became popular — perhaps more as a prose writer than a poet. His main theme both in prose and poetry is his love for rural Russia. Another representative of neo-Slavophile views, he is best known for his sketches of country life. His collection, *Black Boards,* deals with his love of icons and his dismay at the systematic destruction of country churches in Russia. On occasion his statements are so critical of official policy in this area that one wonders how the censor permits them. *Black Boards,* for example, creates much the same overall impression as Turgenev's *Sketches of a Hunter* did in the nineteenth century, painting an extremely negative picture of rural conditions. Soloukhin's poetry is anecdotal, almost prosaic sometimes, sometimes rather naively lyrical; and he is unusual among Russian poets in often writing in free verse, which suits his relaxed style well.

The case of Yury Galanskov (1939–72) is a tragic one. Aside from his poetry, he was involved in such underground publications as *Boomerang, Phoenix, Syntax,* and the *White Book* on the Sinyavsky-Daniel trial. A pioneer of civil rights activism, he took part in a number of political demonstrations. He was arrested in 1967 and sent to a forced labor camp. Although suffering from a duodenal ulcer, he was forced to work and was given a diet that was largely inedible. His mother's requests that she be allowed to send him medicine and vitamins was refused, as were requests from his friends and supporters to send him food products. Finally a hasty operation in the prison hospital failed to save his life. Galanskov knew he would die, predicted his death, and his poems are a piercing expression of his sense of outrage and horror. In many ways they are reminiscent of certain of Mandelshtam's political verses written in his moments of greatest despair.

Other poets, such as Burich, Nekrasov, Sabgir, Khomin, Chudakov, Bobyshev, and Morozov, published in *Syntax* (with which Galanskov was associated) and also in *Phoenix* magazine in the mid-1960s. Their voices are angry and direct, often openly rebellious and scornful.

Natalya Gorbanevskaya (b. 1936) is known to have published only nine of her poems in officially authorized Soviet journals, although her verse was circulated privately and two collections were published abroad. Gorbanevskaya has been a leading civil rights activist and was one of the seven to demonstrate in Red Square on August 5, 1968, against the Soviet invasion of Czechoslovakia. Because of her infant child, she was not tried along with the other demonstrators, and she continued to agitate on their behalf, compiling an account of their trial which was published in the West. In December 1969 Gorbanevskaya was herself finally arrested, and in April 1970 was declared to be suffering from schizophrenia and placed in a psychiatric prison hospital, first in Moscow, then in Kazan, where a course of drug treatment was administered. There has recently been a good deal of publicity in the West about the misuse of psychiatry in the Soviet Union as a means of dealing with dissenters, and whether for this reason or for some other, Gorbanevskaya was released in 1972 and finally permitted to emigrate in 1975.

Gorbanevskaya's verse reflects her political activity, but usually only in the most oblique way. Intensely personal and nonpublic, it transcends politics, not accusing, but describing the psychic reality of her situation. Gorbanevskaya, perhaps more than any other poet of her generation, has had the capacity to transmute and concretize her suffering in imagery that is both of the day and universal, as, for example, in the following, single-sentence lyric: "In my own twentieth century/ Where there are more dead than graves/ to put them in, my miserable/ forever unshared love/ among these Goyan images/ is nervous, faint, absurd,/ as after the screaming of jets,/ the trump of Jericho." The nervous pulse of her work, the intensity bordering on hysteria, recall the poetry of that other poet of suffering, Marina Tsvetayeva. In her love lyrics too, Gorbanevskaya evokes the old Russian mystique of regeneration through suffering: "Why talk of disaster or beauty/ when the oblivious body, happy,/ naked as the thief's upon the cross,/ wants to be deceived." Hers is a poetry of pain, of separation, of isolation, of despair, of threatening disaster, of disaster present.

Having touched upon this most recent émigré poet, let us return briefly to the older émigré poetry which we left in a state of disarray on the eve of World War II.

During the war, émigré poetry ceased to be published. By the end of the war, the émigré community had been so scattered that it never fully reconstituted itself in Western Europe. Perhaps the most conspicuous feature of the history of postwar Russian émigré poetry was the emigration of a large number of Russian poets to the United States. Just as America had provided a haven for German writers such as Thomas Mann and Bertolt Brecht during the war, it continues to do so in the postwar period with regard to Russian writers and, especially, poets. Over fifty Russian poets have settled in America, making the U.S.A. the major center at present for Russian poetry abroad.

The Russian emigration is traditionally divided into "First Wave" (after the Revolution) and "Second Wave" (after World War II). The recent Jewish exodus has on occasion been referred to as a "Third Wave." Although Russian poets in America represent all three of these, the bulk of them are drawn from the Second Wave. Most of the First Wave literary figures are no longer alive. The problem of an aging generation faces even the Second Wave. This is a crucial problem since, in the past, "replacement" has occurred only through emigration from the USSR. Except possibly in Yugoslavia and China up to the end of the forties, Russian émigré culture has not proved able to continue itself through its children, and the Russian diaspora has often seemed on the verge of total assimilation.

Material conditions for Russian literature outside the Soviet Union are not propitious; the reading audience is so small that the best journals often sell no more than a few hundred copies. In spite of these circumstances, however, postwar poetry has been developing in a number of directions and now appears very promising.

Igor Chinnov (b. 1909), one of the most talented of modern Russian poets (either here or in the Soviet Union) has been in the United States since 1962 and retired from the faculty of Vanderbilt University in 1977. His poetry has attracted relatively wide attention and has been the subject of more than forty different articles and reviews.

Chinnov's early poetry has much in common with the "Parisian Note." It is characterized by an economy of means, a sense of restraint, and a strong underlying aestheticism. His later poems, while using the same system of formal devices, are more ironical, with elements of surrealism and the grotesque. Chinnov quite properly considers himself a modernist. The world for him is absurd, and the individual can only hope to enjoy a few

1 Russian Poetry Since the Revolution

isolated moments of aesthetic pleasure in a universe which is essentially cruel and meaningless. As is true of much of modernism in general, Chinnov's art is characterized by a strong anti-psychologism. He is an epicurean poet, the majority of whose poems are dedicated to sensual perception. He plays, not on emotions, but on sensations. People as individuals appear relatively rarely, while inanimate objects tend to predominate. Verbs of being are more frequent than verbs of motion, and objects (nouns) simply accumulate one on the other. As a result, visual images play an unusually large part in his poetic scheme. Colors in particular stand out, preference is given to bright, metallic effects. In spite of the strong sensual element, this imagery carries considerable symbolic weight as well.

Nostalgia is present in Chinnov's verse too, but it is at most a minor theme. The poet's interests transcend temporal and spatial borders. Significantly, the titles of all his collections are taken from foreign languages: a former representative of the "Parisian Note," he is now a truly cosmopolitan poet.

Yury (George) Ivask (b. 1896) is another well-known poet and scholar, on the faculty of the University of Massachusetts. Like Chinnov, he began to write poetry in a rather conservative fashion — somewhat in the manner of the "Parisian Note." Later, he abandoned this Acmeistic simplicity and clarity in favor of a more intimate, personal associative verse and phonic experimentation, involving even "trans-sense language." The strongest influence here is undoubtedly that of Marina Tsvetayeva.

Ivan Elagin (b. 1918) is currently on the faculty of the University of Pittsburgh. His verse is sharply differentiated from that of the "Parisian Note." He holds to a fundamentally odic tradition rather like Yevtushenko, who is, incidentally, an admirer of his. There is a marked urbanism in his work, war and machinery supplying much of his imagery, with minimal use of the idyllic natural landscapes so often encountered in the work of émigré poets. Instead of the exquisite half-tones and delicate perceptions of Chinnov, there is a tendency to hyperbole in Elagin, on which, in his chanting, emphatic readings, he lays even further stress. Much of his verse is topical; one of his anthologies is even entitled *Political Feuilletons in Verse*.

Nikolay Marchenko, another important émigré poet, writes under the pseudonym of Nikolay Morshen. Like so many of the Second Wave poets, he comes from the Ukraine, and on occasion he successfully inserts Ukrainian into his Russian verse, creating a sort of macaronic effect. Morshen's early poetry is fraught with a sense of time. It reflects the life and movement of an age in which the individual is swept along by events over which he has no control. The war and the "Cult of Stalin" are confronted in his verse, which is often pessimistic and somberly philosophical.

Morshen makes wide use of irony, resembling in this respect Igor Chinnov. The two poets are, however, very different. Morshen's irony contains no humorous element; it is a compound of nostalgia and the bitterly grotesque. The grotesque in Morshen, however, is not, as it is in Chinnov, the component of a fantastic, chimeric world, but descriptive of a real city of asphalt and concrete; and where Chinnov shrugs his shoulders and jokes, Morshen engages in heated protest.

Morshen's more recent poetry, however, has shown some very interesting developments. His former, pessimistic, politically-oriented, thematically urban manner has given way to nature poetry and also to formal experimentation: sound associations, verbal games. The predominant mood is one of joy, and a new sense of humor is evident.

A certain general tendency is observable here: the "more recent" the poet, the fresher his memories of the Soviet Union, the greater his bitterness (and nostalgia), and the stronger his inclination to introduce political elements into his verse. With the passing of years, specific or local political considerations often assume less prominence, and more transcendent moral or aesthetic concerns become evident.

Joseph Brodsky (b. 1940), on the other hand, presents the odd spectacle of an essentially nonpolitical poet from the start, whose case was turned with a great deal of trouble into a political *cause célèbre* by the Soviet government. He was criticized in the Soviet press in 1963 as a "literary parasite" and actually tried and convicted in 1964 for "idleness" (an offense indictable under Soviet law), although really on account, probably, of his unorthodox, nonconformist style of life. In a ludicrous mockery of a trial, the judge refused to recognize poetry-writing as a legitimate occupation (at least in Brodsky's case), and exiled the poet to a remote collective farm in Siberia for five years. After twenty months, however, he was allowed to return to Moscow. In the meantime he had been published in the United States, and his reputation subsequently grew rapidly in the West. The government deported him in 1972 in the hope of reducing his status to that of just another émigré who would no longer attract the attention of Western observers or perhaps act inadvertently as a source of discontent and rebellion for Soviet dissident writers. He is presently on the faculty of the University of Michigan.

Though technically extremely complex, Brodsky's poetry is accessible to translation; Brodsky has experimented with a number of genres — from large, loosely structured philosophico-metaphysical narratives to sonnets or sonnet cycles. The philosophical and meditative content of his verse represents an important stratum which is not inevitably violated; some of his poems, moreover, are very plot-oriented, and this is also conducive to translation. The late W. H. Auden, in his Foreword to Brodsky's *Selected Poems,* translated by George Kline, wrote: "Mr. Brodsky commands many tones of voice, from the lyric . . . to the elegiac . . . to the comic-grotesque . . . , and can handle with equal ease a wide variety of rhythms and metres, short lines, long lines, iambics, anapestic, masculine rhymes and feminine." It is remarkable, and indeed a tribute to the translator, that Auden, without any knowledge of Russian, was able to glimpse all this, plus the diversity, linked to profound traditionalism, of Brodsky's talent. Brodsky is certainly one of the most promising figures for Russian poetry today.

One of the most recent forced émigrés is Lev Mak. His work, in its philosophic and metaphysical preoccupations, has something in common with Brodsky's. However, his is a very different poetic personality, lacking perhaps the discretion Brodsky displays in maintaining an economy of imagery. Mak makes broad use of paradoxes and sudden thematic shifts, attempting to dissolve that hierarchical order by which we normally organize our perceptions. He freely mixes classical, Biblical and Slavic mythology with the realities of twentieth-century existence, attempting to recreate the sense of high tragedy we associate with antiquity. The resulting tension between myth-making on the one hand, and the tawdriness of our age on the other, produces a powerfully grotesque effect. Mak is an original and highly promising poet, although he is still virtually unknown either in this country or in Russia.

This survey has necessarily been brief. Inevitably, we have had to omit many poets and much poetry we would have wished to include, and we were anxious not to take up any more space than was absolutely necessary with introductory material. We have tried here to represent the diverse tendencies and talents of Russian poetry since the Revolution as fairly as possible. We have sought to re-establish Russian émigré poetry in this period in its rightful place alongside the rest of Russian poetry because, in the final count, there is no "Soviet" poetry or "émigré" poetry; there is only "Russian" poetry. We have also, we think, considered objectively both established and nonestablished *samizdat* poets. This collection is not a document, but an anthology of what, in our judgment, constitutes some of the best Russian poetry of the period without regard to political creed or activity. Nevertheless, as any survey of modern Russian poetry seems inevitably to turn into a chronicle of disaster, we suppose ours has not escaped a similar fate. The facts of murder, imprisonment, and exile are overwhelmingly evident and cannot be dismissed as irrelevant. Poetry, however, is what survives. It is the record of the speaking voice which continues after the destruction of the body. That it should survive in such overtly savage and inimical conditions is the wonder of it all.

This anthology covers basically the period since the Revolution of 1917, but on occasion draws upon poetry written just before the Revolution so as to provide, as it were, the background against which the poetry developed.

The broad division of poets into prewar and postwar is a clear one; yet in a few instances (e.g., Akhmatova, Selvinsky), this classification has been problematic. War-time poetry, either retrospective or actual, is represented in these two sections. Further difficulties have arisen with regard to poets who wrote poetry both in Russia and while in emigration. Rather than scatter an individual writer's work over several sections, we felt it was important to present each poet in one place as a totality.

We have set ourselves the goal of presenting poems that both function successfully as poetry in English (not reading as "translations") and are representative of the period. Often the first of these considerations has led us to exclude familiar anthology items, but it has also been our conscious policy to make this selection as fresh as possible. A continuing concern has been the reconfirmation of the importance of émigré poetry in the modern period.

John Glad
Daniel Weissbort

A NOTE ON TRANSLATION

We believe that the secret of successful translation may lie as much in the selection of the text as in the actual translation itself. In selecting the poems for this anthology, we therefore have tried to test their potential, and realize it, in translation; and we have resisted the impulse to assume that their qualities in the original must somehow magically survive the linguistic transference. Broadly speaking, poems in which the primary emphasis was phonic or linguistic tended to lose out in the process, whereas imagistic poetry or poetry with an explicit narrative or philosophical content presented fewer problems. Thus, many justly admired anthology pieces will not be found in this collection because we could not secure adequate translations — which is not to say that they are not translatable, but simply that, in our view, satisfactory translations have not yet been achieved.

We believe that a poetic translation, while referring back constantly to its model, should also have a separate existence. The translation is a commentary on the original poem while, in a sense, aiming at an organic equivalence of effect; difficult as it may be to define, it is an "aesthetic experience" that both the original and the translation seek. In the words of Dudley Fitts, "the translation of a poem should be a poem, viable as a poem, and, as a poem, weighable" ("The Poetic Nuance," in *On Translation*, Cambridge, 1959, p. 35).

This view is by no means shared by all. Fitts himself confesses that he once held to the literal, word-for-word approach. It is our feeling, however, that while the reader may find the latter useful, it is unlikely that he will be able, on the basis of a literal rendering, to reconstruct the poem. The literal translation is essentially an aid to reading in the original language. Literary or poetic translation is a far more complex act of criticism and reinterpretation than the approximate verbal matching of so-called "literal translation."

Of course, there are many poems in which wordplay is so specific to the given language that they can be adequately translated only by providing the elaborate sort of notes favored by Nabokov. Mandelshtam's poem "January 1, 1924," is one example: the poem is structured around chains of association triggered by dual meanings of individual words. Mandelshtam writes that he is riding in a sleigh and is trying to button up a heavy horsehair blanket, which he compares to fish fur. The word used for "blanket" (*polost'*) also means "hollowness." Later, he develops the dual meaning when the *polost'* becomes simultaneously a hollowness and a heavy blanket resonating with its horsehair against the frozen runners — like a bow against a stringed instrument. The fish-fur analogy is later clarified by the phrase "court of the pike" (*shchuchiy sud*). This phrase is part of a Russian folk saying indicating the arbitrary and predatory. Thus, when the typewriter clicks out a "Soviet sonatina" (*sovetskaya sonatinka*), it transpires that the typewriter's keys are lies wrapped around a pike bone and that the sonatina is really a court order.

"January 1, 1924," a major poetic achievement, is a complex jigsaw puzzle of double meanings in which the chain of associations is merely one piece. A literal translation with voluminous notes would be an invaluable aid to any student struggling with the Russian; nevertheless, no translation standing on its own can do justice to such an original, and we feel that this type of poem lies beyond the scope of the anthology.

In contrast, consider Pavel Antokolsky's poem "Son." This poem verges on prose and is an impressive example of poetry in which direct communication predominates. What is being communicated is the thought and feeling of a father who has lost his son; the formal elements of rhyme and meter are supportive rather than primary. Consider also this poem by Akhmatova:

> There is a boundary in the heart's land
> That lovers, loving passionately, may not cross,
> Though lips meet in terrible silence, and
> The heart through loving breaks in pieces.
>
> Here, friendship too is powerless, as are the years
> That blaze with a sublime happiness —
> Then is the soul free and clear
> Of all dependence on langorous flesh.
>
> They are insane who try
> To reach that point, and those that go beyond
> Are torn by anguish.
>   Now you know why
> My heart does not flutter beneath your hand.

Here there is a far greater degree of stylization than in Antokolsky's poem, but the emotional content is still central and distinct enough to survive the process of translation more or less intact, within a fairly loose, even impressionistic, formal approximation of the original poem.

Imagistic poetry is certainly fertile ground for the translator, for images are generally transferable interlingually, even though meter and rhyme may be lost or diminished. Note the following example in which Mandelshtam writes of falling asleep while reading Homer:

Homer falls silent
And foam swirls from the heads of kings.
Only the black sea rages
And a heavy surf thunders against my pillow.

Again, poetry in which the philosophical content is dominant can be quite productive. In "Metamorphoses" Zabolotsky confronts with great power the problem of identity. Also working in a philosophical vein is Lev Mak, whose poetry functions, at least on this level, equally well in Russian and English:

The biologist studies filaments, the stomatologist — cavities.
What does the locust not devour?
                                    To destroy a man
Is much easier than to cure a toothache. It is simpler
To stifle our souls than to know them.
                                    The devil again
Makes a clock out of a mincing machine, cuts
A new banner out of cloth impregnated with poison;
We kiss it, swearing an oath . . .

                        At midnight,
His study windows are ominously alight.
The pure breeze
Enters impure lungs and leaves them impure;
The souls
Of our children, forged by us out of the resonant,
Shining copper of good intentions,
Are recast as soldiers' buckles, rocket cases, radar antennae.
                        from *"Behind the Slaughter-House, Evening"*

Although Russian and English are both Indo-European languages, they differ radically in almost every respect. Phonetically, Russian is structured along quite different lines from English. Virtually none of the sounds of

Russian has more than an approximate English equivalent. As for vocabulary, Russian, compared to the Romance or Germanic languages, has an insignificant number of recognizable cognates with English.

Russian is an inflected language, like German and Latin, and has six cases. Thus, most nouns, adjectives, and pronouns have twelve possible forms each, counting singular and plural forms. This eliminates the need to indicate the grammatical function of words by their position in the sentence, as in English; therefore Russian possesses a very free word order.

In place of the complex system of tenses in English, Russian has only past, present, and future; further distinctions are made by what is called "aspect." Most verbs have two aspectual forms, the use of which is a source of considerable agony to foreigners studying the language.

Thus, on all linguistic levels — phonetic, lexical, and grammatical — the Russian and English texts of a poem must necessarily differ more radically than in the case of English and the Romance or Germanic languages.

The most frustrating area of translation from Russian is that of stylistic levels. To understand the problem one must look at the origins of the Slavic languages. All the Slavic languages derive from an original Slavic language now referred to as "Proto-Slavic." Proto-Slavic was an Indo-European language which split into three separate dialects in approximately the middle of the first millennium A.D. These dialects in turn gave rise to three families of languages: South Slavic (Bulgarian, Serbo-Croatian, Slovenian, Macedonian), West Slavic (Polish, Czech), and East Slavic (Russian, Ukranian, Byelorussian). In the ninth century the Greek missionaries, Cyrill and Methodius, translated the liturgical texts into a South Slavic dialect, and this language became the official language of the Russian Orthodox Church; it is now referred to as "Old Church Slavonic." Since the Church was for many centuries the principal bearer of literacy, this imported South Slavic dialect exerted an enormous influence on the modern Russian literary language. In fact, modern Russian is a hybrid composed of the former East Slavic vernacular and Old Church Slavonic. Thus, there has arisen a hierarchy of styles in modern Russian in which Old Church Slavonic forms are perceived as relatively formal, while the indigenous Russian forms tend to be more colloquial. These two categories coexist under extremely complex circumstances along with such features as dialect, obsolete forms, etc., common to any language. Faced with a poem in which the author has chosen to ring the changes with these stylistic levels, the translator can attempt to make his translation more formal or colloquial, as the case may be; but the multiplicity of levels is so specific to Russian as to be untransmittable in another language.

An extreme example would be "Conversational Melody," by Nikolay Klyuev, in which the poet imitates the speech of the "Iron Tsar" (Wilhelm II):

1 Golova moya — umok lukavy,
2 Porazmysli ty, poraskumekay,
3 Mne kogo b v zhelezo zakovati?
4 Ozhelezil zemlyu ya i vody,
5 Polonil ogon' i par shipuchiy,
6 Veter, svet kolodnikami sdelal,
7 Nyne zh ya kak kuropot' v lovushku,
8 Svetel Mesyat s Solnyshkom poymayu:

Klyuev has deliberately moved as far as possible from the literary language in the direction of popular or peasant speech and primitive or archaic usages. Line 1 reads, "My head — clever mind." This type of repetition (head=mind) is characteristic of orally transmitted folk poetry; furthermore, the word used for "mind" here is *umok* — a diminutive of the sort widely used in Russian folklore. Line 2: "Ponder, figure (it) out." The word used for "ponder" is *porazmysli* — an obsolete form, and "figure (it) out" is *poraskumekay* — a substandard form characteristic of peasant speech. Line 3: "Whom can I shackle in iron." The predicate (*zakovati*) is an Old Church Slavonic form perceived as substandard in modern literary Russian. Line 4: "I have made the earth and waters into iron." *Ozhelezil* (Made into iron) is a neologism. Lines 5–6: "I have captured fire and hissing steam; I have made the wind and the light into slaves." *Polon* ("captured") is taken from a form characteristic of the original East Slavic vernacular but now regarded as archaic (as opposed to *plen*, the form taken from Old Church Slavonic); *shipuchiy* ("hissing") is colloquial. Lines 7–8: "Today, like a partridge in a snare, I will catch Bright Moon and the Sun." *Kuropot'* ("partridge") is a substandard form characteristic of folk speech; the word for "bright" (*svetel*) is a short-form adjective which is used attributively only in peasant speech; also "Sun" is put in the diminutive (*Solnyshko*) — something characteristic of the Russian folk tradition.

Such a multiplicity of stylistic levels can be discussed illuminatingly enough in the form of notes, but the attempt to transmit it directly in English translation is clearly as hopeless as attempting to describe a symphony in terms of a painting.

The basic, although not invariable, strategy adopted here in dealing with Russian verse forms has been the flexible use of free verse; free verse, however, should not be taken as a synonym for loose, undisciplined, or formless verse. Although Russian poets experimented in the eighteenth century with syllabic verse, the bulk of nineteenth- and twentieth-century Russian poetry provides a more or less regular alternation of stressed and unstressed syllables. The most popular type of Russian poetry has been syllabo-tonic (the same binary and ternary meters traditional in much of English poetry), and some tonic poetry (reintroduced into Russian by Mayakovsky).[1] Moreover, Russian is an inflected language, and the limited number of conjugational and declensional endings makes rhyme considerably easier than in English — the equivalent of a Russian rhyme is not necessarily a rhyme of equal strength in English. Thus, more often than not, we have attempted to reproduce metered, rhymed poetry in rhythmic but unrhymed verse. We offer these translations, not as improvements of the originals, but as minimal violations of, or intrusions into, them. That is, in selecting the poems, we have attempted to pick those in which it was possible to render the linguistic stratum in the most transparent manner possible. In this way, we felt we could best serve the dual purpose of presenting poetry which was not obtrusively "translation" and which at the same time allowed the reader access to at least some of the original excellence of the poem.

Our basic criterion in selecting for this anthology has been to determine what seemed "to work" as poetry in English, which we have tried constantly to reconcile with "fidelity" to the Russian original. We have tried to maintain a flexible approach to translation, not falling back on contemporary trends, such as universal rejection of rhyme and meter. We hope too that the use of a variety of translators has helped us to maintain a diversity of approach and effect. We have further sought to reflect the range and

1 "Syllabic" poetry — a specific number of syllables per line; "tonic" poetry — a specific number of stresses per line; "Syllabo-tonic" — a specific number of syllables and stresses per line.

diversity of modern Russian poetry by casting our net wide, while trying to represent major figures with adequate samplings of their work. We hope, finally, that we have given some indication in this "Note on Translation" of how intimately involved with the whole process of assembling such an anthology are the innumerable problems and challenges of translation — which has been described as the most complex human activity of all.

THE TRANSLATORS

Bohdan Boychuk
Pamela Davidson
Olive Dehn
John Glad
Emmett Jarett
Denis Johnson
Joseph Kiegel
Sharon Leiter
P. Lemke
Peter Levi
Kathy Lewis
Dick Lourie
Bernard Meares
Alec Merivale
Robin Milner-Gulland
IWP
Bob Perelman
Alexander Petrov
Carl R. Proffer
Shirley Rihner
Mark Rudman
Anthony Rudolf
Paul Schmidt
Gerry Smith
Nigel Stott
Geoffrey Thurley
William Tjalsma
Theodore Weiss
Daniel Weissbort
Mary Jane White
Bertram D. Wolfe

I
PRE-WORLD WAR II POETRY IN RUSSIA

ALEKSANDR BLOK 1880–1921

NIGHT: A STREET, . . .

Night: a street, a streetlight; drugstore;
A meaningless dim luminance.
Go live for twenty-five years more —
Nothing will change. There's no way out.

You'll die, and start again, while all
Recurs, identically: the night,
The chill ripples on the canal,
The drugstore, the street, the streetlight.

Denis Johnson & Kathy Lewis

ON THE PLAIN OF KULIKOVO

I

The river stretches wide. It flows on tiredly,
Sadly, washing its banks.
Above the lifeless clay of yellow cliffs, the hay
Stands sadly on the steppe.

O Russia! O my wife! Our long road lies ahead,
Terrible and clear.
Our road runs through our chests like an arrow
Of the ancient Tartar power.

Our road goes through the steppe, it runs through boundless grief
— Your grief, O Russia.
And even the dark night that lies beyond the border
I do not fear.

Let night arrive — we'll ride on. We'll light the steppe
With fires as it stretches
Into the distance. And shining above the smoke on the steppe,
The Khan's sword, and the sacred banner.

And the battle just goes on! In the blood and dust, our peace
Is only something we dream.
The mare of the steppe is flying on and on, and tramples
The feather-grass.

There isn't any end . . . The miles of cliffs flash by,
And all the clouds,
Frightened, billow down among us, nearer and nearer,
And the sunset is washed with blood.

The sunset is washed with blood. Blood gushes from the heart.
Weep, heart, weep.
There isn't any peace, the mare of the steppe flies on
At a terrible gallop!

2

At midnight you and I paused on the steppe.
There is no going back, no looking back.
Beyond the Nepryadva River the swans
Were weeping, and again they weep.

Along our way, the white and burning stone,
And past the river, the barbaric hordes.
The flaring banner never will again
Fly gaily in the wind above our forces.

And lowering her head toward the ground
My friend addresses me: "Sharpen your sword,
That you may not set down your life in vain
For the holy cause, against the Tartar horde."

Aleksandr Blok   3

I'm not the first to fight; and not the last:
The country will be troubled for a long time.
So pray for your beloved at the first
Liturgy, O fair and shining wife!

3

The night when Mamai and his hordes were spread
On the steppe and on the bridges
You and I were there on that dark field
Together — did you know this?

Before the dark, portending Don I heard
Within my all-too-knowing
Heart your voice along the plain at night
Among the cries of the swans.

From midnight on, the Prince's forces billowed
Upward like a cloud,
And in the distant mist our mother pummeled
The horse's stirrup, and wailed.

And in the distance, night birds, circling, coasting,
While up above our Russia
The soundless lightning that comes in summertime
Kept watch over the Prince.

The eagles' scream above the Tartar camp
Threatened disaster
And the Nepryadva was decked in mist
Like a princess in a veil.

And with the mist above the sleeping river
Directly down to me
You came, in clothes radiant with light,
Not frightening the horse.

Like a silvery wave you flashed
On your friend's steel sword
You refreshed the dusty chain mail
On my shoulder.

And when, in the morning, like a black cloud
The horde set out
Your image, not made by human hands,
Shone forever on my shield.

4

Now again the feather-grass
Is bent to earth with ancient pain,
Again, from past the river's mist,
From the distance, I hear you call my name.

The herds of horses on the steppe
Have vanished, leaving none behind;
Terrible passions have escaped
Under the yoke of the waning moon.

And I, with ancient pain myself,
A wolf beneath the waning moon,
Do not know what to do with myself,
Which way to fly within your wake.

I listen to the battle roaring,
The trumpet-calls, the Tartars' shouts,
I see a stretching conflagration
Raging silently over Russia.

In the grip of awful pain
I wander now on my white horse . . .
I meet the clouds that freely range
High up in the night of mists.

Luminous thoughts begin to rise
Within my lacerated heart
And luminous thoughts begin to fall,
Engulfed in a dark fire.

"Appear to me, my marvellous marvel,
Teach me to be luminous!"
My horse's mane begins to shiver . . .
In the wake of the wind, the cries of swords . . .

Aleksandr Blok 5

5

And the dawn was covered
with the shadow of inescapable misfortunes.

6

Soloviev

Over the plain of Kulikovo
Again the mist ascends
And like a lowering cloud bank covers
The field, and darkens the dawn.

Beneath the silence and the mist
One cannot hear the battle
Roaring terribly, nor see the flash
Of lightning in the struggle.

But I can see you, dawn of holy
Days immersed in violence!
Above the enemy camp again
Swans' cries, the flapping of their wings.

The heart can never rest in peace;
The clouds drawn down today
Like heavy armor before the battle.
Your hour has come — Pray!

Denis Johnson & Kathy Lewis

VISITOR

She came in glowing
from the frost,
and filled the room
with cold breath
and fresh air;
with a tinkling voice
she chattered about things

6　Aleksandr Blok

utterly irrelevant
to anything.

Right at the start, she dropped
a fat art periodical on the floor . . .
immediately there began to seem
too little space in the big room.
All this was irritating enough,
and a little ridiculous.
When I read her *Macbeth* aloud
she started to laugh.

No sooner had I got to "The earth's bubbles"
(which I can't speak about without
excitement) than I noticed
she too was excited, staring,
attentive, out of the window . . .

It turned out a big tabby cat
was crawling along the roof edge,
stalking a pair of blue birds,
which were kissing . . .

What riled me most was,
the bluebirds were kissing,
not us; and,
the age of Paolo and Francesca had passed.

Geoffrey Thurley

VLADIMIR MAYAKOVSKY   1893–1930

A CLOUD IN TROUSERS

Your thought
musing in those brains of oatmeal
like a bloated functionary on an oily sofa —
I'll mock it to death with a dripping shred of my heart
and nourish my biting contempt.

No gray hair in my soul,
no doddering tenderness.
I rock the world with the thunder of my voice,
strolling, looking good —
twenty-two.

Sensitive ones,
your love is a violin solo,
cruder ones use a drum.
But you can't be like me,
inside out, all lips.

Come out and learn,
cambric-prim officialdom
of the angelic leagues!

You too, ladies, thumbing your lips like a cook
his cookbook.

If you prefer,
I'll be pure raging meat,
or if you prefer,
as the sky changes tone,
I'll be absolutely tender,
not a man, but a cloud in trousers!

Flowery Nice doesn't exist!
Again I sing to praise
men used as hospital beds,
women wornout as clichés.

I

You think I'm crazy? It's malaria?

It happened.
It happened in Odessa.

"See you at four," Maria said.

Eight.
Nine.
Ten.

Then the twilight
spun around from the window
and stomped off into nightmarish darkness,
frowning,
decemberish.

Behind its dilapidated back,
snickering candelabras.

You wouldn't recognize me,
a sack of gristly meat,
moaning,
writhing.
What can such a jerk want?
A lump's desires are infinite!

Who cares
if I'm made of bronze,
if my heart is lined with iron?
At night I only want
to muffle my clang
in soft woman.

And so,
huge,
I hunched by the window,
my forehead melting the glass.
Love, no or yes?
And what kind,
big or teeny?
From my body how could it be big?
It would have to be a quiet little lovelet
that's shy of noisy traffic,
that loves horse-tram bells.

On and on,
my face muzzling
the rain's pocked face,
I wait,
drenched by the city's splashing surf.

Midnight races,
grabs,
stabs,
get rid of him!

The twelfth stroke fell,
a chopped-off head.

Gray raindrops on the windowpanes
howling,
a heap of grimaces,
like all the gargoyles of Notre Dame
in concert.

That's it!
The hell with her.
I'll yell till my mouth busts.

Quietly,
I heard
a nerve
twitch like a sick man hopping out of bed;
at first
it barely stirred,
then pattered around,
uneasy,
strict;
then a few more,
tap dancing
frantically.

The first floor ceiling crashed.

Nerves!
Big,
little,
millions!
Galloping like mad
till their knees give!

Through the room, night oozed on and on,
ooze the heavy eye can't heave out of.
The hotel doors
suddenly banged,
chomping unevenly.

In you rushed,
sharp as "Here!"
torturing your suede gloves
you said,
"Guess what?
I'm getting married."

Vladimir Mayakovsky 11

Go get married.
Big deal.
Who cares?
I'm perfectly calm,
pulse:
zero.

Remember
you used to say,
"Jack London,
money,
love,
sex."
I only saw
a Giaconda
that had to be stolen!

You were stolen.

I'll gamble for love again,
my brows a fiery arch.
So what!
Hobos can live
in burnt-out houses.

You mock me?
"A beggar has no money,
and you have no 'emeralds of madness.'"
Now listen!
They mocked Vesuvius,
and Pompeii was destroyed!

Attention
gentlemen,
dilettantes
in sacrilege,
crime,
slaughter —
have you seen
the epitome of horror,

my face
when
I
am quite calm?

And I feel
"I"
is too small for me.
Some other body is bursting out.

Hello?
Who is it?
Momma?
Momma!
Your son is wonderfully ill!
Momma!
His heart is on fire.
Tell Lyuda and Olga
their brother is trapped.
Each word,
even the jokes,
that his scorching mouth pukes up,
hurls itself out like a naked whore
from a burning brothel.

A whiff
of burning flesh!
Here they come!
Glittering
helmets!
But please, no heavy boots.
Tell the firemen to climb
tenderly on a burning heart.
Here, let me.
I'll pump barrels of tears.
I'll push against the ribs.
I'm jumping! I'm jumping! I'm jumping! I'm jumping!
They fell in.
You can't jump out of your heart.

Vladimir Mayakovsky 13

Through cracked lips,
from my smoldering face,
cindery kisses leap up.

Momma!
I can't sing.
In the church of my heart the choir's in flames.

Charred images of numbers and words
rush from my skull
like children from a flaming building.
Fear,
grabbing at the sky,
lifted high,
the Lusitania's burning arms.

Into quiet apartments
where people are trembling,
a hundred-eyed fire roars from the docks.
My last cry —
groan through the ages,
I'm on fire!

2

Praise me!
I am greater than the greatest.
On everything before me
I stamp *nihil*.

I won't read anything
at all.
A book?
What's that?

Here's how I used to think
you made a book:
a poet comes along,
mouth half open, inspired,
then suddenly the idiot bursts into song —
fancy that!

But, it seems, before he starts his song,
he tramps around, calloused from fermentation,
with the dull fish of imagination
flopping about in the heart's swamp.
And while his soup of love and nightingales
is boiling, thrumming with rhyme,
the tongueless street's in torture,
unable to make a sound.

We're proud,
We lift up towers of Babel,
but god
scatters all speech,
grinds
cities into fields.

Quietly the street shoves pain along.
Out of its gullet a yell sticks up.
Fat taxis and bony cabs
swell, stuck in its throat.
Its tubercular chest
is pedestrianed flat.

The city barricades the street with night.

But still,
when the street coughed up its phlegm
onto the square,
shoving that porch off its throat,
it seemed a choir
of archangels cried
god was plundered, now he comes to punish!

But the street sat down and yelled,
"Let's stuff our bellies!"

Krupps and baby Krupps
paint war brows on the city,
but in its mouth
dead words rot,

only two grow fat:
"bastard"
and I think the other
is "borsch."

Poets,
sopped with lamentation,
rush from the street, their long hair matted,
"how can those two words sing
of maidens
and love
and tiny flowers in the dew?"

After the poets
come thousands
of students,
whores,
contractors.

Hey gentlemen!
Stop!
You're not beggars,
don't beg!

We're strong
and take huge strides.
We mustn't listen, must rip them apart,
those who are glued
as a special bonus
to every double bed.

Should we kneel and beg them
"help me!"
beg for hymns
and oratorios?
We who are the creators in a blazing hymn —
in the noise of factories and laboratories.

Who gives a damn for Faust
in his occult rocket

slithering along the parquet of heaven with Mephistopheles!
I know
a nail in my boot
is worse than Goethe's fantasies!

I,
the extreme golden mouth,
whose every word
gives birth to the soul,
and christens the body,
I say to you,
the least living speck
is worth more than anything I'll ever do.

Listen!
Today
brasslipped Zarathustras preach,
rushing around,
moaning and wailing.
We,
our faces crumpled like sheets,
our lips dangling like chandeliers,
inmates of leper city,
where dirty gold breeds leper's sores,
we are far purer than Venetian azure,
washed by sea and sun!

Damn Homer and Ovid
for not having made
characters like us,
pocked and sooty.
I know
the sun would dim
seeing the golden sparkle of our souls!

Muscle and sinew work better than prayer.
Do we have to beg time for charity?
We —
each of us —

hold the world's reigns
in our five fingers.

Saying this brought me to my Golgothas in the auditoriums
of Petrograd, Moscow, Odessa, and Kiev,
where there wasn't one
who didn't
yell:
"Crucify him!
Crucify him!"
But,
people, even you who have wounded me,
you're closer and dearer than anything.

Haven't you seen a dog licking
the hand that whips it?

I,
mockery of my tribe,
like some long
dirty joke,
I see the one no one sees
crossing the mountains of time.

Where men's vision fails,
I see 1916 come,
leading hungry masses,
wearing the thorny crown of revolution.

I am with you, I, his precursor,
I am wherever there is pain,
I nail myself
to every tear.
There is no more that can be forgiven,
I've cauterized once-tender souls,
a thing far more difficult
than taking a million Bastilles!

And when
he arrives,

announced by rebellion,
and you greet your saviour,
then I'll
rip out my soul,
stamp on it
to make it big,
and hand it to you,
bloody, for a flag.

3

Ah, what's this?
Why
do dirty fists
shake at clear joy?

It came
the thought
of insane asylums came
and hung its curtains in my head.

And —
like a battleship, sinking,
men choking,
diving out open hatches —
so Burlyuk,[1] terrified,
crawled
out of his own gashed eye.
Nearly dirtying his teary eyelid,
he drawled out,
stood,
walked,
and unusually tender for one so fat,
proclaimed,
"Good!"

Good, when a yellow shirt
keeps the soul from having to answer questions.

1 David Burlyuk (b. 1882) Russian artist and Futurist poet.

Good
to yell
when thrown to the gallows,
"Drink Van Houten's Cocoa!"

That
thunderous
flash
is worth more
than anything . . .

Lurching through cigar smoke,
like a liqueur glass,
here comes Severyanin's [2] drunken face.

You call yourself a poet,
squeaking like a little gray quail!
Today
brass knuckles
will smash the world inside your skull!

You,
troubled by only one thought,
"Is my dancing smooth enough?"
Look at me enjoying myself,
me —
an ordinary pimp and gambler.

On you,
pickled in love,
wetting the centuries
with weeping,
I turn
my back, using the sun
as a monocle
for my bulging eye.

Dressing up incredibly,

2 Igor Severyanin (1887–1941), Russian Futurist poet.

I'll strut over the world,
spreading ruin or joy,
and in front of me,
like a pug on a leash, my pet, the Emperor Napoleon.

The world will lie on her back,
meat quivering, eager,
things will come to life,
lips
prattling forever,
Umm umm *ummm!*

Suddenly,
clouds
and various cloud-like things in the sky
will kick up a fuss,
as if white-suited workers were dispersing
after calling an embittered strike against the sky.
Enraged thunder crawled out of the clouds,
its huge nostrils snorting friskily,
and for a second, the sky's face twitched
like the iron Bismarck, grimacing.

And someone,
tangled in cloudy chains,
held out a hand to the cafe
and somehow it seemed feminine,
and gentle somehow,
and somehow like a gun carriage.

You think
the sun's kindly
patting the cafe's cheek?
No it's General Galliffet [3]
coming to cut the rebels down!

Take your hands out of your pockets!

3 · Marquis Gaston Alexandre Auguste de Galliffet (1830–1909), a French general known
for his harsh treatment of Communard prisoners.

Grab a rock, a knife, a bomb,
and if you don't have any arms,
use your forehead!

Come on, you little starving,
sweating,
timid,
moldy, lice-infested clods!

Come on!
We'll paint Monday and Tuesday with blood
and make them holidays.
At knifepoint let the earth remember
those she tried to vulgarize!
The earth,
fleshy
as Rothschild's overpetted mistress.

As on an official holiday,
let the flags fly, in a delirium of gunfire,
you street lamps, raise up higher
the bloody carcasses of merchants.

Swearing —
begging —
knifing —
biting
each other's flesh —

The sky was red as the Marseillaise,
a final shudder and the sun set.

This is crazy.

There won't be a thing left.

Night will come,
chew you up,
gobble you down.

Look —
is the sky turning Judas again,

with its handful of treachery-stained stars?
Night came.
Mamai [4]
squatting down on the city to feast.
You can't break through this night,
black as Azef. [5]

I slouch in the corner of a bar,
getting wine on the tablecloth and on my soul,
and I see
in another corner the round eyes
of the madonna piercing my heart.
Why give this crowd in a bar
such radiance of painted cliché?
See?
Again they spit on the man from Golgotha
and choose Barabbas.

On purpose, perhaps,
my face is no newer
among this human garbage heap,
perhaps I'm your handsomest
son.

Give them
in their mildewed joy
a time of fast death,
so the children will grow,
boys becoming fathers,
girls — pregnant.

And let the new born
have the keen grizzle of the magi.
And in their turn

4   Mamai — Khan of the Golden Horde. He was defeated by Russians under Prince Dmitry
Donskoy at the Battle of Kulikovo, Sept. 8, 1380.
5   Yevno-Meyer Azef (1869–1918) dual agent and terrorist in employment of the Socialist
Revolutionary Party and the Tsarist police.

they'll baptize
their infants with the names of my poems.

I, praiser of England and machines,
perhaps am merely
the thirteenth apostle
in a common gospel.

And wherever
my dirty voice sounds,
then, minute by minute,
day and night,
maybe Jesus Christ
is sniffing the forget-me-nots of my soul.

4

Maria! Maria! Maria!
Let me in!
These streets drive me nuts!
No?
You'll wait
for my cheeks to collapse
and me to arrive,
squeezed,
stale,
toothless, muttering
that today
I'm "amazingly honest?"

Maria —
look,
my shoulders are sinking.

On the streets
men poke at the blubber of four-story craws,
little tiny eyes stick out,
worn out in forty years,
to sneer

at me gnawing —
again —
the stale crusts of old caresses.

Rain pours its tears down
on the sidewalk. A wino in the puddles
soaked, licks the dead street's cobbles,
but on his faded eyelashes,
yes! —
on the eyelashes on the grizzled icicles
tears pour down,
yes! —
from the lowered eyes of the waterspouts.

The rain poked and licked
everyone on foot,
but athlete after fat athlete gleamed by in carriages.
Stuffed down to the bone,
people cracked open,
and the grease dripping out,
plus the old chewed hamburger,
plus the gummy used bread,
flowed down in a cruddy river from the carriages.

Maria!
How can I jam a delicate word into those fat ears?
A bird
sings
for charity,
hungry — but he sings sweetly.
But I'm a man, Maria,
ordinary,
one that the tubercular night
coughed up onto Presnya's dirty hand.

Maria, do you want a man like me?
Let me in!
Or I'll have a fit and squash the doorbell.

Maria!
The pastures of the street are a jungle.
They've got their hands around my throat.

Open up!

It hurts!

Look, they're sticking
hatpins in my eyes!

I'm in.

Sweetheart,
never mind
the damp mountain of sweaty-bellied women
I carry on my oxy neck —
I lug
a million pure endless loves through my life
and a billion foul little likes.
Never mind
if again
in storms of betrayal
I kiss thousands of pretty faces
"Mayakovsky's girls!"
They're just the dynasty
that rules from a madman's heart.

Maria, come closer.

Naked and shameless
or trembling in fear,
give me your beautiful mouth.
My heart and I never live in May,
we're stuck
in a hundred Aprils.

Maria!
The poets trill sonnets to Diana,
but I
am pure flesh,

100% man.
I ask for your body,
simply, as Christians pray,
"Give us this day
our daily bread!"

Give, Maria!

Maria!
I'm scared I'll forget your name
like a poet's scared he'll forget
a word
born at night in pain,
equal to god.

I'll cherish and love your
body
as a soldier,
mutilated by war,
useless,
alone,
cherishes his one leg.

Maria —
You don't want to?
You're not going to?

Ha!

So again,
dim and dull,
I'll take my sobbed-on heart
and carry it
as a dog
carries
to the kennel
his paw a train crushed.

I give joy to the road with my heart's blood.
Blood sticks in flowers on my dusty shirt.

The sun, Salome, will dance a Herodiade
a thousand times
around the earth, the Baptist's head.

And when my time
has danced itself out,
a million spots of blood
will be spread along the path to my father's house.

I'll climb up, filthy,
(from sleeping in ditches)
and I'll stand
beside him and bend down
and shout in his ear,

"Listen, sir god,
aren't you bored
daubing your puffy eyes
in cloudy jelly every day?
Why don't we
rig up a merry-go-round
around the tree of good and evil?
You'll be omnipresent in every cupboard
and we'll set the tables with such wine
that even the Apostle Peter, the puritan,
will dance the kickapoo.
We'll put little Eves back in Eden.
Say the word —
and by tonight
I'll get you the best girls
from the boulevards —

how about that?

Why not?

You shake your head, Curly?
You frown, Santa?
You think
this thing

with wings
behind you knows what love is?

I'm an angel too, I was one —
I used to stare gently as a sugarlamb,
but I'm not going to give old mares
ornamental vases of tormented Sevres anymore.
Almighty, you made hands,
gave
everyone a head,
so why couldn't you manage
to let people, painlessly,
make love and make love and make love?

I thought you were Mr. Big once,
but you're a jerk, a dwarf.
Watch now,
I'm getting my knife
out from my boot.

You winged fools,
huddle in your heaven,
better start shaking your feathers!
I'll slit you, full of incense,
from here to Alaska!

Let me in!

I can't be stopped!
Wrong
or right,
I'm quite calm.
Look —
they've chopped up the stars,
the sky's dripping blood!

Hey you!
Heaven!
Get that hat off!
Here I come!

Vladimir Mayakovsky   29

Not a whisper.

The universe sleeps,
a paw on its huge ear
lousy with stars.

Bob Perelman & Kathy Lewis

A GOOD ATTITUDE TO HORSES

Hoofbeats pounded.
As if to sing:
   "Clip.
Clap.
   Clomp.
Clump."

Stripped by the wind,
shod in ice,
the street skidded.
The horse
fell on its ass,
clattering clumsily,
and suddenly
after every
idle, gaping fancy-pants
out to bell-bottom on Kuznetsky

crowded around,
laughter began
ringing, snickering:
"A horse has fallen!"
"Fallen — a horse!"
Chortled Kuznetsky Bridge.
I alone
would not fuse my voice with its howling.
I walk over

and see
the eyes of the horse . . .

the street convulsed,
turned over, and
flowed on in its fashion . . .
I walk over and see —
swelling drop after drop
roll down its cheek,
hide itself in the hair . . .

And some universal
vague animal
anguish
wells from me and
spills spreading a pool,
gurgling.

   "Horse, you mustn't.
   Horse, listen —
   you think you're more worthless than they?
   Ahh, my little one,
   we're all part horse,
   each is horse in his own way.

It may be,
   old-timer,
that you don't need a nurse —

or perhaps my sentiment
thought he
ludicrous —

anyway
the horse
gave a shrug,
got back on his feet,
whinnied, and
went on,
switching his tail.

A chestnut-haired child.
Cheering up, went
and stood in his stall.
And took the whole incident
like a young colt —
and to live seemed worthwhile,
and to labor,
worthy.

P. Lemke

VELEMIR KHLEBNIKOV 1885–1922

ME AND RUSSIA

Russia set thousands of thousands free.
That's nice! It will long be remembered.
But I took my shirt off
And each glassy skyscraper of my hair,
Every pore
In the city of my body
Hung rugs and red bunting out,
The he and she citizens
Of me,
Olgas and Igors,
Were crowded at my curls' thousand windows,
No one ordered them to,
They looked out of my skin, rejoicing in the sun.
The shirt-prison had fallen!
But all I did was take off my shirt
And give sun to My people!
Standing undressed by the sea,
Thus I gave the people their freedom,
The masses their sunburn.

Bob Perelman & Kathy Lewis

THE BURNING FIELD

Selections from "The Laundress"

We are sheepskin coats. Burrowing moles: born stupid.
On autumn evenings we roll in the hay
While the partying gentlemen
Adjust their armlets.
They dress — they preen,
No fly, watch it, better land on them.
They preen!
It's said they're dressed up even in the middle of the night,
A bit of winter, fresh and white.
They help themselves to a little darling's kisses.
Let's see, what do you look like naked?
Bowlegged,
A pot belly,
Forget the comb, there's nothing to comb!
Dance, naked gentlemen,
Dance!
Joy to the soul,
Joy to the soul!

We didn't live in palaces,
No one pampered us,
Unskilled workers.
We grew like puppies.
— Our knife,
— Feel that!
Nice knife!
Hey, everybody!
The knife's nice!
Get it,
Cut it
Into your brain.
And fall in love
With me, a dark girl
With me, a sweet girl!

The beauty, the long knife,
Fine in the gentleman's heart!
I'll feel you with the knife,
I am just a simple girl,
A laundress, an unskilled worker!
So fine! So fine!
The knife,

You women opened your wombs generously,
Sick and scabby,
To the kids of the rotted cities
And year after year you stole their lives.
Serving freedom incorruptibly
With your dirty, illegal fame,
You chopped off the aristocracy's branches
And stripped the wealth from their skeletons
Like a crowd of gulls
Around a whale's ribs.
You are the tribe of murderers
Who sent the rich sons
Off to bleed, in foreign countries, foreign lands,
As you exchanged love for money
And got fancy hats:
Hats with needles — the fallen capital,
Hats — eclipses of the sun —
With long black needles,
You burst out laughing in the street
When a good girl becomes a lush,
A flock of birds, you fly
Along the streets of the capital
From the hospitals, from the hospitals.
You who hacked the nobility's branches off,
Wear flea-market silks and furs
And snow white underwear,
And throw away the clothes, smelling of sweat
And semen,
The rot.

Velemir Khlebnikov   35

Hey little cuties,
For sale, bought,
Break into private homes,
Dance in front of the mirrors!
Foolish little heels!
Oh so sweet, so sweet!
The storm has covered up the tracks
Of the rich in flight.

Oh lips, my lips,
And purchases of the night!
Oh legs, my legs,
So fine!
Along the carpeted road
You pranced down the Nevsky
Like fleas,
Searching for gentlemen!
Oh wonderful little arms
Covered with white rash, white rash!
Why should I, a towheaded girl,
Balding . . .
Buy myself a wig,
Wear a scarlet belt,
I'll be luscious, luscious!
In the nightly flood of whores, virgins and sluts,
Where the fairytale rich man prowls like a beast,
A novice-degenerate tries for a prize
And the fool wins a firecracker.

We write with a knife!
We think with our bellies,
Scholars of black bread,
Soot, sweat,
Priests of desire.
We are the peddlers of heavenly black eyes,
Prodigal with the gold of fall leaves,
We're rich, our yellow money grows on trees,
We're the violinists of toothache,

In love with rheumatic pain,
In love with chills,
Dealers in laughter,
Soloists of famine,
Gluttons of last year,
Drunks of yesterday,
Lovers of the drainpipe,
Sages of breadcrusts,
Artists of soot,
Accountants of grackles, crows,
Rich men of the dawn —
We're all, we're all tsars today!
Amateurs of the stomach,
Prophets of dirty pants,
Ditchdiggers of last night's dinner —
Children of god.
The beggars are here.
We sleep through savage frost in burrows of snow.
We are night tsars on a convoy
Of palace filths.
Ours is the second capital city in manure.
Our palaces are in warm feces.
With our girls,
Mothers, fathers, and children
We sleep in hundred-year-old horse manure.
And you, tsars, sleep in glory.
We are the tsars on a line of sleds.
We'll live
Decaying,
Glowing,
And you have gone to sleep in glory.
If I don't dance through
The dance of tailor's scissors
I, the bloody jester,
Old atheist,
Am caught in the noose of my joke.

  Bob Perelman & Kathy Lewis

I WENT OUT . . .

I went out in the night,
Young and alone,
Covered to the ground
With stiff hair.
Lonely night
Stood around me.
I wanted friends.
I wanted myself.
I set the hair on fire,
Threw shreds of flame in a ring,
Set the fields and trees on fire —
That was more cheerful.
The fields of Khlebnikov burned.
"I" blazed in the darkness.
Now I'm leaving,
The hair is burning.
And, instead of I —
Stood — We!
Go, stern Varangian! [1]
Carry the law and honor.

Bob Perelman & Kathy Lewis

TO EVERYONE

There is revenge — writing.
My lament is ready,
And the snowstorm moves in flakes,
And the spirits rush without sound.
I am pierced by the spears
Of spiritual hunger,
Studded with the spears of empty mouths.

1 Varangians, Norsemen who, according to the chronicles, founded the first Russian dynasty of Rurik in the 9th century.

Your hunger asks to eat,
And in the pot of tasteful plagues
Your hunger asks for food — here's a free breast!
And afterwards I'll topple like Kuchum
Full of Yermak's spears. [1]
It's the hunger spears feel to pierce
That comes to weed a manuscript.
Oh, to recognize on a woman selling things on the street
Pearls from people I love!
Why did I throw those pages away?
Why was I a clumsy eccentric?
It wasn't the pranks of cold shepherds —
Executing burning manuscripts —
Everywhere the serrated kitchen knife,
The knifed faces of poems.
Everything these three years gave,
Counting songs to the nearest hundred,
The circle of familiar faces,
Everywhere, everywhere, the knifed bodies of tsareviches,
Everywhere, everywhere, goddamned Uglich! [2]

Bob Perelman & Kathy Lewis

ONCE MORE, ONCE MORE

Once more, once more
I am your
Star.
Woe to the sailor who mistakes
The angle between boat
And star:
He will smash against stones

1 Kuchum, last Khan of Siberian Khanate. Fought against Cossack troops of Yermak. Died ca. 1598.
2 Uglich, ancient Russian city where, in 1591, the heir to the throne Dmitry was murdered.

And hidden shoals.
And woe to you who mistook
The angle from your heart to me:
You will smash against stones
And the stones will laugh
Down on you,
As you laughed
Down at me.

Bob Perelman & Kathy Lewis

TRUMPET, SHOUT, CARRY!

You who rest your belly on a pair of fat pilings,
Who stagger out of a Soviet dining hall,
Do you realize that this whole land
Could become one big mortuary?
I realize you're as thick-skinned about the ears as the mighty buffalo
And only a stick can draw any response from you,
But will you really trot away from Hunger Week
When the claw of death
Hangs over the whole land?
There'll be corpses, male and female, and corpselings
Staring at the starry sky,
While you go to buy
A big hunk of white bread for after dinner.
You think hunger is a pesky fly
Easily brushed away,
But listen — there's a drought on the Volga,
One very good reason for giving, not taking.
Carry big loaves
To the Hunger Week collections:
Give some food away,
Save those who are turning gray!
The Volga was always your wet-nurse,
Now she's almost in the grave.

The disaster can get terribly worse —
Shout and shout, put the trumpet to your lips!

Bob Perelman & Kathy Lewis

THE ONE BOOK

I have seen the black Vedas,
The Koran, The Gospels,
And the books of the Mongols
In silken boards
(The Mongols themselves being dust
Of the steppes and odorous
Manure shaped each dawn
By Kalmyk women)
Start a bonfire
And lay themselves on top.
White widows hiding in the smoke,
Hastening the coming
Of The One Book,
Whose pages are big seas,
Fluttering with wings of a blue butterfly,
And there is a silk thread to mark
Where the reader has stopped.
Great rivers in one blue current:
The Volga where Razin[1] is sung at night,
The yellow Nile where they worship the sun,
The Yangtse-Kiang with its thick wash of people,
And you, Mississippi, where Yankees wear
The starry sky for pants,
And the Ganges where people are dark mental trees,
And the Danube where white people,
White in white shirts, stand over the water,

---

1 Stenka Razin, Don Cossack who led a peasant revolt in 1670. A popular hero of Russian
folklore. Executed 1671.

Velemir Khlebnikov 41

116166

And the Zambezi where people are blacker than boots,
And the stormy Ob where god is flogged
And made to stand in the corner
When he eats something rich,
And the Thames where it's boring.
The family of man reads the book,
And on the cover, the author's name,
My name, baby blue letters.
But you read carelessly,
Pay attention,
You're too distracted, you look as if you're lazy,
As if the mountain chains and big seas
Were this catechism's lessons.
Soon, soon, you'll be reading
This one book.
On these pages a whale leaps
And an eagle, skirting the edge of the page,
Lands on seawaves, the breasts of the seas,
Resting on the sea-eagle's bed.

Bob Perelman & Kathy Lewis

IRANIAN SONG

Down along the Iran River,
By its green streams,
By its deep pilings,
Near the sweet water,
Two eccentrics walk
And shoot at pike.
They aim between the eyes,
Stop, darling don't!
They walk, they chitchat.
I'm sure I remember right.
They boil up fish soup.
"What a crummy life!"

42   Velemir Khlebnikov

An airplane up in the sky,
The cloud's daredevil pal;
But where's the flying tablecloth,
The airplane's wife?
Late, by some chance,
Sunk in jail?
I believe fairytales in advance:
What was fairytale will be fact,
But when that happens
My flesh will be dust.
And when the cheering crowds
Are carrying their banners, wholesale,
I'll awake, trampled into the dirt,
Pining, a dusty skull.
Or perhaps I should throw my rights
Into the stove, a gift for the future?
Hey, meadow grass, blacken!
Turn to stone forever, river!

Bob Perelman & Kathy Lewis

HEY . . . Y! UH . . . HM! . . .

Hey . . . y! Uh . . . hm!, covered with sweat,
He drives the gray-horned ox,
And the plow dives like an otter into a muddy lair,
The plow's teeth have chewed the spring pudding up.
The bull was proud of the fat folds of his neck,
And took his horns from the new moon.
Frogs were at prayer, making bubbles,
A fat priest sat in front,
Gold goggle eyes,
And read from the book of weather.
Turtles stretched their necks, surprised.
A machinegun of spring odors and winds
Hit frowning foreheads and nostrils,

A quick ta-ta-ta.
Flowers using pollen
Fought wars of odor,
The sweetest wins.
And the machinegun of spring odors,
The evening like dusk's high priest,
Gave instructions for a different battle.
Flowers fought wars of odor,
Fragrant bullets were flying,
The frogs' song was strong and harmonious
Honoring clear weather.
People, learn of a new war
Where shots are sweet air,
Trenches, wedding flowers,
The honeyed sky gives the command to fire.
And liturgical bubbles
Rose, as the prayerbooks
Of the frogs
Worshipping quiet weather.

Bob Perelman & Kathy Lewis

LONELY MASQUERADER

And while the song and tears of Akhmatova
Streamed over Tsarskoye Selo,
I unwound the skein of the enchantress
And dragged myself like a drowsy corpse around the desert
Where improbability was dying;
Tired of masquerading,
I stepped into the gap.
Meanwhile, a bull with a curly brow
In dark caves, underground, gnawed and feasted on people
In the smoke of immodest threats.
And wrapped in the will of the moon
Like a sleepy wanderer in his cloak,

I leapt from cliff to cliff
Above abysses.
I went along blind, while
The wind of freedom pushed me
And beat me with slanting rain.
And I ripped the bull's head from his strong sinews and bones
And put it near the wall.
Like truth's crusader I brandished it over the world:
Look, here it is!
Here is the curly brow, for which the masses once burned!
And with horror
I understood that no one saw me,
That one must sow the eyes,
That a sower of eyes must keep moving.

Bob Perelman & Kathy Lewis

NIKOLAY KLYUEV   1887–1937

OCTOBER, A COPPER-CRAWED COCK

October, a copper-crawed cock,
Crows in the wind's forest.
In these drifts of fallen leaves
I'll lay an egg of snow.

The forest gapes with holes
From a rooster's beak. Pigeon droppings
Swirl in a drafty chicken coop of clouds.
Trouble not, they whisper, the Spirit of God.

Once a year it is given to you
To lay your egg in the snow's new road.
In a day the woman river
Wove a sky-blue strip of blanket.

Near are cow weddings, horse scratchings,
The leather-cured holiday of Assumption,
And a cloudy wagon train limps
To a starry smithy for reshoeing.

  John Glad

46

CAN I TELL YOU MY LOVE WITH A PORTRAIT

Inscription on a portrait
dedicated to Nikolay Ilich Arkhipov

Can I tell you my love with a portrait,
You unknown, yet mine as my blood?
Already the carrots have blushed,
And cods bask in brine.

The sweet lard of beef kidneys
Snaps gopher-like in candles
And beyond the double pane
A mosquito savors the widow's feast.

The sled dreams that winter
Is spinning the rabbit-down snow . . .
Beyond the window, darkness has flung down
The mourner's burden of rags.

Calico lisps at half-blind brocade:
"What Lenten trash has the poet
Scattered about the portrait?
How bitter the wax of his lines!

His letters are hunchbacked
Like old beggar women . . ."
A dead man's pillow
Longs for a loving hand.

Harmonies roil like drunken bees.
I would marry them to love
When carrots bleed
And tubs cry brine.

John Glad

YOU TWIST YOUR DEATH IN NOOSES

You twist your death in nooses
And hone swords in the night.
I search, but find among you
No thirst for dawn.

You've crossed land and water,
flung ships at the constellations,
And ignored only me — the soul of the world —
As pitiful trash.

I am clothed in sackcloth,
Shoed in bast,
But bliss and happiness
Stream from my violated eyes.

You mix ashes in my bread,
Spill bitter poison in my wine,
But I am bright, wise, unknown
Like the sky.

A free worker
In this field of life and labor,
How can I not pluck you out
Like a worthless thorn — forever?

John Glad

THE SKY LIES BLUE — LIKE A SEA

The sky lies blue — like a sea.
Basked in by a cloudy whale.
Beyond the window drizzle
The dress beads of dampness.

The yard is an owl wing —
eyey, ornate.
This restaurant kitchen is no village,
Its obscenities aren't magpie calls.

48   Nikolay Klyuev

In the town as in dream
People shrink into plant lice,
Huts swell into Mountains.
But I dream of White Sea skies,

The bustle of gulls, the splash of an oar,
The free trade of a hunter.
On the·island of Solovetsk
The northern dawn dies;

A water spirit weaves
A woolen tow of wave.
While I boil beef
For the draymen's guild.

The celestial whale rolls its tail
Toward the warmth, the spring floods,
And I am eaten away at by salt,
Like a net abandoned on the shoal.

No fisherman will come for it,
Plodding through the knee-deep foam . . .
Dusk keeps the watch, searching
Like a homeless tramp for a bed.

John Glad

A CONVERSATIONAL MELODY, A GOOD VERSE

"To be sung in the evening interlude
with domra or lute."

From "Otpusk" — the secret scroll
of the Olonetsk hermit folk narrators

On the birthday of our most Pure Savior,
During the life of the wise Planida [1]
And on the assumption of the old man of Poddubnoy,

1 Pagan goddess of fate.

It was not a mountain that bent to the ground,
But the bald waters that surged up in stone.
In the land where the sun sleeps
On a felt mat behind a scarlet curtain,
Where the hunchbacked night boils her herbs,
Blackens her braids with soot
And fires her cauldron with fallen trees,
There was born the iron kingdom
Of Wilhelm,[2] the heathen tsar.
He is strong — this heathen.
His people believe in the Luther-god.
They make no cross on themselves,
Observe not the Great Fast,
Decorate no branch on Semik-Day,[3]
Do not steam themselves in the bath hut,
Washing off the unclean spirit.
And afterwards they do not cry out to the goddess Udilyona:
"Udilyona, mother of the rye,
Comb out your gold hair from the straw
And plunge each ear in mead and molasses . . ."

It is no hawk shrieking beyond the gully,
Calling its young to the kill;
It is no forest lynx meowing into the night,
Full from warm blood;
It is an evil tongue that preaches,
The iron tsar spewing molten words:
"Head, head of mine, clever head,
Whom can I bind in iron?
I have cast into irons the land and the waters,
Enslaved fire and hissing steam,
Shackled the wind and the light.
Today I will trap the bright Moon and Sun
Like partridges in a snare.

2 Wilhelm II (1859–1941), last German emperor (1888–1918), abdicated.
3 Pagan holiday.

50   Nikolay Klyuev

The Moon will preen his feathers on the prison fence
Like a cock on a pole,
His craw beaming into stone holes
As he keeps the watch unsleepingly.
For his haughtiness and disobedience
I will strip off the Sun's red boots,
Shear his yellow hair and shaggy moustache
And have the wool workers beat them into felt.
That bulging gold piece he has bound to his neck
Will dangle from my dog's collar.
And I'll strap him — red and haughty —
To a scabby country woman on the stove's warm shelf.
We'll see how the falcon likes bedding with a crow.

But what's salt pork without wine?
What I do I'll do to the end:
Harvest the rye from the fields of Chernigov,
Rake off profits from the drunks, dispensing
Mother-Volga in bottles.
I'll knock off the iron hat
From the great hill of Stenka Razin.
And from Moscow — that corpulent boyarinya —
I'll strip her sable five-stitched gown,
Plait from her braids a gold-threaded headdress
And rip the heavy rings from her pudgy fingers.
I'll grind up the sacred relics of Makavey in an iron mortar
And with its sifted dust whitewash the stoves.
And from the beards of Moscow priests
I'll fashion gleaming black brooms!"

*　*　*

It is not the flower of the lungwort
Drunk with dream and the honeyed dew of evening,
It is not that cemetery dweller, the cross,
Peering like a pillarite into the unknown,
It is Mother Planida in this our baptized Russia
Drowsing from the labors of her cell.

Drowse, dream, daydream
Of blessed Peter and the virgin Piatenka.
"Mother Planida, sleep no more
Beneath that twenty-stone skull cap,
For with you you have lulled Mother Russia to sleep.
Call out, warn her of the enemy.
Do not take Vihor, the whirlwind, as a messenger,
Nor the Sutyomka's, black-braided sisters of twilight,
Nor Moroz[4] nor the rumbling Zoy.[5]

Better than Vihor's wild cossack dance and whistling
Is the tender roll of the balalaika.
The Sutyomka's have no time. At God's command
They sew a headdress for Zarya.[6]
They must not confuse pearls with fish eyes,
But decorate her forehead with a basket stitch.
Moroz's skis are rough;
Behind him the snow crusts and drifts.
His deer-skin boots and coat have the fur turned inward;
From running his sweat would flow heavy
Through the gulleys and lowlands,
Splashing like a swollen river in spring.
Don't take the bell ringer Zoy either.
Without him the forest thicket would be desolate
As a monastery without a bell.
Zoy hangs the cuckoo's call, the forest's clatter
Like rattles on the branches.
In the evening, a sweet-voiced monk,
He reads his prayer book behind the pines . . .
Take into your fingers, Mother Planida,
The golden keys of paradise.
Awake, unlock the blue, indivisible stone[7]
And free from its rock prison the world's best herald:

4 Frost.
5 God of insect hums and ringing air.
6 Dawn.
7 Symbol of the Trinity.

The blessed bird, the sparkling Paskaraga."[8]
From these apostolic words Planida shuddered
Like a grouse in the swamp.
She threw back her reckless head,
Casting her skull cap beyond the great Onega.
The cap swelled into a mountain
Overgrown with the black firs of its edging.
Its cord became the Soroga River . . .

* * *

Oh you baptized
Learned folk!
Keep the women off the street,
The kids on the bench.
Let the biddies in bed
Talk off their heads.
But listen, listen
To the end of my song.
Czar David, help me,
Ivan the Baptist,
Give words to my fable,
Melodies to my finger joints.
And may the stingiest of you
Give a ruble for beer! . . .

For a thousand years Makosha Marok[9]
Has been stealing the tracks of man,
Setting snares behind the pines,
Trapping human souls.
For a thousand years Lembey[10] has ruled the thickets,
Gathering tribute from creation:
From the rabbit — fur, tawny down from the eagle-owl,
Handfuls of silver rubles from the aspen tree.

8 Bird of Paradise.
9 Pagan god of deceit and illusion.
10 Unclean forest spirit to whom are subject animals, monsters, and the souls of children cursed by their parents.

But for a thousand winters and springs
No one has listened to the song of Paskaraga!
The prophetic Planida unfolded
The indivisible stone — like a triptych,
And the angelic bird began to sing,
Calling out to Russia of adversity.

Its first cry was headier than a girl's braids.
The Znobyanik blossom heard and grew white
As the cheeks of a maiden painted
On bed sheets together with her warrior lover:
A prophetic sign there would be many widows in Russia.

Its second call was like the crack of sea ice,
The steel whistle of many sabres.
It was like Yarost[11] puffing up his cheeks
And blowing on the blood in the furnace of his smithy,
Like Death the treasure hunter
Ripping souls from the fallen with a pick axe.

The third cry was like the peal of water in the baptismal fount
When the Spirit descends upon the firstborn
Of a father of twenty years and a mother of seventeen.
From his warm shelf above the stove
The old man who is called A Hundred Tribes in One
Glowered at the armies of the enemy and muttered:
"Like a louse under the belt
This filth must be steamed out in the bathhouse."
He scooped up the Don, the Onega, the Kama
And splashed the three rivers from his dipper
Over the stove's live coals.
The Ugrian shelves hissed,
The Ural's granites billowed steam,
The Valdai Hills sharpened the teeth of their comb.
And like young firs, like cliffs above the sea
A hundred tribes grew up from under the stones . . .

* * *

11 Rage.

54 Nikolay Klyuev

A story's not a woman's spindle;
An end is no beginning.
As for "Where from?" and "What then?"
Ask Kuva — the red raven.
He traded nests with Thunder
To lay an egg — a masculine lot.

John Glad

MOTHER SABBATH

To Nikolay Ilich Arkhipov who is my last joy

The angel of simple human affairs
Flitted into my hut like a lark.
The stove and bench smiled,
The rain barrel honked,
And a fly mumbled in darkness at the cat:
"Sir, wash the black from behind your ear."

The angel of simple human affairs
Crowned with a wreath
The old women behind the spinning wheel,
Anointed the door frames,
Spilled beads and red cinnabar into crocks
And passed his staff to the purse with a whisper:
"Thou shalt be filled with harmonies in paradise."

The angel of simple human affairs
Is blue at dusk, white at dawn.
He lit a candle before a round loaf,
Wove a cornflower into the beard of twilight
And strummed cricket-like from the hearth:
"Peace to you, sown field and hunchback barn,
Peace to the hearth where nets are always rich
With sunfish of the years!"

Impassive are the meadows of silence —
The pasture of secrets and a sheepskin moon.
There the skies are warm as a bunk,
Sheep are pancakes and oxen — round loaves;
Flocks of food are led by the hearth broom,
And a stove's forehead is your father's home.

The angel of simple human affairs
Bestowed upon bread fat and measure.

Inky judges loathe verse
Where roosters shriek in the commas,
Cows stray knee-deep through heavy dashes,
And lines peer with big eyes like foxes from a den.
What difference does it make if your father's purse
Was a meadow where Egory played a reed pipe?
Elijah and Medost, Frol and Pantelemon,[1]
The sacred synod of a peasant hut,
Water from their palms
A meadowed family of bays, chestnuts, and roans.

What difference does it make
If evening shouted down a rain barrel,
Calling for the sun?
She won't lead out her ginger ducklings
Till the oven prong falls asleep against the stove.
The bench will spread mats for its mistress
And blacken her braids with darkness's ebony stain.

The angel of simple human affairs
Ordered the singing mash to boil.

The hut drowses like an old grouse
In a pine hollow. With a log paw
The heather spirit presses to its breast
The cross of the Solovetsk Islands,
Stronger than any gate.
A heart and cross are a mark for oblivion . . .

1 Peasant names.

The midwife's fingers of Ivan Kalita[2]
Rage at death, embroider gossip,
Erect Moscow in thickets of haystacks . . .

Do you hear, brothers, a muffled clamor —
The paternal calls of icons behind the stove?
The steeds of Elijah, the garment of Odigitria,
The wings of Sophia, the trampling of the gates,
Groom and Bride, an interceding Queen —[3]
All these open their lips in an ear of grain!

The angel of simple human affairs
Foamed in harvest from the breast of the earth.

The womb of a barn, the small of a haystack's back:
Forefathers of memories, fathers of visions.
The threshing rod gulps from grain breasts
Sweet milk — whiter than new snow —
And plunges teeth through violated flesh:
The skull of a sheaf, the banquet hall of God.
The millstone caresses the grain as a peasant lad his wife:
Its stone navel grinds into flour
The sickle's sigh, the anguish of the harvest feast
While the crop's bosom ferments deep in a wooden tub.

The midwife fingers of Ivan Kalita
Set sieve traps for ground grain.
The catch sours in brilliant pots:
In an agate chalice lie the eyes of many worlds,
A crucified swan and above it a rose . . .
Fire proffers a bride-price
And in ringing logs embryos of souls
Scatter gold and pearls.

2 Ivan I. Despotic tsar (1328–40) who played a large role in the establishment of Muscovy
as a power.
3 Traditional scenes depicted on icons. Odigitria is the name used for Mary in her role of
guidance; Sophia, the symbol of wisdom, is often depicted with wings; the "trampling of the
gates" refers to a visit to Hell by Christ in which the gates of Hell are ripped from their
hinges.

Nikolay Klyuev   57

Fragrant and tanned,
A loaf enters the chambers of warmth.

Myriads of seraphims hover above the stove,
Hearken to a sacred rite: the scrubbing
Of the dough tub. Crumbs decorate the scouring pad
Like wedding flowers in the maid-of-honor's hair.
The cricket game of interludes sings fairy tales,
Amazing the gossip fly, the opportunist cat.

The angel of simple human affairs
Breathed warmth into thinking beasts.

An aging ram, a prophet-cock,
The shaggy burdock guard of empty lots
Promise rain, swing their beards . . .
A cloud drapes its kerchief over the fields
And offers drink to a garden radish,
Quickening whiteness and strength.
The cloud is a sign — of early warmth,
Of thick green leaves, of cow weddings
And the crackling pancake of a summer sun.
Having spilled the dough of tillage into pots,
The nurse of the fields became a drake.

The hut peers keenly through the honeyed rain,
Pecking eagle-like at the blue with a gargoyled roof.
She begs fate to cover her ribbed joists
With finely feathered timber.
She knows that gray corners will spread
Forty wings from the darkness to aid her in flight.
For the housewarming, Eleon has plunged
Through the window's seas his cedar face,
The bast sandal of Exodus, the Sabbath of the Living . . .

A cloth is spread for golden bowls,
Bread is broken for winged guests.
Sergunka waits on Pud, Avdey on Vasiatka.
Our Sabbath is bluer than the lakes!

The angel of simple human affairs
Unfolded his wings in Vasiatka's dance.
The wedding dance is the flight of a ship
To agate and moon light, to Christ's land.[4]

The black agate of life's sea
Splashes verse from raging heels.
Herds of unicorns — spiritual poems —
Can't be counted at milking time;
The snares of grappling words
Catch but tracks, glints of horns.
Spiritual poems give suck
Only to light-foot castrati.
Melhisador and John the Baptist
Guard a caravan of singing horns.

The Father is sweet, but sweeter yet is the Spirit.
A shepherd, the hawk of a woman's brood,
Rips with claws of passion a heron,
The mother for whom he lusts.
His beak beats at her liver, her bloodied womb,
That the poet might be born.
She thinks this hawk's catch in the cradle
Is a sheaf of corn flowers.
The blossoms are guarded by a six-headed steed
Whose mane streams in sounding strings,
Whose eyes are songs.

This turquoise sheaf, this purse of smiles
Swaddles April in chirps and caws,
Clings to the young wife: "Tonight
An oak will burst into flame on the stove.
Rage that the combs of your breasts
Might breed wasps and stinging bees.
. Curly Fedot, the humming tree,
    Will give them resin and burning honey!"

4 Ecstatic prayer meetings of the Khlyst sect during which the souls of the dancers are
carried to heaven by the ship of Christ.

Nikolay Klyuev 59

For two hundred and seventy days the hive
Fosters swarms of honeyed lights . . .
Life the beekeeper taps at the hive's entrance:
Spots of melted earth warm the flowers!
Hollowness sickens the cradles' hive;
In each, beauty hums like a bee.
Poppy lips and mica eyes —
A female kingdom, My turn has come.

Rejoice, brothers, for I am pregnant
From kisses and horse testicles!
A scarlet spouse, the gelding of song
Tramples a meadow of joints and buttocks.
He gnaws at my members as if they were his stall
And digs his hoof into the obsessed belly of my life.
A baby born is a herd of colts
With music in their withers and measure in their neigh.

The angel of simple human affairs
Longed to shepherd the hurricane drove.

Glory to the loaf, praise to the stove
For baking the Blue Sabbath,
For breeding an elk with cymbals for horns,
For cradling the shores of the soul.

Know, friends, that a merchant
Rides a white eagle to the animal land!
He brings chests packed with miracles,
Cages of future, bales of glory!
The hut-dock blooms with hope,
The cat meows magically at the milking pan,
And grain fledglings in a mouse hole
Dream of the sowing's bright day.

If only the gray mouse who guards the door
Is frightened away by the squeak of March skies,
The grain will have guests: a beetle,
A ray of light and her baby — a water droplet.
The piebald heap will weave the sun's heat

And drive out into the stubble a barley navel.
See, like a snipe lover the ear of grain
Is fed precious bread by Christ's violet face.

The angel of simple human affairs
Flamed crimson in a bookish twilight.

Brothers, hearken with love
To the Earth's Sabbath:
Only in the bosom of the hut
Will you find peace.

But the loaf's nipples
Are hunters of semi-precious eider ducks.
The raging spring pelican of thought
Lays eggs near the pot's trivet . . .

Behind the stove are the bright skies
Of Kitezh,[5] Mamelf and Arin
Where a goat with a fleece of words
Rubs against a grandmother's skirt.

There is an icon of Moses' shrub,
A cup of rye depth;
Brother in light,
Eat, drink
The body and blood of Russia!

The Lord of the threshing floor,
The keeper of the grain
Licks the earth's sides
As an elk cow her calf.
This swarthy God of the hut[6]
Waters the ploughed fields with his spit.

Before his Oneness
I am drunk from the sheepbarn's wine

5 A legendary idyllic city which God supposedly made invisible to evil persons by covering
it with his hand.
6 Icons normally darken from the candles burning beneath them.

And spill my verse
As a catfish its milky sperm.

I am echoed
By a noisy catch
Of pike and sturgeon.
And enchanted words.

The depths of the Zaonezhye[7]
Cast pearly gifts:
Mental mirages,
Gardens of sound.

Paleostrov, Vyga,
Kizhi, Solovki[8]
Splash over my book
Dippers of rainbow.

I hear the psalmic grief
Of church bells and gull cries.
My polar face
Burns above the sea.

The angel of simple human affairs
Flitted into my heart like a lark.
He found its chambers clean as a tablecloth.
Marigolds blossom everywhere.
White-toothed labor mends a miner's sack
For ingots of the mind.
The girl conscience pokes at the needle's eye
The thread of shame, the darkness of eyelashes . . .
The heavenly weaver who shook our hearts
Is palamino at noon, blue-eyed toward evening.
He's woven a backwater where melodic whales
Drowse in expectation of the storm's beauty . . .
This is the Sabbath at the death bier,
This is the Sabbath after the cross . . .

7 The Trans-Onega region in the far North of Russia where Kliuev lived.
8 Places in northern Russia.

Russia's lips swell from brown blood;
The stone has been cast back,
Night has fallen on the universe
And a sobbing Peter stands at the gates . . .

From birch lip
We render aromas
To smear the water shoots
Of Mary's hut.

We'll whiten towels with grave
And in a bluebird dawn
Take alabaster
To a Christ of rye.

Your face of wheat
Sleeps in cornflower foam . . .
Shirts smell
Of Veronica's sweaty shawl.

The pancake orchard is fragrant . . .
We step through time
To taste in the new Cana
The fire-fingered wine.

The pigeon of dream
Coos at cave gates,
And on a rock, Mother Sabbath
Has finished weaving
Her blue flax.

   John Glad

SERGEY YESENIN 1895–1925

WINDS, WINDS, WINDS

Winds, winds, winds,
Wrap all my life in your flying snows.
I want to be the golden lad I was
Or a flower of the meadow lands.

I want to die for everyone and myself,
While the herdsman pipes his flock.
My ears are filled with starbells
By the white of snow and the dark.

The unclouded trilling of it is good, good,
As it drowns suffering in the blizzard.
I'd stand on one leg if I could
Like a tree by the wayside.

And neighboring bushes would embrace me
And snorting horses pass me by.
The moon's hands reach down to me
And hoist my sadness to the sky.

Nigel Stott

64

FOR MY SISTER SHURA

The world is full of cats,
More than we could ever count.
In my dream I can smell the sweet peas,
In the sky a pale star sounds.

Whether walking, feverish or half asleep,
All I recall from those far-off days
Is a kitten purring on the stove
Eyeing me unconcernedly.

I was still a kid at the time,
But while granny hummed he leapt,
Pounced like a tiger cub
Onto the ball she dropped.

It's all over now. First granny died,
And a few years after that
They turned the cat into
Headgear for granddad.

Nigel Stott

FIELD UPON FIELD UPON FIELD

Field upon field upon field,
The provinces' dead hand.
Yesterday lights on my heart,
Within — bright Russia stands.

The miles come whistling
Off my horse's hooves like birds
And the sun is casting
Handfuls of rain on my head.

O land of savage flood
And gentle springtime pressures.
For schooling all I had
Was dawn and the stars.

Sergey Yesenin 65

And the winds for me were a bible
To read in and to muse,
While by my side Isaiah,
Tended his golden cows.

Nigel Stott

THE GOLDEN BIRCH GROVE'S

The golden birch grove's
Happy tongue is still,
And cranes flying sadly past
Seem not concerned at all.

No wonder. We're all travelers here,
Passing through, visiting, leaving home again.
The hemp field and the broad-faced moon
Over the pond dream of those who have gone.

On the bare plain I stand alone,
And the wind carries the cranes far off.
Memories of my happy youth flood back
Yet I have no regrets for what is past:

Neither the years of idle dissipation,
Nor the lilac blossoming of my soul.
In the garden a bonfire is burning
Of rowan twigs which warms no one at all.

Rowan berries won't catch fire,
Nor will the grass fade and die.
As the tree gently shed its leaves
So I shed my sad words.

And should time and the wind
Rake them together in a useless pile,
Just say that the golden grove's
Sweet tongue is still.

Nigel Stott

66   Sergey Yesenin

I REGRET NOTHING, . . .

I regret nothing, neither do I complain nor weep.
All will pass, like mist from white apple trees.
The gold of fading tightens its grip —
I shall never be young again.

My heart grows chill within.
It will never beat as before.
The birch print of the countryside
Will tempt me out barefoot no more.

Vagrant spirit, less and less
Do you stir the flame of my lips.
Oh, the lost freshness of my youth,
Storminess of eye, passion welling up.

Oh my life, do my desires grow narrower,
Or was it all a dream?
It's as though, in the vibrant spring early hours,
I had passed by on my rose-colored steed.

We are all, all of us, mortal.
The copper drains silently from maple leaves.
May you be blessed for evermore
That you put forth buds, then died.

Nigel Stott

MYSTERIOUS, ANCIENT WORLD OF MINE

Mysterious, ancient world of mine,
Like the wind your fury has abated.
Stone macadam hands entwine
The village's throat.

Horror hurtles through the white
Of snow, braying like a startled beast.
I greet my gray, unlovely death.
I go out to meet it.

Sergey Yesenin 67

Town, town! In the grim struggle,
Wretches, you called us, scum of the earth.
The field shivers in ox-eyed desolation.
Telegraph poles stick in its throat.

The devil's neck is sinewy.
The iron track is no great burden
For him to bear. What does it matter anyway.
It's not the first time we've lost everything.

Let the heart's anguish linger on.
Here is a song of the rights of beasts.
Thus it is when the wolf is hunted down,
When the hunt has him in its vice-like grip.

The animal crouches low. A gun
Flashes in the undergrowth. Suddenly
Something leaps — fangs
Savage the two-legged enemy.

Beloved beast, I hail you!
Yours is no meek surrender to the knife.
Like you, I'm everywhere pursued.
I walk among enemies of iron.

Like you, I'm ever on the alert.
And even as the arrogant horn resounds,
I make one last, deadly leap.
And my enemy's blood stains the ground.

And though I sink back then through whiteness,
Though I dig my own snowy grave,
In the other world, a song of vengeance
Will be sung to mark my death.

Nigel Stott

68 Sergey Yesenin

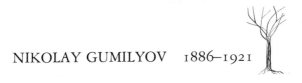

NIKOLAY GUMILYOV 1886–1921

THE STREETCAR THAT LOST ITS WAY

While walking down a strange street
I suddenly heard the cawing of crows,
Distant thunder, and the tones of a lute —
Here came a streetcar flying past.

How I managed to leap to its step
Is beyond me — even in the bright
Daylight it spewed behind itself
In the atmosphere a trail of fire.

It moved forth like a dark, winged storm,
This streetcar losing itself among
The depths of time — "Conductor, stop!
Conductor, stop this car at once!"

Too late. By now we had already
Rounded the wall, crossed through a grove
Of palms, and thundered across three bridges
Over the Neva, the Nile, the Seine.

Then, his face flashing by outside,
An old bum peered in through the window —
He was, of course, the one who died
In Beirut just a year ago.

69

Where is this? Answering, my heart
Beats listlessly yet anxiously:
"Is this the station where you buy
Your way to the India of the Soul?"

A billboard: drawn in blood, the letters
"Grocer's"; here, I know, instead
Of cabbages and rutabagas
One may purchase lifeless heads.

And then the executioner,
In red shirt, with face like an udder,
Chopped off my head: it lay with others
In this slimy box, just at the bottom.

Down the alley, a wooden fence,
A house with three windows, and a gray lawn.
"Conductor, stop the car at once!
Conductor, stop the streetcar!"

Mashenka, here you lived and sang,
Wove rugs for me, whom you would wed.
Where is your body, the voice that sang?
Is it possible you are dead?

How you wept inside your room,
While I, with powder in my hair,
Went off to present myself to the Empress,
And never beheld you again.

Now I see it all: Our freedom
Is just a small light breaking through
From another world: people and shadows
Loiter by the gate to the planets' zoo.

A lush, familiar wind begins
To blow, and beyond the bridge, the hand
Of a rider in a glove of iron
And two horse's hooves come flying on.

The great stronghold of Orthodoxy,
St. Isaac's dome, commands the sky.

70 Nikolay Gumilyov

A prayer of intercession for Mashenka,
Her health; a requiem for me.

But still my heart is always shadowed;
It's hard to breathe; it hurts to live.
Mashenka, I never thought that one could
Have such love, or feel such grief.

   Denis Johnson & Kathy Lewis

CHILDHOOD

As a child I loved
Honeysmelling meadows,
Withered grasses, thickets,
Ox horns in the grass.

Every dusty roadside shrub
Shouted: "It's a joke,
Dance around me,
And you'll see who I am!"

The autumn wind unruly,
Roaring past, broke off our game —
My heart beat more ecstatically,
I believed I would die

Not alone, but with friends,
With my coltsfoot and burdock;
Soon I guessed what lay
There behind the distant skies.

That's why I relish stormy
Military pastimes, for
Human blood is no holier
Than the emerald juice of grasses.

   Joseph Kiegel

FIRST CANZONE

I've sailed several of the world's oceans,
Ancient, jovial and foaming,
And driven caravans on the steppes
How many incomparable days and nights . . .

How we laughed in the old days
With my footloose Muse . . .
Rhymes, like birds, flew together then.
I don't dare remember how many.

And only this love is left me, a stringed
Harp, its appeal like fine needles,
My soul run through with the deep
Blue lights of paradise.

You alone are left me. In my waking hours,
Seeing the midnight sun, you're the reason
I live on this earth
And make my earthly case.

You're my uneasy lot —
I'm that Jerusalem pilgrim
Who must speak of you
In the tongues of seraphim.

Mary Jane White

MOON AT SEA

The moon has already left the cliffs
For the transparent sea, full of gold,
Where my friends drink in a small,
Sharp-nosed boat, without hurrying
The fieriest wine.

Look, how the light clouds pass
Through the moon's post, that reflection.

72   Nikolay Gumilyov

One of us considers slowly that
It is a train of Chinese concubines.

Some believe — it leads to the groves
Of Eden to which the devout retire;
But three of us
Wager it is a caravan of swans.

Mary Jane White

FRAGMENTS 1920–1921

1

I often think of my old age,
Of wisdom and of rest.

2

Even now I stand in some other garden
Among bloody roses and humid lilies.
Virgil tells me in hexameter
About the superior joys of earth.

3

The peal of bells
And green maples,
And bats.
And Shakespere and Ovid
For those who listened to them,
For those who see them —
That's why everything under the sun
Is sad for poetry.

4

I'm glad it's gone — that smoke from the samovar
Which clouded my mind twenty years ago
Like the bloody fog in the eyes of a man enraged
And reaching for his knife;
Glad the bodies of women don't excite me,

Nikolay Gumilyov 73

Glad the glory of women doesn't hurt me,
Glad I don't see uplifted hands in branches
Or hear sighs in the rustling grass.

The highest house was built by God Himself
On the border of his light realm
With the leave of Lord-Lucifer . . .

5

That tragicomedy — we called "Man" —
Was the twentieth ludicrous and ghastly century,
Ghastly since, in the full color of his powers,
He looked on the sky as if he were looking
Into his grave, and ludicrous because
He thought to approach the unattainable approaches;
It was an age of heroic hopes and accomplishments . . . .

Mary Jane White

THE PORCELAIN PAVILION

Risen from the artificial lake,
The jasper bridge
Curved like a tiger's spine
Moves our direction.

And in that pavilion several
Friends in light clothing
Drink mulled wine
From cups painted with dragons.

Now conversing pleasantly,
Or jotting out their poems,
Cocking their yellow caps,
Rolling up their sleeves.

It's clear in the clean lake —
The concave bridge like a jasper moon
With several friends of the cup
Turned upside down.

Mary Jane White

PRE-MEMORY

So this is all of life! Whirling, singing,
Oceans, metropolises, deserts,
A desultory reflection
Of what is lost forever.

A flame rages, trumpets trumpet,
And chestnut-colored horses race,
Then the agitating lips
Of happiness, it seems, repeat.

And sorrow and joy, now again,
Again, as before, as always,
The ocean gestures a gray mane,
Deserts, cities arise.

But when, at last, arising
From sleep, will I again be me —
Just a simple Indian, dozing
On a hallowed evening, by a stream?

Denis Johnson & Kathy Lewis

A BABY ELEPHANT

Right now my love for you is a baby elephant
Born in Berlin or in Paris,
And treading with its cushioned feet
Around the zoo director's house.

Do not offer it French pastries,
Do not offer it cabbage heads,
It can eat only sections of tangerine,
Or lumps of sugar and pieces of candy.

Don't cry, my sweet, because it will be put
Into a narrow cage, become a joke for mobs,
When salesmen blow cigar smoke into its trunk
To the cackles of their girl friends.

Don't imagine, my dear, that the day will come
When, infuriated, it will snap its chains
And rush along the streets,
Crushing howling people like a bus.

No, may you dream of it at dawn,
Clad in bronze and brocade and ostrich feathers,
Like that magnificent beast which once
Bore Hannibal to trembling Rome.

  Carl R. Proffer

OSIP MANDELSHTAM   1891–1938

THE VALLEY BLEEDS WITH ROMAN RUST

The valley bleeds with Roman rust,
and time's crystal rapids whirl past
the dry gold of a classic spring.

Trampling the fallen oaken leaves,
I recall Caesar's exquisite features —
the maiden profile, the treacherous hump.

Here, so far from Capitolium and Forum,
through the fading calm of nature
I sense the earth's edge. I hear
the Augustan apple rolling like the years.

I hope for a light grief in old age.
I was born in Rome and it has returned to me.
My autumn was a kind of she-wolf,
And August — the month of Caesars — smiled at me.

John Glad

I AM DEAF

I am deaf,
I am blind,
From my ears trickle ochre and minium,
In my eyes well rust and vermillion.

I dream
Of Armenian mornings.
I wonder,
How do bluebirds live in Yerevan?

I see a baker
Playing blindman's bluff with bread,
Lifting the moist skins of lavash cakes
From a hearth.

Oh Yerevan, Yerevan!
Did a bird draw you?
Or did a childish lion
Color you with crayons?

Oh Yerevan, Yerevan!
You're not a town,
You're a walnut.
How I love the crooked Babylons of your streets!

I have fingered this senseless life
Like a mullah his Koran.
I've frozen time
And spilled no hot blood.

Oh, Yerevan.
That's enough.
Anyway,
I don't want your frozen grapes.

John Glad

BECAUSE I LET GO YOUR HANDS

Because I let go your hands,
Because I betrayed your lips
I must wait for dawn in a drowsing acropolis . . .
How I hate these ancient weeping timbers.

Achean men harness a horse in darkness,
Biting into walls with teethy saws.
I cannot calm this dry bustle of the blood,
I cannot name you with a sound.

How could I think you would return?
How could I leave you
Before even the cock had crowed,
Before hot axe heads bit into wood?

The walls cried tears of transparent resin
And the town felt its wooden ribs
As blood surged to the ladders,
Beckoned on by a thrice-dreamt vision.

Where is dear Troy? Where is the imperial palace?
This lofty bird house of Priam cannot stand.
Arrows fall in dry wooden rain
Where others spring up like alder thickets.

The last star is painlessly snuffed out
And the gray swallow of morning taps at the pane.
The slow day tosses in shaggy haystacks
Like an ox awakened from a long dream.

  John Glad

INSOMNIA. . . .

Insomnia. Homer. Taut sails.
I have read the list of ships to the middle:
this migrant flight
that once winged over Hellas.

What drives this wedge of cranes into alien borders?
What do you seek, Achean men?
Were it not for Helen,
What need had you of Troy?

Homer falls silent
And foam swirls from the heads of kings.
Only the black sea rages
And a heavy surf thunders against my pillow.

John Glad

LIKE GRUMBLING ROMAN PLEBS

Like grumbling Roman plebs
aging ewes sulkily retreat to the hills,
among them black chaldeons —
creatures of the night in hoods of darkness.

Multitudes of shaggy knees
jerkily advance — like sticks.
A fleeing foam of fleece swirls
like lottery tickets in the night's enormous wheel.

This black Aventine, this sheep-like Rome
longs after a ruler of its seven hills.
But only dogs bark near the shed
and the campfire's smoke is bitter in the eyes.

Phalanxes of shrubs lunge in attack
driving regiments of warriors from their tents.
And in the sacred chaos of flight
their common fleece hangs in heavy waves.

John Glad

NOTRE DAME

Where a Roman consul once judged a foreign people
Joyously like Adam stands the first basilica.
The light vault ripples its crossed muscles
And stretches a web of Gothic nerves.

A secret blueprint
Concealed by the strength of pointed arches,
Protecting the buttressed wall,
Supporting an idle battering ram.

This elemental labyrinth, this dumbfounding forest,
This reasoning cavern of a Gothic soul.
Egyptian might and Christian timidity
Ruled by vertical law.

But the more, Notre Dame,
I studied your monstrous ribs,
The more I knew: from evil weight
I too would one day fashion beauty.

John Glad

LENINGRAD

I'm back in my town — excruciatingly familiar
as a child's glands.
Hurriedly I gulp the river lights' fishy grease
and recognize the yolk of a December day
spilling into an evil tar.
Petersburg, I don't want to die!
I still have the phone numbers, the addresses
where I'll find the voices of dead men.
I live just off the back stairs,
in my temple throbs a bell
yanked out with the meat.
All night I wait for precious guests
shifting the shackles of door chains.

John Glad

IN THIS COOL TRANSPARENT SPRING

In this cool transparent spring
Our Slavic Petropolis is clothed in green down.
The waves of the Neva curl Medusa-like,
Inspiring only a mild revulsion.
Along the northern river's embankment
Rush mechanical glowworms
While overhead swarm steel dragonflies and beetles.
Gold needles flash in the sky
But no star can kill
The heavy emerald of a sea wave.

John Glad

I DRINK TO THE ASTERS OF WAR, . . .

I drink to the asters of war, to everything for which I stand accused.
To opulent coats, to asthma, to the bile of a Petersburg day.
To the melody of Savoyard pines, to the reek of petrol on the Champs
  Elysees.
To roses in Rolls Royces and the oils of Parisian paintings.
I drink to the waves of Biscay, to pitchers of Alpine cream,
To the red-headed haughtiness of English women.
I drink . . . . But you know, I just can't make up my mind which to
  uncork —
This fragrant Asti Spumante or the Chateau Neuf du Pape.

John Glad

WHERE CAN I HIDE IN JANUARY

Where can I hide in January
When I am drunk from locked doors
And want to moo at barred gates?
This town is as open as chain links.

82 Osip Mandelshtam

I've had enough of stockings
Stuffed with twisted streets
And boxes packed with barking alleys.
I flick the switch and idiots scurry in the light.

In the pit's warty blackness
I slip toward a frozen pump
And eat the dead air
Of a feverish rookery.

I gasp after them, beating
An icy wooden box.
Give me a reader! An advisor! A doctor!
Or at least . . . a conversation on this spiny stairwell.

John Glad

I HATE THE LIGHT

I hate the light
                    of monotonous stars.
In dreams I rave
                    of the tower's arrow-like growth.
Stone!
        Be of lace,
Become
        a cobweb.
Pierce through
                    the heaven's empty breast.
Wound it
                    with long needles.
My turn
        will come.
I feel
        the wing's beat.
But where
        will it go —

                                    Osip Mandelshtam 83

The living arrow
                    of thought?
My moment,
              my path
                        are past.
There
        I could not love —
Here
        I am afraid.

John Glad

ON STONY PIERIAN SPURS

On stony Pierian spurs
the muses' ring was forged in dance
that blind bards might lay up for us like bees
heavy combs of Ionian honey.
And from the bulging female brow
fell coldness
that distant grandsons might touch
the archipelago's tender coffins.

Spring tramples the fields of Hellas
as Sappho pulls on a red slipper.
And from the cicada's hidden smithy
tiny hammers ring out over the cut grass.
Already beef hides have been stretched
over wedding shoes,
and before the carpenter's door
scamper headless chickens.

Turtle-like
the lyre lies fingerless,
baking its golden belly
in the Epirian sun.
She longs to be flipped over, carressed.

84   Osip Mandelshtam

Where is Terpander?
How long must she wait
for the rape of dry thumbs?

Above the gossiping, bare-headed grass
wasps copulate with honeysuckle
and oaks drink deep from tepid springs.
I would break no bread
and sip but wine and honey
where the creak of labor
does not blacken the islands' sky.

John Glad

LAMARCK

If life is but a blot on a dying day,
If this shy boy, this timid patriarch was right,
Then I will occupy the last rung
On the rubbery Lamarckian ladder.

From my lips will grow tentacles,
My trunk will be hooped in rings,
My suckered fingers will thrash an ocean floor
And I will disappear like Proteus behind a horny mantel.

Behind us float the brandy-glass eyes
Of a crustacean world.
We see for the last time
Life's refraction.

He said:
Of what use was Mozart?
You must denounce hot blood
And be silent as the spider.

Nature has packed away this long brain
Like a sword into scabbard.
She has forgotten those whose grave is green,
Whose breath is red, whose laugh is supple . . . .

John Glad

ANNA AKHMATOVA   1889–1966

SO, I REMAINED ALONE

So, I remained alone,
Counting the empty days.
O, my free companions,
My swans!

And I'll not summon you with song,
Not bring you back with tears,
But in the sad hour of dusk,
Remember you in my prayers.

Struck by the deadly arrow,
One of you has fallen,
And another, kissing me,
Has become a black raven.

But it happens, once a year
When the ice is melting,
I stand by the clear waters
In the Catherine Gardens.

And I hear the splashing of great wings
Over the blue surface of the lake.
I do not know who has opened the window
In the prison of the grave.

Daniel Weissbort

WE DO NOT KNOW HOW TO SAY GOODBYE

We do not know how to say goodbye.
Shoulder to shoulder, we walk and walk.
Already it is dust, and I
Am silent, while you are lost in thought.

Let's go into this church. What will we see?
A baptism, wedding, burial-service.
Without looking at each other, we shall leave —
Why is our life not like this?

Or else, let's go into the graveyard. There
You will pick up a stick and lightly trace
In the trodden snow we crouch on, sighing,
Houses where we shall be together always.

Daniel Weissbort

A DREAM

Is it pleasant to dream
unearthly dreams?
    A. Blok

This dream was either a prophesy or not.
Among the heavenly bodies Mars stood out
Scarlet-faced, scintillating, sinister —
And that night I dreamt of your coming.

It was everywhere . . . In the Bach Chacone,
The roses that bloomed in vain,
And the chiming of the village bell
Over the blackness of the ploughed fields.

It was in the autumn season which drew close
Only to turn about and hide again.
Oh August, how could you bring me such news
On this terrible anniversary of mine!

How shall I repay this royal gift?
Where shall I go, and with whom celebrate?
See, in the burnt notebook I am writing
My poems — as before, immaculate.

Daniel Weissbort

THERE IS A BOUNDARY . . .

There is a boundary in the heart's land
That lovers, loving passionately, may not cross,
Though lips meet in terrible silence, and
The heart through loving break in pieces.

Here, friendship too is powerless, as are the years
That blaze with a sublime happiness —
Then is the soul free and clear
Of all dependence on languorous flesh.

They are insane who try
To reach that point, and those that go beyond
Are torn by anguish.
                    Now you know why
My heart does not flutter beneath your hand.

Daniel Weissbort

THE VISITOR

Always the same fine snow
Beating against the dining-room panes —
And I was myself no different.
It was then my visitor came.

"What do you want?" I asked.
"To be with you in hell," he said.

I laughed. "It would seem your words
Bode neither of us any good."

But then he touched the flowers
With the dry tips of his fingers.
"Tell me how men kiss you.
Tell me how you kiss."

And he did not take his eyes,
Staring blankly, from my ring.
Not a single muscle stirred
In that malevolent face.

And I knew it was his pleasure,
Intensely and passionately,
To need nothing at all, to know
I had nothing to deny him.

Daniel Weissbort

REQUIEM

Instead of a Foreword

In the terrible years of the Yezhov period I spent seventeen months waiting in line outside Leningrad's prisons. On one occasion, someone "recognized" me. Then the woman behind me, her lips blue with cold, who, of course, had never heard of me, emerged from the stupor which held us all and whispered (we all whispered then) this question into my ear:

"Could you describe this?"

And I said: "I could."

Then something like a smile passed over what had once been her face.

I

At dawn they came for you.
I trailed behind — it was like
A funeral. In the darkened room

Children cried. The icon candle died.
The icon had left its coldness on your lips,
And oh, the deathly film of sweat upon your brow!
Like the wives of those who mutinied against the tsar,
Under the Kremlin's towers I shall howl.

1935

2

Quietly flows the quiet Don,
The housebreaking yellow moon

Enters with its hat askew.
A shadow greets the yellow moon.

Whose shadow? See, it is a woman,
A woman ailing and alone.

Dead is her husband, gaol claims her son,
Pray for me, everyone.

3

No, it is not I, it is another who suffers.
I could not have borne such suffering; let what has happened
Be draped in black cloth.
And away with lamps . . .
Night.

4

They should have shown you, little scoffer,
Apple of everyone's eye,
Delinquent of Tsarskoye Selo,
What your life was going to be like,
How you would stand before
The prison, three-hundredth in line,
Clasping a parcel, your tears
Scalding the New Year's ice.
The prison poplar is swaying.
In the soundlessness, we ask how many
Innocent lives will be taken . . . .

Anna Akhmatova   91

For seventeen months I have cried out,
Ceaselessly I call
You home. My son, you are my nightmare now —
At the executioner's feet I fall.
Everywhere is confusion.
How can I tell apart
Man the beast and man the human? —
And how soon is the sentence to be carried out?
Only dusty flowers are left,
A tinkling censer, tracks
Somewhere — leading nowhere;
And looking me straight in the eye,
A menacing presage of death,
This enormous star.

6

Weeks fleetly run on.
I can't believe it happened:
How the white nights saw
Into your cell, my son;
And how what they now see,
With burning hawk-like eye,
Of your tall cross, they tell —
And of your agony.

1939

7   The Sentence

And the stone word
Struck my still living breast.
No matter — I was prepared.
Somehow I shall last.

Today there is much to be done.
I must kill off memory,
My heart must be changed into stone,
I must learn to live again.

Or else . . . . Hot summer rustles
Festively outside my window.
Long ago I had a premonition
Of this bright day, this empty house.

Summer 1939

8   To Death

You'll come anyway — so, why not now?
I am expecting you — life is an ordeal.
I've put out the light and opened the door
For you, so simple, so wonderful.
Take any form you like for this,
A shellburst leaking poison,
Or like a seasoned criminal, neatly dispatch me,
Or poison me with typhoid fumes,
Or, as in that tale you dreamt up,
So sickeningly familiar to all,
The top of your blue cap
Peeking behind the palefaced janitor.
I don't care any more. The Yenisey
Swirls, the North Star shines.
And an ultimate horror overlays
The blueness of my dear one's eyes.

19 August 1939
The House on the Fontanka
Leningrad

9

Already madness has taken
Half my soul under its wing,
Giving me heady wine to drink,
Into a dark valley beckoning.

And I have come to terms with this:
The battle's lost. I listen to
My ravings, and it seems as if
They come from some place far removed.

Anna Akhmatova   93

And it is not permitted me
To take away anything. Although
I importune madness with my pleas —
The answer's always 'No.'

Not my son's agonized look,
His suffering wrought in stone,
Nor that day the storm broke,
Nor the visiting hour in prison,

Nor the cool feel of your hands,
The agitated shadows of the lime trees,
Nor the faint distant sounds,
The last few words consoling me.

4 May 1940
The House on the Fontanka

10   Crucifixion

"Weep not for me, Mother,
I am in my grave."

I

A choir of angels hymned the hour,
The heavens were on fire, and he
Said, "Why have You forsaken me, oh Father?"
And, "Mother, weep not for me."

II

Sobbing, Mary Magdelene writhed,
His favorite disciple stiffened,
And no one even dared to cast his eye
Upon the Mother, standing silent.

1940–1943

Epilogue

I

I learnt how faces crumple, how fear
Gazes from under eyelids, how
Suffering's hard cuneiform
Is etched on cheek and brow;

How black or ashen locks turn
In moments, not in years, to white,
How the smile fades on uncomplaining lips
And dry fearful laughter vibrates.
I pray not for myself alone,
But for those who stood with me, for all
Who in July heat or cruel cold
Stood by the blinded red-brick wall.

2

Again the dead hour has come, I remember
The dead: I feel, I cry, I hear:

The one who could scarcely be led to her end,
The one who no more trod her native land,

The one who tossed her beautiful head:
"I come here as if to my home," she said.

I should like to recall each one by name
But cannot — the list has been taken away,

And so, instead, I have woven a shroud
Out of their poor words overheard.

I remember them always and everywhere,
I shall not forget, beset by new cares.

And if my tormented mouth is shut,
My mouth, through which millions cry out,

Let them likewise remember me
On the eve of my memorial day.

And if some day in this country it's thought
To raise a memorial in my honor,

I'll give my consent to this accolade —
But on one condition: let it not be raised

Either by that sea where I was born —
The last link with that sea has been broken —

Or in the park at Tsarskoye, close
By the cherished tree stump with its stricken shadow,

But here, where I've stood three hundred hours
And where they never unbolted the doors.

For even in blessed death I fear
To forget the rumble of Black Marias,

Forget how that vile door slammed in the face
Of the old woman howling like a wounded beast.

So let the snow flow down like tears
From my bronzen eyelids motionless,

And let the distant call of the prison dove
Boom, and silent boats sail the Neva.

                                March 1940

Daniel Weissbort

MARIA PETROVYKH   b. 1908

THE AIR IS MOTIONLESS WITH HEAT

The air is motionless with heat,
The trees as if asleep.
What's happening in the stillness
To that solitary tree?

No breeze disturbs the garden.
From root to leaf it shakes.
What is this — fear or yearning,
Anxiety or shame?

But what's the matter with it?
What possibly could be?
Look how the trembling surfaces
Do bark from deep within.

A tree is going crazy there
And I do not know why.
A tree is going crazy there.
The reasons pass me by.

Does it want to forget something,
Cast out a memory?
Or is it powerless to seize
Some long-forgotten thing?

97

It quakes as if beneath the axe.
Branches can bear no more.
Delirious with silver,
They bend low in the dark.

The tree has not the strength to calm
Its palpitating leaves,
And gladly would it run away
But that its roots go deep.

A tree is going crazy there
In utter soundlessness.
I understand it no more
Than I understand myself.

Sharon Leiter

MAXIMILIAN VOLOSHIN 1877–1932

HOLY RUSSIA

Now didn't Suzdal and Moscow
Gather the land up just for you,
Bit by bit, and store
Your dowry gold in a little bag
And rear you carefully for marriage
In a thin, frescoed tower?

And didn't the mighty Carpenter-Tsar
Build you a mansion by the river
With the world's five seas
In view? And didn't your radiance
And strength make you the perfect bride
For any king's son?

But from your early youth you dreamed
Of wooden monasteries deep
In the forest, the wandering tribes
Of the steppes, ascetics' chains, jails,
Cheats, thieves, bad priests, and the high wail
Of Nightingale The Robber.[1]

1 Figure from Russian folklore.

You didn't want to be the Tsar's
And this is how the thing transpired:
The enemy whispered: Yield
Your treasure to the rich, your power
To slaves, your might to foes, your honor
To serfs, give traitors your keys.

You were persuaded by this advice
And gave yourself away to thieves,
And burned your cities and fields;
Your ancient home was devastated,
You left as a beggar, humiliated,
Slave to the lowest slave.

Dare I stone you or condemn
Your urgent flame? Shall I not bend
Before you with my face
In the mud and bless the print of your
Bare foot, you homeless, drunk, impure
Russia, Christ's holy fool!

Bob Perelman & IWP

BORIS PASTERNAK   1890–1960

A SULTRY NIGHT

It drizzled, but didn't bend
the grass in the storm's sack.
Dust gulped down pills of rain
like iron in a muffled powder.

The village was past healing,
and — dazed — a poppy swooned.
Rye flared hairy and red
and God trudged, delirious.

In the orphaned, sleepless,
damp universal waste,
groans tore from their posts,
the whirlwind dug in, abated.

Drops squinted in blind
pursuit. Wet branches and pale
wind bickered at the fence.
I held my breath — they spoke of me!

And then I thought that garrulous garden
could jabber on into eternity.
I'm still invisible from the street,
hidden by the babble of shrubs and shutters.

Once they spot me, no way out:
they'll talk, talk, talk me to death!

Mark Rudman & Bohdan Boychuk

TO LOVE, . . .

To love, to go in endless thunder,
to stamp out anguish, wear no shoes,
to spook hedgehogs, to pay good
for evil to cranberries in cobwebs.

To drink from branches that whip your face,
snap back and slash the azure:
"Yes, it's an echo!" And at the end
to lose your way in kisses.

To ramble through a world of turnips!
To know at sunset that the sun
is older than those stars and carts,
older than Margarita and the Innkeeper.

To lose your tongue like a subscription
to a storm of tears in Valkyries' eyes,
to grow as numb as the sweltering sky,
to drown the forest masts in ether.

Stretched out in thorns, rake up
the residue of years like pine cones.
On the highway; entering an Inn;
dawn; frozen; eat some fish.

Scrambling down to sing again:
"Old and gray, I walked and fell,
the town was choked with weeds
washed by the tears of soldiers' wives.

In the shadow of a moonless barn,
in the flames of flagons and groceries,
maybe even this old husk of a man
will perish in his time."

And so I sang, sang and died,
died and circled back to her
embraces like a boomerang, and —
as I recall — kept saying goodbye.

Mark Rudman & Bohdan Boychuk

102   Boris Pasternak

STORM, AN ENDLESS INSTANT

Summer waves goodbye to the wayside
station. The thunder removes
his cap, and recites a hundred
blinding photographs.

A lilac cluster darkens.
The thunder plucks a sheaf
of lightnings, to expose,
from far fields, the overseer's house.

And when terror drums
on the roof, and a stockade
of rain falls like charcoal
strokes on a drawing,

the mind's ravine flickers,
and it seemed there'd be more light
even in those recesses
where it is already day.

Mark Rudman & Bohdan Boychuk

THE MIRROR

A cup of cocoa steams in the mirror;
  sheer curtains stretch and yawn.
Down the garden path, past storms and chaos
  the mirror dashes for the swings.

There pines rock and impregnate
  the air with pinegum; the garden
scatters its spectacles in the grass;
  the shadow reads a book.

In the distances past the gate, the dusk,
  into the steppes, odor of drugged air,
hot quartz shimmers and flows
  laced with snails and branches.

Boris Pasternak   103

The garden wrestles in the room,
    in the mirror — but doesn't smash the glass!
Like collodion it spread from dressers
    to the rustlings in bark.

The mirrored tide glazed the world
    with sweatless ice, knocking
bitterness out of knots, scent out of lilac,
    breaking the reign of mesmerism.

The weird world walks in its sleep
    and only the wind can bind
what breaks into life, breaks in a prism
    and gladly plays in tears.

The soul won't be blasted with saltpetre,
    or unearthed like a treasure.
The garden wrestles in the room,
    in the mirror — but doesn't smash the glass!

In this rich hypnotic country
    you can't blow out my eyes.
Slugs come unplugged after rain and riddle
    the eyes of garden statues.

Water murmurs in the ears, the siskin
    shrees, and tiptoes daintily.
Go smear their lips with blueberries,
    they don't get high on mischief.

The garden wrestles in the room,
    shakes a fist at the mirror,
dashes to the swings, grabs, shakes,
    muddies them — but doesn't smash the glass!

    Mark Rudman & Bohdan Boychuk

DON'T TOUCH

"Don't touch. Wet paint." the sign said.
   But soul paid it no mind,
now memory's stained by calves and cheeks
   and hands and lips and eyes.

More than for any loss or gain
   I loved you because
you caused this white and yellow world
   to turn a whiter white.

My friend, I swear that this dust
   will be whiter than
fever, lampshades, or the white
   bandage on a brow.

   Mark Rudman & Bohdan Boychuk

MOOCHKAP

The spirit sweats — the horizon's
tobacco tinged — like thought.
Windmills image a fishing village:
boats and weathered nets.

The village of frozen windmills
hovers like a motionless harbor.
All smells of a weary stasis:
nothing, nothing stirs.

The hours skip past like stones,
richochet across the shallows,
not drowning, keeping afloat,
tobacco tinged — like thought.

There was time before the train
to see her, but now it's sunk

Boris Pasternak   105

in the hellish limbo, the nervous
roiling in the gut before a storm.

Mark Rudman & Bohdan Boychuk

AS WITH THEM

The face of azure beams on the face
of this breath-taking, beloved river.
A catfish surfaces — a splash —
a deafening echo.

Sheaved eyes grieve like eaves,
like two hearths reddening.
The face of azure beams on the forehead
of the breath-taking lady of the deeps,
of the breath-taking stepchild of sedge.

The wind lifts alfalfa laughter,
blows a kiss down the valleys,
gorges on marshberries, crawls,
smears its lips with ferns,
tickles the river's cheek with a branch
or — turning sour — ferments in the reeds.

Maybe a sunfish will fan a fin?
The day swells and reddens.
The Shelon's a tray of black lead:
can't tie the ends, can't raise a hand.

The face of azure beams on the forehead
of this breath-taking, beloved river.

Mark Rudman & Bohdan Boychuk

LET THE WORDS . . .

Let the words be shed like amber
and lemon peel from orchards,
thoughtlessly, profusely,
sparely, tersely, sparsely.

Who needs to explain
why the leaves are so
ceremoniously sprayed
with lemon and madder?

Who shed tears on pine needles,
jetted between railings,
threaded jalousies and filled
notes on music stands?

Who dappled the doormat
with beads of mountain ash —
a blanket of diaphanous
quivering italics?

You want to know who ordains
that August should thrive,
to whom nothing is trivial,
who dwells in the trimmings

of maple leaves
and held by his column
during the hewing of alabaster
since Ecclesiastical times?

You want to know who ordains
that the lips of September
asters and dahlias should grieve,
that spindly broom leaves
should topple from gray caryatids
onto the dank gravestones
of autumn's hospitals?

You want to know who ordains?
Almighty God of details,
almighty God of love,
of Yagailos and Yadvigas.

The dark beyond the grave
may still remain a riddle,
but life, like this autumn stillness,
lives in its details.

Mark Rudman & Bohdan Boychuk

TO BE FAMOUS ISN'T DECENT

To be famous isn't decent, there's
Nothing noble about it.
One shouldn't start archives,
Tremble over manuscripts.

Creation is self-giving, and not
Success, not sensation.
To be a parable on people's lips
Is nothing, is shame.

Live without pretenses, live
So that, finally,
You draw towards yourself the love
Of space, hear the future.

And leave gaps in fate, rather
Than have, marking the margins
Of your papers, places and chapters
Of a whole life.

Sink into obscurity,
Hide your steps in it,
As a place hides in fog
When you can't see a thing.

Others will live their lives inch
By inch, along your path.
But you yourself should not distinguish
Victory from defeat.

And do not, in any thing
Retreat from yourself.
Just be alive, only that, alive,
Alive, only that, to the end.

Bob Perelman & Kathy Lewis

NIKOLAY ZABOLOTSKY   1903–58

THE FACE OF A HORSE

Animals never sleep. At night when it's dark
They stand like a stone wall over the world.

A cow's sloping head has smooth horns
And makes noise in the straw; holding
Primaeval cheekbones separate,
The heavy stony forehead presses down
To inarticulate eyes
That barely can roll in circles.

But the face of a horse is sharp and fine.
He hears the talk of leaf and stone.
He listens! He knows the cries of animals,
From the ragged woods, the nightingale's call.

And being so wise, whom should he tell
All the miraculous things he knows?
The night is deep, constellations
Are lifting over the dark skyline.
And the horse is calmly standing guard,
The wind rustling his silky hair,
Each of his eyes like a huge burning world,
His mane spread — royal purple.

And if a man could see
The magic face of a horse
He would rip out his own silly tongue
To give to the horse. The magic horse
Is the one who really deserves a tongue!

Then we would hear words.
Words as big as apples, thick
As honey or curds.
Words that have the thrust of fire,
That fly into the soul and there make light,
Like fire shining on the wretched objects
Of some poor hut. Words without death,
Words that let us sing.
But now the stable is empty
And the trees can no longer be seen.
Morning, the miser, has covered up the mountains
And opened the fields for work.
The horse, from his cage of shafts,
Drawing a covered cart,
Looks with the eyes of a prisoner
At the mysterious, unmoving earth.

   Bob Perelman & Kathy Lewis

SNAKES

The cool, damp forest shakes,
Here are the varying blossoms
And the shining bodies of snakes
Entwined among the stones.
The warm, simplistic sun
Pours down on them its rays.
Arranged among the stones,
The snakes are sheer as glass.
Although a bird makes noise
Or a beetle bravely wails

Nikolay Zabolotsky   111

The snakes sleep, hiding their faces
Within their bodies' warm folds.
And mysterious and poor
They sleep, their mouths unclosed,
While time floats in the air
Above them, scarcely noticed.
A year goes by, two years,
Three years. And finally
A man comes on the bodies —
Severe models of sleep.
What are they for? From where?
Can they be justified?
A pile of lovely creatures
Sleeps, in disarray.
The wise man leaves to ponder,
And lives as a hermit, alone,
And instantly bored nature
Stands over him like a prison.

Denis Johnson & Kathy Lewis

ALL THAT MY SOUL POSSESSED, . . .

All that my soul possessed, it seemed that again I had lost it all,
As I lay emptily in the grass, wretchedly sad and bored.
And a flower rose up over me, a body, living, beautiful,
With a grasshopper standing in front, a sort of miniature guard.

And then I opened my book, which was thick and heavily bound,
On the first page was an illustration of a plant.
And dark and dead, stretching from the flower to the book
Was either the flower's truth or else the lie shielded within.

And the flower seemed amazed at the sight of its reflexion,
As if it tried to comprehend a quite outlandish wisdom;
Its leaves were trembling, stirred by thought to an unaccustomed
   motion,
Trembling with that effort of will, which cannot be expressed.

112 Nikolay Zabolotsky

The grasshopper raised his horn and nature suddenly awoke,
And the sorrowing creature started to sing a praise of thought.
And then the image of the flower engraved in my old book
Began to move, and to compel my heart to move toward it.

Bob Perelman & Kathy Lewis

THE LOOP CANAL

Out my window, the loop canal
Holds the neighborhood in thrall.

Teamsters, having snared their horses
In copper-plated harnesses,
Stroll in their jackets like padishahs,
With the low-life's preposterous lordliness.
All around the taverns stand;
The teamsters are sitting in taverns,
The assembled horses' faces stare
Minutely through the windows there.
And there, past where the faces linger,
For a quarter mile the crowd spills forth:
The blind men stretching out their fingers
Like steel rods, crying out in chorus.
A vendor, clapping, throws a pair
Of trousers upward in the air —
A screaming falcon: he is lord
Of trousers, the movements of planets and crowds
Are his; the twirl of pants commands
The crowd suspended: There it stands,
Its pride forgotten, quite unable
To turn from such a miracle,
Ecstatic in exhaustion.

Shriek and whistle like a stooge,
Vendor, fling them to the sky!
But before this packed human deluge

Another current passes by:
One man lifts a boot on a tray,
Another one praises his poodle for sale,
A third, a fearsome, ruddy man,
Beats a saucepan with his hands.
And there is no resistance now:
The crowd is wrapped up and subdued,
Moving like a sleepwalker,
Its hands stretched out before it.

And the dark factories stand like castles
Around us, and the sound of hawking
Is in the sky; again on the columns
Of their splendid legs the mustangs are walking.
The carts moan sadly through it all,
The furrowed mud is thrown about,
The cripples sleep by the canal,
Lying down on empty bottles.

Denis Johnson & Kathy Lewis

AT THE FISHMONGER'S

And here, forgetting human wisdom,
We enter quite another kingdom . . .
A rosy sturgeon's corpse suspended
(Loveliest of all the sturgeons he)
Hangs from a hook, his fins extended,
Pierced through the tail — a sight to see!
Below him salmon smoke in butter
And eels, like links of sausage, sputter,
In smoking gravy twist and bend
And join each other end to end,
And midmost, like a yellowed bone,
Sits the smoked sturgeon on his throne.

O sumptuous ruler of the belly,
O God and master of my guts,
The secret leader of my spirit
And formulator of my thoughts, —
O give yourself to my desire,
And let my throat absorb your savour!
My lips are trembling — all on fire,
Like hottentots my innards quaver.
My guts are all inflamed with greed
And tortured by the juice of hunger,
Now seeming to contract at need,
Now like a dragon growing longer;
The spittle in my mouth tastes stronger,
My jaws are double-locked with wire —
O give yourself to my desire!

On each side jars of spices clatter,
While gang-fish bellow all around
And butcher knives, with blood bespattered,
Quiver and twist within the wound.
Here glows a small sub-aqueous garden,
Where, past a green translucent wall,
Bream swim in sad hallucination,
Oppressed by frenzy, filled with gall,
With doubt and — can it be, with panic?
Above, the hawker, death, prevails
And threatens with his spear titanic.

"Our Father," read the brazen scales;
Two quiet weights, in saucer standing,
Define the road of life and death;
The portal creaks, the fish responding
With waving gills draw in their breath.

Alec Merivale

NOCTURNAL GARDEN

O nocturnal garden, secret organ,
Forest of long trumpets, refuge of cellos!
O nocturnal garden, sad procession
Of motionless firs and oaks without voice!

All day there was rushing and noise, the poplars —
A shock, the oaks — a turmoil. One hundred
Thousand leaves like one hundred thousand bodies
Entangled in the autumn wind.

An August made of iron in tall boots,
His plate piled with game, stood far away
And the meadows were filled with the thunder of shots
And birds' bodies fluttered in the air.

The garden was still, and suddenly the moon
Appeared. Below, long shadows lay in tens
And crowds of linden trees raised their hands,
Hiding birds beneath clusters of green.

O nocturnal garden, poor nocturnal
Garden, o things asleep for a long time!
O the flaring just above the gaze,
A starry fragment's momentary flame.

Bob Perelman & Kathy Lewis

POEM ABOUT RAIN

Wolf:
Honorable woodland snake,
Why do you creep, when you know not
Where to go — why do you make haste?
Can one live life in such a hurry?

Snake:
Most wise wolf, a world that does not move
Is not comprehensible to us.

116 Nikolay Zabolotsky

And so we run, that's all,
Like smoke escaping from a peasant's house.

Wolf:
Your answer is not hard to grasp.
How feeble is the snake's intellect!
My light, you are running from yourself,
Understanding truth to lie in movement.

Snake:
You are an idealist, I see.

Wolf:
Look: a leaf falls from a tree.
The cuckoo, shaping his song
From two notes (the naive fellow!),
Sings in the noble grove.
The sun shines, bright rain descends,
The water falls for a minute or two,
Peasants scatter barefoot,
Then it is bright again,
The rain has stopped,
Tell me the meaning of this scene.

Snake:
Go discuss it with the wolves.
They will explain
Why water flows from heaven.

Wolf:
Yes, I shall go to the wolves.
The water pours over their flanks.
The water sings like a mother
When it falls gently upon us.
Nature, in a smart sarafan,
Leaning her head upon the sun,
Plays all day on an organ.
We call this — life.
We call this — rain.
The splashing of little ones through puddles,

The rustle and dance of trees,
The laughter of forget-me-nots.
Or, when the organ's note is sullen,
The sky trembling to the sound of drums,
And an army of ponderous clouds
Covering all from edge to edge,
When a great gush of water
Knocks the woodland beast off its legs,
Not believing our own eyes,
We call this — God.

Daniel Weissbort

POPRYSHCHIN

When roads are covered with ice
And the wind shakes the graveyard crosses,
Gogol, with twitching fingers,
Leads out his hunchbacked dreams.
And numbed by the bitter cold,
Beyond endurance oppressed,
The stony monsters reel,
As the wind aims straight at the head.
The wind is a tearer of wings,
Exploding the ashen snows,
And suddenly, lower and lower,
Prostrates itself at your feet.
Where is such majesty from?
No longer a demon, but this —
Popryshchin's [1] eyebrows are raised,
He lifts his face to the front.
Wind, blow through the offices,
Sweep the pens off the desks,
Spreading its pearly fan
Spain will rise at your feet.

1 Popryshchin is the character from Gogol's story "Diary of a Madman," a poor clerk who imagines himself to be Ferdinand, King of Spain.

It will flourish a purple mantilla
Over our native fields,
And clamorous Seville will come out
In a body to greet its king.
And he, slender and drawn,
His suffering eyes aglow
Will rise . . .
                    Then darkness again.

A bed, a warden, a mattress,
The shirt cutting under the arm,
Medzhi's[2] desolate whine,
Outside the first glimmer of dawn.
Wind, rage through the offices,
Drive the snow down the avenue,
Overturn the great man's coach,
Bury it in the drifts.
By windows, columns, porches,
By arches of concrete, flow;
Pluck the general's stars from his tunic,
Bury bridges under the snow.
Stretching its limbs it whirls,
Sets up an icy howl,
After it snow fiends tumble,
Racing over the roofs.
They grapple
The bell towers,
Explode in a peal of bells,
Lie down in brick slaughterhouses,
And again leap out from a corner,
Where in the blind hurricane,
Making a last brave stand,
In a white shirt there sways,
Dead-faced,
Ferdinand.

Daniel Weissbort

2 Medzhi is a dog belonging to the daughter of the director of the department where
P. works.

YESTERDAY REFLECTING UPON DEATH

Yesterday reflecting upon death,
My soul suddenly grew bitter.
Sad day! Age-old nature
Gazed at me from the forest's depths.

And the anguish of separation
Pierced my heart, and in that moment
I could hear all — the evening grass,
The water talking, and the stone's dead cry.

And over the fields I wandered, a living being,
Entered the forest without fear,
And the thoughts of dead men rose about me
In limpid columns to the sky.

And Pushkin's voice was heard above the foliage,
The birds of Khlebnikov [1] sang by the water's side.
I met a stone; the stone was motionless;
And in it Skovoroda's [2] face appeared.

And all creatures, all the nations,
Guarded their indestructible life,
And I myself was not a child of nature,
But its thought, its unsteady mind!

Daniel Weissbort

METAMORPHOSES

How the world changes! How I myself change!
I have a single name, but actually —
in that which is called me — I am not alone.
Alive, I am a throng of many deaths.
So many are the lifeless twins cast off by my own body!

1 Khlebnikov (1885–1922) was a Futurist poet.
2 Skovoroda (1722–94) was a poet theologist, pantheistic philosopher.

If only my mind's eye could see beyond itself,
peering deep into the cemetery loam,
it would perceive my own prone figure.
I would show me — to me —
a me dissolved in the surging salty ebb,
a me drifting through the air to some invisible kingdom,
my wretched dust — once so beloved.

Yet I live on! More purely and more fully
this gathering of odd creatures engulfs the spirit.
Nature lives. Alive among the stones
is the grain and even my lifeless herbarium.
Link to link and form to form,
singing organ, orchestral sea,
die not in joy — nor in storm.

How all things change! That which was a bird
lies on my desk — a written page.
Thought — once a simple flower —
now lumbers bullishly along.
And that which was me will one day
grow again, adding to the world of plants.
And thus, plucking at the tangled yarn of existence,
you suddenly see that which should be called immortality.
Oh, our superstitions!

John Glad

WARNING

Where ancient music weaves its shapes,
Where the keyboard battles with the dead,
Where notes fight with the silence of space,
Poet, do not seek furnishings for the soul.

Uniting mindlessness with mind,
Among barren meanings we will build a house —

A school of worlds unknown until this moment.
Poetry is thought constructed in the body.

It flows invisible in the water
That we celebrate with our zealous labors.
It burns in the midnight star,
The star that rages like a flame before us.

May the troubled sleep of cattle, the shallow reason of the birds,
Gaze out from your wonderful pages.
May the trees sing and the bull astound
With his dread conversation — that same bull
In whom is locked the soundlessness of worlds
Linked to us by strong ties.

Pelted with stones and mud-bespattered,
Have patience. And remember all the while:
If you listen carefully to music,
Your house will go to ruin, and the schoolboy,
Thirsting for knowledge, will mock us.

Daniel Weissbort

DANIIL KHARMS   1904–42

DEATH OF THE WILD WARRIOR

The clocks strike.
The clocks strike
Dust flies over the world.

In the towns people sing
In the towns people sing
In the deserts the sand is ringing.

Across the river
Across the river
The whistling lances fly.

The wild man fell
The wild man fell
And sleeps with his amulet glittering.

Like a light vapor
Like a light vapor
Upward flies his soul,

And in the sun's disc
And in the sun's disc
It thrusts with a rustle of tresses.

Four hundred warriors
Four hundred warriors
Blink and threaten the skies.

123

The slain man's wife
The slain man's wife
Crawls on her knees to the river;

The slain man's wife
The slain man's wife
Breaks off a piece of a stone,

And hides the slain man
And hides the slain man
Under broken stone in the sand

Four hundred warriors
Four hundred warriors
Are silent four hundred days.

Four hundred days
Four hundred days
No clocks strike over the dead.

Robin Milner-Gulland

124   Daniil Kharms

ALEKSANDR VVEDENSKY 1904–41

WHERE

Where he was standing leaning against a statue. With a face charged with thoughts. He himself was turning into a statue. He had no blood. Lo this is what he said:

farewell dark trees
farewell black forests
revolution of heavenly stars
and voices of carefree birds.

He probably had the idea of somewhere, sometime going away.

farewell field-cliffs
hours on end have I looked at you
farewell, lively butterflies
I have hungered with you
farewell stones farewell clouds
I have loved you and tormented you.

With yearning and belated repentance he began to scrutinize the tips of the grassblades.

farewell splendid tips
farewell flowers. Farewell water.
the postal couriers rush on
fate rushes past, misfortune rushes past.
I walked a prisoner in the meadow
I embraced the forest path
I woke the fishes in the mornings

scared the crowd of oaks

saw the sepulchral house of oaks

horses and singing led laboriously around.

He depicts how he habitually or unhabitually used to arrive at the river.

River I used to come to you.

River farewell. Trembles my hand.

You used to sparkle, used to flow,

I used to stand in front of you

clad in a caftan made of glass

and listen to your fluvial waves.

how sweet it was for me to enter

you, and once again emerge.

how sweet it was for me to enter

myself and once again emerge

where like finches oaktrees rustled.

the oaks were crazily able

the oaks to rustle scarely audibly.

But hereupon he calculated in his mind what would happen if he also saw the sea.

Sea farewell farewell sand

o mountain land how you are high

may the waves beat. May the spray scatter,

upon a rock I sit, still with my pipes.

and the sea plashes gradually

and everything from the sea is far.

and everything from the sea is for

care like a tedious duck runs off

parting with the sea is hard.

sea farewell. farewell paradise

o mountain land how you are high.

About the last thing that there is in nature he also remembered. He remembered about the wilderness.

farewell to you too

wildernesses and lions.

And thus having bidden farewell to all he neatly laid down his weapons and extracting from his pocket a temple shot himself in the head. And hereupon took place the second part — the farewell of all with one.

126   Aleksandr Vvedensky

The trees as if they had wings waved their arms. They thought that they could, and answered:

You used to visit us. Behold,
he died, and you all will die.
for instants he accepted us —
shabby, crumpled, bent.
wandering mindlessly
like an icebound winter.

What then is he communicating now to the trees. Nothing he is *growing numb*.

The cliffs or stones had not moved from their place. Through silence and voicelessness and the absence of sound they were encouraging us and you and him.

sleep. farewell. the end has come
the courier has come for you.
it has come — the ultimate hour.
Lord have mercy upon us.
Lord have mercy upon us.
Lord have mercy upon us.

What then does he retort to the stones. — Nothing — he is becoming frozen. Fishes and oaks gave him a bunch of grapes and a small quantity of final joy.

The oaks said: we grow.
The fishes said: we swim.
The oaks said: what is the time.
The fishes said: have mercy upon us.

What then will he say to fishes and oaks: He will not be able to say thank you. The river powerfully racing over the earth. The river powerfully flowing. The river powerfully carrying its waves. River as tsar. It said farewell in such a way, that. that's how. And he lay like a notebook on its very bank.

Farewell notebook
Unpleasant and easy to die.
Farewell world. Farewell paradise
you are very remote, land of humans.

What had he done to the river? — Nothing — he is turning into stone. And the sea weakening from its lengthy storms with sympathy looked upon death. Did the sea faintly possess the aspect of an eagle. No it did not possess it.

Will he glance at the sea? — No he cannot. In the night there was a sudden trumpeting somewhere — not quite savages, not quite not. He looked upon people.

When

When he parted his swollen eyelids, he half-opened his eyes. He recalled by heart into his memory all that is. I have forgotten to say farewell to much else. Then he recalled, he remembered the whole instant of his death. All these sixes and fives. All that — fuss. All the rhyme. Which was a loyal friend to him, as before him Pushkin had said. Oh Pushkin, Pushkin, that very Pushkin who had lived before him. Thereupon the shadow of universal disgust lay upon everything. Thereupon the shadow of the universal lay upon everything. Thereupon the shadow lay upon everything. He understood nothing, but he restrained himself. And savages, and maybe not savages with lamentation like the rustle of oaks, the buzzing of bees, the plash of waves, the silence of stones, and the aspect of the wilderness, carrying dishes over their heads, emerged and unhurriedly descended from the heights onto the far-from-numerous earth. Oh Pushkin. Pushkin.

All.

Robin Milner-Gulland

128   Aleksandr Vvedensky

JOSEPH UTKIN   1903–44

THE TALE OF RED-HAIRED MOTELE,
MISTER INSPECTOR,
RABBI ISAIAH AND COMMISAR BLOKH

First Chapter

Until the Time Without A tsar and a Little After

Both grandfather and father worked,
And in what way is he better than others?
Little red-haired Motele
Also worked
For two.

What he wanted didn't come,
(But he had his dreams!)
He thought he'd study in kheder [1]
But they turned him
To tailoring.
"So what?
You want me to cry?
No means no!"
And he put ten patches
On a vest.

1 School (Yiddish)

And . . .
(This, it's true, is far in the past,
But even what is passed
Can't be forever hushed.)
On Fridays
Motele davnel [2]
And on Saturdays
Ate fish.

Once Upon a Time

The number of houses passed through
Is the number of countries passed through.
Each house — its own motherland,
Its own ocean.

And under each weak
Little roof,
No matter how weak —
Its own happiness,
Its own mice,
Its own destiny.

And rarely,
Very rarely —
Two mice
In one crevice!

Now: Motele is mending vests,
And the inspector
Carries a briefcase.

And everyone in town knows
Some tailoring need.
And the inspector has
A fine beard
And a fine
Wife.

2 Prayed (Yiddish)

Happiness comes in different shapes,
In different shapes
In different places:
Motele dreams of chicken
And the inspector
Eats chicken.

Happiness — it's skittish.
Catch as catch can.
Now: Motele loves Riva
But . . . Riva's
Father — a rabbi.

And the rabbi often talks
And about the same thing always:
"She needs big happiness
And a big
House."

There is so little the heart wails,
Wails like a steam engine.
The only big thing Motele has
Is merely
His nose.

"Well so what?
You want me to cry?
No means no!"
And he puts a patch
On both trousers
And vest.

*　*　*

Yes, under each weak little roof,
No matter how weak it is —
Its own happiness, its own mice,
Its own destiny.

And however stubborn life is
It can't give less than a little,

Joseph Utkin　131

And Motele
Has a mama,
An old Jewish mother.

Like everyone's, of course. Loved.
(Aha! We don't talk about that!)
She cooked
Tsimmes[3] well
And bore
Children well.
And he remembers an annual
And semi-annual . . .

But Motele lives in Kishinev,
Where there are many police,
Where many masses are sung
For the Tsar's family,
Where lived . . . Mister . . . Inspector
Of the lovely beard.

It's hard to talk of a whirlpool,
And a whirlpool
Stands by the mouth:
Just . . .
Two . . .
Pogroms . . .
And Motele becomes
An orphan.

"So what?
You want me to cry?
No means no!"
And he puts a patch
On a vest
Instead of on trousers.

＊　＊　＊

And someone drew and drew the days by.

3 Prunes (Yiddish).

132 Joseph Utkin

And in the sky
Nonsensically
Hung buttons of stars
And a moon
Yermolka.[4]

And in the drowsy, miserly silence
Mice started with squeakings.
And someone
Sewed
For someone
A takhrikhim.[5]

"What Matters" and "What Doesn't Matter"

That day was so new.
Young, like the dawn!
For the first time in Kishinev
For the Tsar there was no singing!

Such days are rare,
And there was only one just like that one.
Then came no more to the synagogue
Mister
Rabbi.

Trousers,
Vests,
Laugh!
Rejoice in my day!
Mis-ter Chief of Po-lice
Has gone
To jail!
But this is too wonderful,
My Lord!

But why doesn't he laugh,
This Mister

4 Skullcap.
5 Shroud (Yiddish).

Joseph Utkin 133

Policeman?
A rare wise word
From the cobbler, Ilya:
"Motele, here Jehovah is beside the point,
What matters is you
And me."

*　*　*

And the days began jabbering
Like Med, the peddler-woman.
And the Jews argued:
"Yes" or "no?"

So were issued many
Wise words.
Any head
Was a synagogue.
The past is not much in the present:
Just howl and moan.

"No" —
The inspector concluded.
"Yes" —
The tailor said.

*　*　*

And someone drew and drew the days by.
And in the sky
Nonsensically
Hung buttons of stars
And a moon
Yermolka.

And in the drowsy, miserly silence
A bloody-mouthed dog barked.
And someone
Deliberately
Sewed
A takhrikhim

134   Joseph Utkin

For Nikolas!
That day
Was so new.
Young, like the dawn!
For the first time in Kishinev
The singing
Was not for the Tsar!

Denis Johnson & Kathy Lewis

ILYA EHRENBURG 1891–1967

OUR GRANDSONS WILL BE ASTONISHED

Our grandsons will be astonished,
Browsing through the pages of texts:
"1914 . . . '17 . . . '19 . . .
How did they live? . . . poor things! . . . poor things! . . ."
The children of the new century will read of battles,
Will learn the names of leaders and orators,
The number of the dead
And dates,
They will not discover the roses smelled sweet on the battlefield,
That among the voices of cannons was the clear song of swallows,
How beautiful in those years
Life was,
Never, never did the sun smile so joyously
As over the destructed cities,
When those creeping from the basements
Marvelled: The sun has survived! . . .
The impassioned speeches echoed,
Ardent multitudes were dying,
But soldiers discovered that the snowdrops have a fragrance, now
An hour before the attack.
They were led away in the morning and shot,
And they alone discovered what an April morning means.

136

In slanting rays the cupola shines,
But the wind begged: Wait! one minute! a minute more! . . .
Kissing, they could not tear themselves away from the sad lips,
They could not let go of tightly clasped hands,
They loved — I will die! I will die!
They loved — burn, flame, in the wind!
They loved — Oh, where are you? Where?
They loved — as they could only here, on a passionate and loving star.
In those years there were no gardens of golden fruit,
But only an instantaneous flower, a single doomed May!
In those years there was no "until we meet again,"
But a ringing, brief "goodbye."
Read all about us — be astounded!
You did not live among us — be saddened!
Guests on the earth, we came only for an evening,
We loved, destroyed; we lived in the hour of death,
But over us the constant stars were standing,
And beneath them you were conceived.
In your eyes our desire is still burning.
In your speeches our rebellions still cry out.
Far away, we spilled into the night and the centuries, the centuries,
Our lives as they died away.

Denis Johnson

NIKOLAY TIKHONOV   b. 1896

FIRE AND ROPE, BULLET AND AXE —

Fire and rope, bullet and axe —
These faithful servants at our backs.
In every drop there slept a flood,
From every stone a mountain loomed.
And in each trampled twig
Black-handed forests sighed and moaned.

Falsehood gorged itself from our plates,
Bells sounded only out of habit,
Weightless coins lost their ring,
And children had no fear of corpses . . .
Only then did we learn
Words beautiful — bitter and cruel.

John Glad

II
PRE-WORLD WAR II ÉMIGRÉ POETRY

MARINA TSVETAYEVA 1892–1941

THE HORN OF ROLAND

Like a poor buffoon, of his deformity —
the tale of my orphanhood I tell:
behind the prince — his lineage, seraphim —
a host, behind everyone — thousands
upon thousands just like he, so,
faltering, he falls upon a living wall
and knows of thousands to take his place.

The soldier is proud of his regiment, the devil —
of his legions; behind the thief — his gang,
behind the buffoon — his hump, forever.

So, finally too tired to stand firm, held up
by the realization: alone, destiny — to fight:
To the whistling of fools and the laughter
of the crowd, for — out of — against — all,
I stand and, from the blast, struck —
turned to stone — send heavenward
this thunderous call to emptiness.

And this fire in my breast is pledge
that a King will hear you,
                              Horn!

William Tjalsma

TO KISS A FOREHEAD IS TO ERASE
WORRY —

To kiss a forehead is to erase worry —
I kiss your forehead.
To kiss closed eyes is to give sleep —
I kiss your eyes.
To kiss lips is to give water —
I kiss your lips.
To kiss a forehead is to erase memory —
I kiss your forehead.

John Glad

AN ANCIENT SONG

Yesterday his eyes stared into mine;
Today they squint to the side.
Yesterday he stayed till the birds sang;
Today every lark's a crow.

I'm stupid, you're wise;
I'm stone, you're alive.
I wail the wail of all women:
"My love, how have I wronged you?"

Her tears are water, her blood
Is water; she bathes in blood and tears.
Love is a cruel stepmother
Without justice, without mercy.

Love sails away on ships,
Departs on white roads . . .
And a groan sweeps the earth:
"My love, how have I wronged you?"

Yesterday he lay at my feet,
Swore he wouldn't give me up

Marina Tsvetayeva 141

For all of China. But then his hands unclenched,
And life fell from them like a rusty copeck.

Unloved, frightened, a murderer of children,
I stand accused.
But even in Hell I will say to you:
"My love, how have I wronged you?"

I'll ask the table, the chair:
"Why, for what reason do I suffer?"
He's through kissing . . . me.
Now others respond.

He taught me to live in fire . . .
And threw me on an icy steppe.
Tell me just one thing, my love:
"How have I wronged you?"

There's no need to shake a tree;
A ripe apple picks its own time . . .
Forgive me — for everything.
"My love, how have I wronged you?"

John Glad

AN ATTEMPT AT JEALOUSY

How is it with another woman?
Easier I bet.
One oar stroke! Did the memory
Of me (an island floating

In the sky not the sea) grow dim
Quickly like a coastline?
O souls, you will be sister and
Brother, not lovers!

How is it with a *normal* woman,
Rid of the divine?

Now that you've dethroned your queen
And given up your throne,

How is it? Do you keep busy?
Getting smaller? How
Do you get up? How are you able,
Poor man, to pay the cost

For her eternal boorishness?
"Enough of your hysterics,
I'm moving out!" How is it with
A woman who's just like

Any other, my chosen one?
Do you like her cooking?
When you're sick of it, don't whine!
How is it with a statue,

You who walked on Sinai?
How is it with a stranger,
A mortal? Tell me, do you love her?
Does shame, like Zeus's reins

Not lash your brow?
How is it? How's your health?
Still singing? Tell me, what do you do
About the wounds, poor fellow,

Of your stinking conscience? How is it
With a commodity?
Not easy, eh? Plaster of Paris
Isn't as good as marble

Of Carrara? (God was hewn
From it but he's smashed
To dust!) How is it with one
Of a hundred thousand,

You who have known Lilith? Are
You satisfied? Magicless?
How is it with a woman of earth,
Using five senses

Only? Well cross your heart, are you
Happy? No? In an endless pit
How is it, my love? Worse than for me
With another man?

Bob Perelman, Shirley Rihner, & Alexander Petrov

POEMS TO BLOK

I

Your name — a bird on my hand,
Your name — ice on my tongue.
A single movement of the lips.
Your name — so short,
A ball caught in flight,
A silver bell in the mouth.

A stone dropped in a still pond
Will splash like your name.
At night, in hooves' light clicking
Your loud name clatters.
It calls to us at the temple
In the clicking of a gun-cock.

Your name — ah no!
Your name — a kiss on the eyes,
On the tender frost of the still lids.
Your name — a snow-kiss,
A gulp from a cold blue spring.
Deep sleep — comes with your name.

2

Gentle ghost,
Blameless knight,
Who called you
Into my young life?

In mist — you stand,
Dove-colored, clothed
In a snowy chasuble.

It's not the wind
Pushing me here and there through the city.
Oh, already for the third
Night, the scent of the enemy.

His eyes are blue —
The snow-singer threw
A charm on me.

The snow-swan
Spreads feathers for my feet.
They sail and slowly
Drop into the snow.

So, on feathers,
I go towards the door,
Behind it — death.

Behind blue windows
He sings to me,
With far off bells
He sings to me.

With a long cry,
A swan call,
He calls.

Gentle ghost,
I know I'm dreaming it all.
Do me a favor,
Amen, amen, evaporate,
Amen.

3

You're going by, west of the sun,
You will see the evening light.

Marina Tsvetayeva   145

You're going by, west of the sun,
And snow will cover your tracks.

By my windows, free of passion,
You'll go past through the quiet snow,
My wonderful righteous godly man,
The soft light of my soul!

I do not covet your soul!
Your path is inviolable.
Into your hand, pale with kissing,
I will not drive my iron nail.

And I will not call your name aloud
Nor will I stretch my hands out,
Only from afar will I bow
To a holy image of wax.

And standing under the slow snowfall,
I'll kneel down in the snow
And in your holy name, I will
Kiss the twilight snow.

And there, with a king's step,
You go by — in the quiet, still
As death, quiet light, glory of heaven —
Ruler of my soul!

4

A den — for the beast,
A road — for the lost,
A hearse — for the dead,
To each — what's his.

To woman — cunning,
To the tsar — ruling,
To me — praising
Your name.

Cupolas flame, in Moscow where I live,
Bells clang, in Moscow where I live,
Tombs stand in rows where I live,
Kings and queens asleep in them.

Didn't you know, in the Kremlin at sunrise,
It's the easiest place in the world to breathe,
Didn't you know, in the Kremlin at sunrise,
I pray to you till dawn.

And while you're walking along your Neva,
That is when, beside the river Moscow,
I'm standing with my head down, seeing
All the streetlights lined into one.

I love you, in total insomnia,
I listen to you, in total insomnia,
Oh, that is when, on all sides of the Kremlin
The bell ringers awaken.

But my river — and your river,
But my hand — and your hand,
Will never touch, dear love, until one
Dawn catches another dawn.

6

They thought: Human!
So they made him die.
He's dead and gone.
Mourn the dead angel.

At twilight
He sang evening beauty.
Three wax fires
Flutter, superstitious.

He radiated
Hot lines across the snow.

Marina Tsvetayeva   147

Three wax candles
For the sun. The light bringer.

Oh see how
The dark eyelids are sunken.
Oh see how
His wings are broken.

The black reciter
Reads, the bored people shift.
The dead singer
Rests, celebrating Sunday.

Bob Perelman, Shirley Rihner, & Alexander Petrov

ANATOLY STEIGER 1907–44

IT IS AN ANCIENT CUSTOM

It is an ancient custom
That certain people lie
And others help them
                to lie
(Even though they see through everything),
And all this together is called love.

John Glad

THEY WILL NOT ASK US: . . .

They will not ask us: have you sinned?
They'll ask us only: did you love?
With heads hanging,
Bitterly, we'll say: yes . . . Oh, yes,
We loved . . . Again and again . . . .

Paul Schmidt

NOBODY WAITS . . .

Nobody waits at the foot of the stairs any more
Or takes our hand crossing a street, the way they did
When we were young. Nobody tells us about the mean
Ant and the Grasshopper. Or teaches us to believe in God.

149

Nowadays nobody thinks of us at all —
They all have enough just thinking of themselves,
So we have to live as they do — but alone . . .
(Impotent, dishonest, and inept.)

Paul Schmidt

HOW CAN I SHOUT, . . .

How can I shout, to be heard in that prison,
Beyond those ramparts, through those walls,
That not everyone has betrayed him,
That he is not abandoned, alone in the world?

I dreamed that I broke in to see you,
Sat on your bed and held you in my arms.
(Though he's long lost the habit, surely,
Of tenderness and soft, familiar words.)

Yet friendship exists, it really exists,
And tenderness of male for male as well . . .
It is not obligation, but particular nobility
To say so, with unwavering eyes.

Paul Schmidt

HOW DO WE BREAK THE HABIT . . .

How do we break the habit of big words:
What does "pride" mean? What's "humiliation"?
(When you know perfectly well I'm ready
to respond to the first sign, the first call,
the first slight gesture.) . . .

Paul Schmidt

. . . NOT AN EPILOGUE, . . .

. . . Not an epilogue, but everything coming to an end.
We'll meet. I'll grow very pale.
Your arrogant face will flicker
With annoyance: "What a silly idea!"

At my arrival — a meaningless arrival,
Because I can't behave like all the rest —
What is this constant wanderlust?

Suppose, a variant: (The thought drives me mad)
A clumsy hug?

Paul Schmidt

FRIENDSHIP

Where is he now, I wonder?
And what's his life like?
Don't let me sit by the door
Expecting a sudden knock:
He will never come back.

Was it to hurt me, or himself?
(Or maybe he was lucky.)

One dream remains — the thought of peace.
— Don't need friendship, all words are empty,
And that word's the emptiest of all.

(For friendship you need to have two.
I was one, the other was air: you.)

Paul Schmidt

Anatoly Steiger 151

THE DULL RATTLE OF SHUTTERS . . .

The dull rattle of shutters being lowered
So the cottage looks like someone blind,
And then, like a shot point-blank —
The roar of a motor in the garden out in front.

. . . And an endlessly accompanying glance:
Hopeless, melancholy, spaniel-eyed.

Paul Schmidt

UNTIL THE SUN SINKS . . .

Until the sun sinks into a green
Smoke and twilight starts to spread
We speak of nothing but summer.

Yet autumn will soon tell us
The truth, in a cold voice.

Paul Schmidt

WE BELIEVE BOOKS AND MUSIC

We believe books and music,
We believe verse and dreams,
We believe words . . . (Even when
They're said to us in consolation
From the window of a railroad car) . . . .

John Glad

BORIS POPLAVSKY 1903–35

ANOTHER PLANET

To Jules Laforgue

With our monocles, our frayed pants,
our various diseases of the heart,
we slyly think that planets and the moon
have been left to us by Laforgue.

So we scramble meowing up the drainpipe.
The roofs are asleep, looking like scaly carp.
And a long-tailed devil, wrapped in a thundercloud,
struts around like a draftman's compass on a map.

Sleepwalkers promenade.
House-ghosts with sideburns lounge sedately.
Winged dogs bark quietly;
we fly off softly, mounted on dogs.

Below, milky land glistens.
A train belching sparks is clearly visible.
A pattern of rivers ornaments the fields,
And over there is the sea, its waters waist-deep.

Raising their tails like aeroplanes,
our pilots are gaining altitude,
and we fly off to Venus — but not the one
that wrecks the charts of our life.

A motionless blue mountain, like a nose.
Glassy lakes in the shadow of mountains.
Joy, like a tray, shakes us.
We head for a landing, our lights fading out.

Why are these fires burning on the bright sun's surface?
No, already they fly and crawl and whisper —
They are dragonfly people, they are butterflies
as light as tears and no stronger than a flower.

Toads like fat mushrooms come galloping,
carrots buck and rear and quiver,
and along with them toothed plants
that cast no shadows are reaching for us.

And they start to buzz, they start to crackle and squeak,
they kiss, they bite — why, this is hell!
Grasses whistle like pink serpents
and the cats! I won't even try to describe them.

We're trapped. We weep. We fall silent.
And suddenly it gets dark with terrifying speed.
Frozen rain, the snowy smoke of an avalanche,
our dirigible no longer dares to fly.

The insects' angry host has vanished.
And as for us, we have stretched out to die.
Mountains close us in, a deep blue morgue shuts over us.
Ice and eternity enchain us.

Emmett Jarrett & Dick Lourie

DON AMINADO   1888–1957

OUR SUNDAY REST

Throw open the window,
Look out the door,
Scratch your belly
And say: Alors!
Let's live a little,
At least some more,
That is, assuming,
We've lived before.
The air is bliss,
The sky is blue;
Not only artists
Love its hue.
So unbutton that bathrobe,
Light up a cigar,
Spread out that paper,
Learn all about war.
Blow fat black rings,
Sprawl out in your chair,
They're fighting in China
So grunt "Oh, merde!"
Or maybe: "Ah so."
You know,
If you puff real hard
Your nose gets . . . chaud.

That yellow terror ain't so yellow
When you're feeling really mellow.
So light up that smelly thing,
Get your world-view through the rings.
Let the gentle summer breezes
Kiss and tickle your bald pate.
But just why do all those arabs
Cut their women into pieces?
But then . . . we can't all be cherubs,
And in thoughts of foreign lands
The paper slips out of your hands.
Languor, summer, dreams of war,
A hellenic mighty snore.
Sunday each man's a hellene
Even if he's never seen
Ancient Greece's golden shore.
Rumor has it, at hard labor
Vicious gentlemen who battered
Older ladies, slit their throats
On their Sunday Sabbath dote.
Overhead the sun is beaming
On blue prison caps and gleaming
Bright from chains and cards for whist.
Just picture now such scenes of bliss
Where murderers are pantheists.
Slumber, blue skies, lucid air,
See the universe laid bare.
Let's live a little
At least some more.
It really isn't such a chore.

John Glad

VLADISLAV KHODASEVICH 1886–1939

MUSIC

All night the snowstorm raged, by morning it had cleared.
A Sunday laziness still infects my limbs,
Mass at the Church of the Annunciation
Has not yet ended. I go into the yard.
How tender everything is: the little house, the smoke
Curling above the roof! The frosty vapor
Is silvery pink. Its columns rise
From the houses to the very dome of heaven,
Like the wings of gigantic angels.
And Sergey Ilyich, my portly neighbor,
Seems suddenly so small. He wears
A sheepskin coat, and felt boots. Firewood
Is scattered about him in the snow.
Straining with both arms, he raises the heavy hatchet
Above his head, but — thud! thud! thud! — the blows
Do not ring out: the sky, the snow, the cold
Absorb the sound . . . "Compliments of the season, neighbor!"
"Ah, how are you!" I too arrange
My firewood. He thuds! I thud! But soon
I'm tired of chopping, draw myself up
And say: "Stop, just a minute!
Don't I hear music?" Sergey Ivanych
Stops working, lifts his head a little
Hears nothing, but listens carefully . . .

"You must have thought you heard it," he says.
"What! Listen! It's so clear!"
He listens again. "Perhaps,
They're burying a soldier? Only,
I can't hear a thing." But I do not let up:
"For pity's sake, it's quite clear now.
And the music seems to be coming from above:
A cello . . . and harps, perhaps . . .
How well they play! Don't bang!"
And my poor neighbor, Sergey Ivanych, again
Stops chopping. He can hear nothing,
But does not want to bother me, and tries
Not to show his annoyance. It's a funny sight:
He stands in the middle of the yard, afraid to interrupt
An inaudible symphony. And finally
I feel sorry for him.
I announce: "It's over." Again,
We take up our hatchets. Thud! thud! thud! . . . And the sky
Is as high above as ever, and feathery
Angels shine in it as usual.

Daniel Weissbort

MONKEY

It was hot. The forests burnt. Time
Dragged on. Next door,
A rooster called. I went out through the gate.
There, leaning against the fence, a thin, dark Serb,
A vagrant, dozed on a bench.
A heavy silver cross lay against
His half-naked breast. Drops of sweat
Trickled down. Above, on the fence
Sat a monkey in a red skirt
And hungrily chewed the dirty leaves
Of the lilac. A leather collar,

Pulled on by a heavy chain, bit into its throat.
Hearing me, the Serb came to, wiped the sweat away, asked
For some water. But taking just a sip,
To see if it was cold, he placed
The saucer on the bench, and the monkey,
Dipping its fingers in the water, at once
Grasped the vessel in both hands.
It drank, standing on all fours,
Leaning its elbows on the bench.
Its chin almost touched the boards,
Its back bent high
Above the balding pate. So, Darius
Must have knelt, pressing himself
To a puddle in the road, the day he fled
Alexander's mighty phalanx.
Drinking all the water, the monkey brushed
Away the saucer from the bench, drew itself up,
And — shall I ever forget that moment? —
Stretched out to me a dark and calloused hand,
Still cool from the moisture . . .
I have shaken hands with lovely women, poets,
Leaders of their people — not one hand
Possessed such nobleness
Of contour! Not one hand
Touched my own so fraternally!
And as God is my witness, no one has ever looked
So deep into my eyes and with such wisdom,
Indeed, to the very depths of my soul.
The sweetest legends of extreme antiquity
This indigent creature reawakened in my heart,
And in that moment life seemed complete.
It seemed a choir of heavenly bodies and ocean waves,
Of winds and spheres, burst like an organ
On my hearing, crashed out, as it once had done
In days long gone, days immemorial.
And the Serb left, tapping his tambourine.
The monkey, squatting on his left shoulder,

Vladislav Khodasevich   159

Swayed in time,
Like an Indian Maharajah on an elephant.
A huge crimson sun
Hung in the opaline smoke,
Shedding no rays. The thunderless heat
Poured down onto the stunted wheat.

That day, war was declared.

Daniel Weissbort

THE AUTOMOBILE

We wander in the bleak silence,
Damp night, the empty dark.
And suddenly, a tuneful summons —
An automobile comes round the corner!

It is shot with black lacquer,
It gleams with faceted glass,
It extends into the darkness
Two white angels' wings.

And the buildings become at once
Like the festive walls of ballrooms,
And close to us a passer-by
Courses through these wings.

And the light, glimpsed fleetingly, looms,
Shaking the rain-damped dust . . .
But listen: I began to see
A different automobile.

It passes in the bright light,
It passes like the light of day,
And it has two wings on it, like these,
But they are black.

160   Vladislav Khodasevich

And everything that chances to come
Under the black shafts of those lights,
Vanishes irrevocably from
My fragile memory.

I forget, I lose
My radiant psyche,
I stretch out blind arms
And recognize nothing:

The world stopped here, simple and whole,
But from the time that thing went by,
There were blanks in it, as though
It had been splashed with vitriol.

Daniel Weissbort

THE BRIDE

The grass grew in vain
Over the darkness of this earthly hell:
For the gaze that penetrates,
Stagnant nature is dead.

I do not know the freedom of the creator,
But I know my own distress,
And with the bold freedom of a singer
I come to a bold decision.

You who are vowed to silence, judge:
The maiden is lying dead,
But see, I touch her breast —
She stands, she looks into a mirror.

The beauty raised from the dead by me
I bear, like a precious burden, —
Before your throne I bring
My young bride.

Unknit your frowning brow and gaze
At this creature of purity,
Grant us eternal love
And immaculate union!

And if you cannot give
Your blessing to such a miracle,
Then let my punishment be
Unending death, without resurrection.

Daniel Weissbort

DACTYLS

1

My father was six-fingered. Across the canvas, stretched tight,
    Bruni[1] taught him to guide the soft brush.
There, where the Theban sphinxes[2] sit lost in contemplation of one
        another,
    Wearing a summer jacket in wintertime, he ran across the Neva,
And having returned to Lithuania, a happy and indigent painter,
    He decorated many Polish and Russian churches there.

2

My father was six-fingered. Lucky men are born that way.
    There, where the pear trees stand by the green border,
Where the azure waters of the Vilnya and the Neman[3] are carried away,
    In a poor, poor family he met with his good fortune.
As a child I saw my mother's wedding veil and slippers in the chest of
        drawers.
    Mama! Prayer, love, fidelity and death is what you are.

---

1 Bruni, Fyodor Antonovich (1800–75), a Russian painter.
2 Thirteenth-century B.C. Egyptian statues brought to St. Petersburg in 1832 and placed
on the embankment of the Neva River.
3 Vilnya and Neman, two rivers running through Lithuania.

3

My father was six-fingered. Sometimes we'd play thumbkin
  In the evening, sitting on the favorite sofa.
Here, on my father's hand I bent back, diligently,
  One finger after the other — five. I was the sixth.
There were six children. To tell the truth, he maintained
  These five with hard work — only for me there just wasn't time.

4

My father was six-fingered. Like a tiny, extra little finger
  He was adroitly able to hold closed in his left hand,
So, uniquely hidden, latent, in the soul forever
  Lies this memory and the sorrow of his sainted craft.
Turned merchant of necessity — not so much as a hint or a word,
  No mention, no grumbling. He did love to fall silent.

5

My father was six-fingered. In his fine, dry palm
  How many colors and features did he hide, close up and hold?
A painter contemplates the world — and judges it with an impudent
    liberty,
  The demonic liberty of a creator — and then creates another.
He closed his eyes, gave up the brushes and his maulstick,
  Created nothing, judged nothing . . . A hard, sweet lot!

6

My father was six-fingered. And his son? Neither a humble heart
  Nor a large family, nor a six-fingered hand did he inherit.
Like the gambler on an unlucky card, he stakes it all,
  Soul and fortune, on a word, a sound . . .
Now, on a January night, drunk, in six-fingered meter
  And six-fingered stanzas the son remembers the father.

Mary Jane White

Vladislav Khodasevich 163

ON THE DEATH OF MY TOMCAT MURR

In amusements he was so cagey and in his caginess amusing —
My conciliatory friend and inspiration!
Now he's in those gardens beyond the fiery river
With the sparrows of Catullus and the martins of Derzhavin.

O, the good gardens beyond the fiery river,
Where there are no foul crowds, where in blessed laziness
The best-loved shades of poets and beasts
Enjoy the well-earned rest of the ages.

When will I go there? I don't want to hurry
My earthly term of hard-times.
But to those fished up in the secret net
I fly more frequently in devoted dreaming.

Mary Jane White

A MONUMENT

I have beginning and end.
I have accomplished little,
But I am a firm link:
This much is given to me.

In a new Russia, in a great Russia
My two-faced idol
Will stand on a crossroads
Where there is time and wind and sand . . . .

John Glad

DOVID KNUT   1900–55

I WAS WALKING . . .

I was walking along the Sea of Galilee,
And in a divinely morose joy
(as if my heart were glad and yet not glad)
I wandered among the Stones of Capernaum
Where once . . . Listen, ponder
In the shade, in the dust of this olive garden.

In the bar of the universe
The same unsleeping voice
Howled with sexual desire,
And from the walls of the eternal city
Leered cinematic shouts.
For everyone! Cheap!! Incessant!!!

What can I tell you of Palestine?
I remember deserted Sedzhera,
The orange cloud of the Khamsin,
The dignified voice of an Astrakhan Ger,
The narrow insulted back
Of a murdered Shomer boy,

A haughty camel at the watering trough,
The peyas of mute Zaddik's from Tsfat,
The dry sky of a hungry eternity

165

Hovering over the world's doomed childhood,
The smooth endless tombstones
Of the Josephate's insane dead,
And a girl named Judith
Who for a long time
Waved a tanned hand after me.

John Glad

I REMEMBER A DIM EVENING . . .

I remember a dim evening in Kishinev:
We'd just walked past Inzov Hill
Where a short, curly-haired official — Pushkin —
Used to live. He had hot negroid eyes
Set in a plain but lively face
And they say he was quite a dandy.

I could see a dead Jew being carried on stretchers
Down dusty, frowning, dead Asia Street
Past the hard walls of the orphanage.
Under the rumpled shroud
You could see the bony outlines
Of a man gnawed away at by life,
Gnawed so far away
That the skinny worms of the Jewish cemetery
Had little to look forward to.

Behind the old men carrying the stretchers
Was a small group of wide-eyed Jews.
Their moldy old-fashioned coats
Reeked of holyness and fate.
It was a Jewish smell — of poverty and sweat,
Of pickled herring and moth-eaten fabric,
Of fried onions, holy books, the synagogue.
And especially — of herring.

Their hearts sang with a great grief,
And their step was silent, measured, resigned —
As if they had followed that corpse for years,
As if their march had no beginning,
No end . . . These wise men of Zion, of Moldavia.

Between them and their black burden of grief
Walked a woman, and in the dusty twilight
We couldn't see her face.

But how beautiful was her high voice!

To the slap of steps and faint rustle
Of falling leaves and coughs
There poured forth an unknown song.
In it flowed tears of sweet resignation
And devotion to God's eternal will
And ecstasy of obedience and fear . . .

Oh, how beautiful was her high voice!

It sang not of a thin Jew
Bouncing on stretchers. It sang — of me,
Of us, of everyone, of futility and dust,
Of old age and grief, of fear and pity,
And the eyes of dying children . . .

The Jewess walked smoothly,
But each time the stretcher-bearers
Stumbled on some cruel stone
She would scream and rush to the corpse.
Her voice would wax strong,
Ringing with threats to God,
Rejoicing in raging curses.

And the woman waved her fists at him
Who floated in a greenish sky
Above the dusty trees, above the corpse,
Above the roof of the orphanage,
Above the hard, crusty earth.

Dovid Knut 167

But then she grew afraid
And beat her breast
And begged forgiveness in a husky wail
And screamed insanely of faith and resignation.
She pressed herself to the ground,
Unable to endure the heavy burden
Of severe, grieving eyes staring down from heaven.

What actually was there?
A quiet evening, a fence, a star,
A dusty wind . . . My poems in "The Courier,"
A trusting high-school girl, Olga,
The simple ritual of a Jewish funeral
And a woman from the book of Genesis.

But I can never tell in words
What it was that hung over Asia Street.
Above the street lights on the outskirts of town,
Above the laughter hiding in the doorways,
Above the boldness of some unknown guitar
Rumbling over the barks of anguished dogs.

. . . A peculiar Jewish-Russian air . . .
Blessed be he who has breathed it.

John Glad

VYACHESLAV IVANOV   1866–1949

THE WINTER SONNETS

1

The runners creak. Dead snow broke like day.
The forest, enchantingly, solemnly snowed in.
The sky's vault dark with swansdown,
Clouds quicker than deer on their sublunary run.

Hear how the bell sings of a distant coast . . .
The dream of the fields obscure and immense . . .
Unbroken snow ahead and the inescapable chance:
Holy Night, do you hold this night's lodging anywhere?

And I see as in a telling mirror,
My family in the close asylum
In the honeyed light of occasional fires.

And my heart excited by the hidden proximity
Waits. For a spark among the pines. And the flight
Of the sleigh hurtles on past, past.

2

Invisible guide to my remote roads,
I've been under your examination all along
In deep purgatories whose threshold
We call a chance at the crossroads.

In the end our pride is extinguishable:
In prisons I'm bound to a merely convenient
Lover, until I approach you, whom I can't love,
And shrink away with a kiss of absolution.

So I ran from severe winter;
A voluptuary of midday kisses,
And held the eternal celebration with Nature.

But with this graveyard of snowdrifts,
The darkness of clouds, the requiem of an ice storm
And me my angry mentor has forced an intimacy.

3

Winter of the soul. Skewed and distant
The live sun warms what stiffens
In a mute snowdrift while tedium
Sings of it in the guise of a storm.

An armload of wood dumped at the fire,
Boiling millet, and the hour prevails upon you —
Then sleep as all sets into somnolence . . .
Ah, this grave of eternity is deep!

The spring with its life-giving fluid iced
Over, its unstable fire grown hard,
You won't find me by lifting that shroud.

My double, obedient servant, drags his coffin
While the true I, betraying the carnal, creates
His temple in the distance, and not by human hands.

4

The winter — dark and molten.
In my long vigil I observed the equinox
The women met in their frenzy on the hill.
Sleep leaves my eyes.

This cold prison, changed to a laurel
Forest by the descending Muse,
Wavers between the real and vision and
In both stands the celestial Herself.

"Doubter," I hear her ambrosiac whisper,
"Has your craven murmer been made a song?
You rustle in a branching skeleton

With the remnants of leaves, dry and brown,
Like an oak under snow — wind whistling in the shrubbery.
As a star I failed to attract you or your sullen gaze."

5

Roving Magus, fierce thief, gray wolf,
I compose these winter verses to your glory.
And hear your hungry howl! The earth has
Welcomed me and human speech is kind.

But not for you, despised. What the host's dog knows
Is a slavish debt and the seers of Polyhymnia will know
You, more magical and kindred than the Delphic
Beast, as one of their own until their voices fail.

Near the place where the dugout of the soul is moored,
Where I was given over to the Fates,
Igor, leader of the wolves, stands his watch.

Your pack of shamen howl. From my childhood
I've known it as a summons, this drawn wailing
Of homeless fire on the frozen steppe.

6

Night. A new moon. And frost, fiercer
Than a she-bear answered the singer of hopes
That he and his Muse had met the damage of the hard frost
Early, as untroubled, gullible children.

Faith is not orphaned without news; given
A continual promise the spirit remains bright,
At this night hour hear how the cock proclaims
The spring finer and holier than any spring.

Vyacheslav Ivanov 171

That trumpeted call which opens the last
Locks on the gates of winter ordains your
Hoarse hymn, leader of the morning.

And the heart which has experienced
The midnight of loss quickens the return of its loved ones
To the face of the earth with a secret beating.

Mary Jane White

ALEKSANDR VERTINSKY

I REMEMBER THE NIGHT

I remember the night,
Your eyes, blue from eye-liner,
The diamond of your tear
As it slid into the wine glass.

I remember a minute passed,
Your blouses — white on the armchairs,
The day — gray and empty after you left,
Your parrot grieving in the corner.
It kept shrieking "jamais"
And crying in French.

John Glad

III
POST-WORLD WAR II POETRY IN RUSSIA

PAVEL ANTOKOLSKY b. 1896

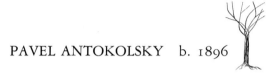

FROM *SON*

We are not always dependent on memory.
The chance cursory track of a pencil,
A chance card in a packet
Of letters — a young soul arises.
Right here it appeared, untouchable,
And smiled, then vanished into the darkness,
Defined absolutely, unblurred, single,
Belonging totally to itself.
Here is his handwriting, punctilious,
Slanting, plain, a bit feminine.
That was when he was living in the east,
Alone, the first time away from home,
Not at the front, in military school.
At first the letters were restrained,
"I'm healthy, satisfied, studying." He was silent
About his troubles, made no mention
Of his feelings. Much later he began to confide
His depression: mother, sister.
But soon his letters started to talk of comrades
And his melancholy grew less acute.
And this is the conclusion of many days,
Served up hot, like a special dish,
"There are remarkable people here, papa."

And again and again, friendship.
Coming to meet people. Being with them
Always. Meeting people — goal
And triumph. Thus little by little my son's
Masculine character was formed.

One small notebook is left. Tidy,
Neat as a lesson,
Is entered the artilleryman's law,
The sacred logic of cannons,
The sacred exactitude of taking aim.
Here's what he lived and breathed that year;
Sincere and purposeful there grew in him
The consciousness of duty, fear
Of overstepping privilege. Undistracted.

Did he foresee the bloody flames
Of death, his soul's disastrous last rest?

Suddenly, from the field, a sketch: a palace
With Venetian arches. Here's a cannon
Under a cypress —
                            But think!
In what pensiveness did he glance
Vaguely at his simple sketch?
What sum, what emotional experience
Is expressed, what gulp of dream?
No total. The mouthful wasn't swallowed.
The signature broke off:
                            V. Antok . . .

      .   .   .   .

You must dig in black ashes a long time.
Not days, not years, but centuries,
Until your dry eyes finally grow blind,
Until the stiffening hand ceases
At the end of its final line. Look now
At the features that you loved.

He's not your successor; you're — his.
You've changed places, he and you.

. . . .

You share your mourning with all Moscow. There
Are no lamps or candles in windows,
Only haze, chilled with all the tears
And so much hard frost. It helps
With its attention. What memories? Rails,
Rails, rails. Poles, flying by, poles.
Those burned-out people, shivering in the wind,
The whine of shrapnel. The metal howl
Of fate. Signifying vengeance? Vengeance.
It is necessary, so
The heart of my son will overgrow his death.
Let it burst into a cannonade. In some
Hearts there is this profession.
                              And if the sky
Is cloudy at the front, if spring
Leaps across the earth, there'll always be
Two of you, on earth, son
And father, without dreams. You have no right
To some special private grief.

Even if, risking the last trump card,
It be placed against your temple. Don't take your life.
Do not flatter yourself. Is this a way out?
For all his cut-short youth, the son
Does not seek indulgence or advantage,
And to battle calls millions of sons.
And into that battle, in indestructible array,
Other beloved sons will go
To replace beloved sons, in the name
Of truth, a greater truth than yours.

Bob Perelman & Shirley Rihner

Pavel Antokolsky   177

ILYA SELVINSKY 1899–1968

I SAW IT!

You don't have to listen to folk stories
    Or read the papers and believe,
But I saw it. With my own eyes.
    Is that clear? I saw. Myself.
Look, here is the path. Over there — the hill.
    Between them
              like this —
                    the trench.
From this trench grief rises still,
    Overflowing its banks.

No! Words cannot tell it . . .
    One has to roar. Sob!
Seven thousand shot down in a frozen pit,
    Rusting over like ore.

Who are they? Soldiers? Not at all.
Partisans perhaps? No.
Here lies lop-eared Kolka —
    Eleven years old.

Here are his relatives. The farmstead "Joyous."
"Self-made" — one hundred twenty peasant households
From neighboring stations,
Neighboring villages,
Thrown down in a ditch like hostages.

178

They lie, sit, slide down from the parapet.
Every one makes a gesture, entirely his own.
Within the corpse, winter has frozen the emotions
Of the living whom death has taken
And the corpses rave, threaten, hate . . .
Like a council, the lifeless quiet makes noise.
The attitudes of the fallen never change —
With their eyes, bared teeth, necks, shoulders
They still quarrel with their executioners,
Crying out, "You will not conquer!"

A man. He is lightly dressed.
One leg in a torn boot,
His chest bared in protest,
The other leg shining with the lacquer of an artificial foot.
A gentle snow falls and falls . . .
The young cripple bares his chest.
Apparently he shouted, "Shoot, devils!"
He chokes. Grows rigid where he falls.

But like a sentry over this graveyard of death
One crutch protrudes from the earth.
And the rage of the dead does not grow cold:
From the rear to those at the front it calls,
Lifting the crutch up like a flag pole,
A guide post, seen from a long way off.

An old woman. This one died standing,
She stood between two corpses at the end,
Her face, sweet and open,
Taken by a dark convulsion.
Her rags flutter as the wind goes by . . .
In the left eye, frozen sealing wax,
But the right looked deep into the sky,
      There where the cloud bank breaks.
And in this reproach to the Virgin Mary
Is the fall of the faith of the years of old:
"If there are fascists alive in the world
      The time has come that there is no God."

Ilya Selvinsky   179

Beside that one, a mutilated Jewess.
Before her a child, as if asleep.
Around his throat with such tenderness
The mother's gray scarf is wrapped.
Oh, maternal strength primeval!
Going to extinction, going under fire,
An hour, half an hour before that fall
The mother saves her child from a cold.
But for them death is no separation:
No enemy has power over them now —
And from the child's ear

     a red stream

Flows down

    into the palm

      of the mother's

        hand.

How terrible to write of this. How strange.
  But it's necessary. Necessary! Write!
Now no joke can shake off fascism:
You measure the fascist soul's corruption,
Recognize its deception,
The "sentimentality" of the Prussian vision,
Now let

   through their

     blue

      waltzes

Burn the hollow of this mother's hand.

Get going! Stigmatize! You confront massacre, butchery,
You've caught them in the act — expose it!
See how with this armor-piercing bullet
  The executioner pierced us,
Let it thunder, like Dante, like Ovid,
Let nature itself begin to cry,
If

  all this

    you yourself

      witnessed

  Yet kept your mind.

I am standing, silenced, before the terrible grave,
And what of words? Words are to ash.
There was a time — I wrote about my love,
    About the trilling of the nightingale.
Would such things appear in a thing like this?
    Truly? And yet
Even for a theme such as this
    One tries to find the true word.

But here? Here are words, like nerves,
But lines . . . they are denser than dried crows' spinal cords.
No, comrades: for these terrors
    Language has no words.
It is too accustomed, therefore plain,
Too refined, thus miserly,
From the implacable grammar depends,
Flown from their lips, each single cry.

It would be necessary . . . to gather an assembly
Of all clans from flag post to flag post
And take from each all its humanity,
All, bursting through the centuries —
Screams, wheezes, sighs, moans,
The echoes of invasions, pogroms, slaughter . . .
Isn't this
        dialect
                of unfathomable torment
    Akin to the words we are after?

But we are possessed of a diction,
Hotter than all our words.
Buckshot sprinkles the foe with damnation.
With the words of prophets the battery thunders.
Do you hear the trumpets at the front?
Confusion . . . cries . . . Thugs grow pale.
They run! But there is nowhere they can run
    Away from your bloody grave.

Relax your muscles. Close your eyes.
Spring up like grass at these heights.

                    Ilya Selvinsky   181

Whoever saw you, forever he carries,
In his soul, all your wounds.
This ditch . . . Can you tell of it with verse?
Seven thousand corpses.

                                Jews . . . Slavs
Yes! But it cannot be told with words.
      With fire! Only with fire!

Denis Johnson & IWP

OLGA BERGGOLTS b. 1910

A WISH

For a long while I have lived with the hope
that the town of Pushkin will return to us —
I shall go there on foot, as in the past
pilgrims used to visit holy places.

I have not forgotten the long, long
journey back, as though through battle.
The road to Pushkin is scorched and sad,
a road to what can never be recovered.

The dear house with its steep green roof,
Nearby the lindens rising high.
Irisha, my daughter, lived in this place —
she was red-haired, like I.

I remember all the paths, every corner
in the mysterious gardens of that town.
I often came here with the one
I still have not ceased to mourn.

I remember all the paths, every corner
in the mysterious gardens of that town.
I often came here with the one
I still have not ceased to mourn.

I shall go on foot to distant Pushkin —
I've heard it's just been taken back.
On the edge of the dark park I shall
prostrate myself before it.

I shall greet everything that I loved here —
do not forgive, do not forget, my heart.
I shall greet all that has been restored to me,
and thrice those who can never be restored.

Daniel Weissbort

TO MY SISTER

I dreamt of the old house
where I spent my childhood years,
and the heart, as before, finds
comfort, and love, and warmth.

I dreamt of Christmas, the tree,
and my sister laughing out loud,
from morning, the rosy windows
sparkle tenderly.

And in the evening gifts are given
and the pine needles smell of stories,
And golden stars risen,
are scattered like cinder above the rooftop.

I know that our old house
is falling into disrepair.
Bare, despondent branches
knock against darkening panes.

And in the room with its old furniture,
a resentful captive, cooped up,
lives our father, lonely and weary —
he feels abandoned by us.

Why, oh why do I dream of the country
where the love's all consumed, all?
Maria, my friend, my sister,
speak my name, call to me, call . . .

Daniel Weissbort

THE BLOCKADE SWALLOW [1]

Through the years of happiness and hardships,
one time will always stand out for me,
the spring of nineteen forty-two,
spring in the besieged city.

On my breast I also wore
a little swallow made of tin.
It was a symbol of good news.
It meant: "I am waiting for a letter."

The blockade invented this symbol.
We knew that only an airplane,
only a bird, could reach us in Leningrad
from our dear homeland.

    . . . How many letters have I received since then!
Why does it seem to me still
that I have not yet received
the letter I want most of all?

Where the life behind each word,
the truth in every line,
my conscience thirsts for, as
parched lips crave the waters of a spring.

Who did not write? Did not send it?
Was it joy? The victory? Some calamity?

1 In the spring of 1942 many Leningraders wore a badge depicting a swallow carrying a
letter in its beak.

Olga Berggolts   185

Or a friend, who forever will
remain unfound, unknown to me?

Or perhaps does this letter that I crave like light
still wander somewhere
seeking my address, not finding it,
and pining miserably for an answer?

Perhaps the day is close when,
in an hour of deep spiritual peace,
I shall receive, unprecedented, imperishable,
the news that sought me back in the war . . .

Oh find me, burn with me, you
who have been so long promised me,
by all that has been, even that absurd
wartime swallow in the siege.

Daniel Weissbort

DON'T TURN AROUND, . . .

Don't turn around, don't look back
into the ice,
        the darkness;
there, someone eagerly
               awaits your gaze,
and you'll not know how to withhold your answer.

Today I turn . . . Suddenly
I see, gazing at me from the ice,
bright-eyed, my friend, alive —
my one and only one . . . forever and forever.

For I did not know it was like this.
I thought it was another I loved.
But my punishment, my joy, my dream,
is that I live only under your gaze!

Only in this am I still right.
Only to him am I still true:
for all the living, I am his wife,
for you and me, I am your widow.

Daniel Weissbort

MY INSATIABLE MEMORY . . .

My insatiable memory is like
A melting asphalt roadway:
I remember all who have passed along it,
Every movement of their life . . .
The tracks of iron wheels, of teeth,
The rusty tracks of injury and anguish.
The bird-like prints
Of a dead daughter's little shoes.
Here, friends in succession have passed.
I remember all of them — why?
For they have forgotten me long ago —
And I shall never see them anymore.
There's one that passed along the edge.
The tracks of his reproach are darker.
Where is he living now? I do not know.
Perhaps, only in my memory.
A scoffing fate endowed me with
This memory as a punishment,
To plague me over the long years
With what my heart has burnt to ash.
Unconsciousness were better than a memory
Like melting asphalt, like a path —
An everlasting path under my footsteps
That cannot leave it, cannot be retraced.

Daniel Weissbort

INDIAN SUMMER

There is one season of the year —
the sun is pale, the air so mild —
An Indian summer
                    it is called,
and the springtime is no more lovely.

Already the delicate cobweb
brushes lightly against your face.
The late birds' voices ring out!
Splendidly the flowerbeds blaze!

The strong showers are long since over.
From the dark, quiet fields the wheat has been gathered . . .
More and more suddenly does my heart start
at a look.
            Jealousy plagues me more.

Oh the wisdom of this bounteous season,
with joy I accept you . . . And yet, my love, where
are you — we call to each other — where are you?
But the woods are silent, the stars austere . . .

For you see, the time of starshowers is over,
and it seems it is time to part forever,
. . . And only now do I understand how
we must love, pity, forgive,
                          say farewell . . .

Daniel Weissbort

BORIS SLUTSKY b. 1919

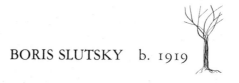

THE BATHHOUSE

You've not been to the local bathhouse
In a small provincial town!
Tubs bulk like boars, and the splashing
Is like a summer day's river outing.

Medals are handed in,
While into the soap room are born
The weals and the scars — all those things
I trust a good deal more.

There, two one-armed men cheerfully
Rub each other's backs,
Scrawled over each one's body,
The marks of war and hard work.

There, on Tuesdays, I construe
From the pattern of each injury
Novels without falsification,
Plays without fraud or flattery.

There, the sailor back on dry land
From an ocean-going cruise
Has brought his broad chest covered
With purple tattoos.

Bursting with pride and excitement there,
And forgetting the boiling water,
I read: "We'll not leave you, mother,"
On the arm of a Partisan.

You hear screams and female laughter there,
Behind the wooden partition.
And a feeling of utter euphoria
Sweeps over you in the steamroom.

There, they discuss the games of soccer,
And with lifted head,
The tailor suffers his callouses,
The furnace worker his scalds.

But the years of disaster and battle
Have not been able to bend
This big-boned race of men,
These sons of my great land.

You've not been to the local paradise,
Between the cinema and sports stadium?
You've not sweated in the bathhouse?
Two roubles it costs to get in.

Daniel Weissbort

LAW, . . .

Law, which each citizen knows well,
Is part and parcel of the State.
The congregation of
The anti-State knows no such rules.

Holding in thrall the people, Power
Decrees what usages pertain.
But rebellions are without
Ink or pads of paper.

190   Boris Slutsky

And when the rioters get hold
Of paper, when they seize the pen,
Then is the mutiny shod and clothed
And nurturing its young.

It's giving comfort to the old,
Minting familiar coinage,
No longer singing rebel songs,
But hymns instead.

   Daniel Weissbort

GOD

We all walked under god.
We were by god's very side.
He lived in no heavenly region,
Sometimes we even saw him
Alive. On the mausoleum.
He was cleverer, more evil,
Than the other, that different one,
Who was called by the name of Jehovah . . .
We all walked under god.
We were at god's very side.
One day I was walking along
Arbat — god passed in five cars.
Beside him his guards were shivering
Under their mouse-gray coats,
Almost bent double with fear.
It was both late and early.
An ashen day was dawning.
Cruel was his gaze
                    and wise.
He looked about him with all-seeing,
With all-penetrating
                    eyes.

We all walked under god.
We were almost at his side.

Daniel Weissbort

HORSES IN THE OCEAN

To I. Ehrenburg

Horses know how to swim,
But not well, not far.
There was a ship called *The Gloria* —
It's easy to recall that name.
The ship sailed, exulting in its name,
The ocean tried to gain the upper hand.
In the hold, tossing their fine heads,
A thousand horses hammered night and day.
A thousand horses! Four thousand horseshoes!
And not a piece of luck between them.
A mine blew a hole in the bottom of the vessel
A long, long way from land.
The people crawled and scrambled into lifeboats.
But the horses just had to swim.
What other course was there, what could be done,
If there was no room on boat or raft?
An island of bay horses floated on the ocean,
A chestnut island in the dark blue sea.
And at first they found it easy going,
They thought the ocean was a stream.
But this was a stream without edge or limit.
At the end of their strength, suddenly
The horses began to neigh, accusing
Those who would drown them in the sea.
The horses went down — their neighing did not cease
Until they had all been drowned.
That's the story. And yet I pity them —
Chestnut creatures that never saw the land.

Daniel Weissbort

THE HOSPITAL

Still the 'Messerschmitts' claw at the heart,
Still the needles go out of their mind,
Still the ear rings with hurras,
The Russian "Hurra-rarara!"
In twenty-syllable lines.
Here, in a former village church turned club,
We lie under labor charts,
But in the corner there's a fusty smell of God —
The village priest ought to be about!
Anathema is powerful though belief is not firm.
The curse-invoking priest ought to be here in person!
What frescoes shine in the corner!
Paradise sings here, hell sets up a fearful howl!
On the unheated earthen floor
A prisoner lies with a stomach wound.
Under the frescoes in an unheated corner
An injured Unteroffizier lies on the floor.
Opposite on a low trestle bed
A young battalion commander is dying.
Decorations glitter on his jacket.
He is . . . disturbing . . . the silence.
He cries out.
(In a whisper — the way was the dying cry.)
He demands, as an officer, as a Russian,
As a man, that in this last hour of his life,
The green, red-haired, rusty Prussian
Should not be allowed to die among us!
He fingers, fingers his decorations,
Smoothes, tugs at his jacket,
And weeps, weeps bitterly that
This request has not been met.
And two steps away, in an unheated corner,
Lies the injured NCO on the floor.
And the orderly removes him, unprotesting,
Away to some distant room,
So that he should not disturb

Our bright deaths with his dark one.
And again quiet descends
And the soldiers explain to a new recruit:
"That's what the war's like in this place!
Clearly you don't approve —
Try fighting the war in your own way!"

Daniel Weissbort

MY FRIENDS

My friends in tanks were burnt
to cinders, to ashes, to dust.
Grass, covering half a world,
has grown out of them of course.
My friends,
                    stumbling onto mines,
took off upwards,
                            were blown sky high,
and lots of peaceful, distant stars
from them,
            from my friends,
                                    caught fire.
People recount their deeds on public holidays,
make films out of them for show,
and my fellow students, my classmates,
turned into verse long ago.

Daniel Weissbort

COPPERS

I taught myself poetry for a few pennies,
Resonant copper that I weighed in my hand.
And the ring of those coins has not been still since,
To this day it continues to sound.

Mother would give me a five-kopeck piece
For a loaf, and then later — two.
I held out till dinner, I breakfasted on
Some books that I bought from the stall.
Sugar got dearer, bread went up in price —
But the low price of Pushkin never failed to surprise.
The shelves in the bakeries often were empty,
In the reading-rooms they were crammed
To bursting with poetry, endlessly lovely.
Whole days I spent in those rooms.
Our entire block thought I was crazy, because
I made poems up on the move,
And on the move read my verse out to myself
With gestures — then said: "That'll do!"
Yes, however much nonsense I spun in those days,
Beauty lurked there, as in a cocoon.
For a few copper pennies I taught myself verse.
For large banknotes it's harder to learn.

Daniel Weissbort

MY OLD MEN ARE DYING —

My old men are dying —
My gods, my teachers.
The builders of the smooth road
Where my footsteps were easy.

You who from errors, from threats,
From blandishments shielded our youth,
Is it possible some cheap illness
Has overcome, mastered you?

My old men are dying,
They bequeath me a long, long life,
But not longer than duty requires,
The law of stanza and line.

Daniel Weissbort

Boris Slutsky   195

SEMYON GUDZENKO 1922–53

BEFORE THE ATTACK

When they go to death — they are singing,
but beforehand
           one can cry.
The most terrible part of the fighting
is the waiting, before the bullets fly.
The snow dug everywhere with mines
and blackened by the dust of mines.
A blast —
and one of your friends dies.
This means, death passes nearby.
Now I know my turn has come.
For me alone
           the hunt goes on.
The hard, heavy
           year of forty-one —
the infantry in the snow, frozen.
It seems to me I am magnetized
to draw toward me every mine.
A blast —
a lieutenant's lungs wheeze
and again death passes nearby.
But already for this waiting
           we have no strength.

196

And frozen animal rage
drives us through each trench,
piercing our necks with bayonets.
The battle was short.
                    And then
we choked down icy vodka
and with the blade of my knife I cleaned
from my nails
                    another's blood.

  Denis Johnson & Shirley Rihner

SERGEY NAROVCHATOV b. 1919

IN THOSE YEARS

I walked, gritting my teeth, past charred
Villages, executed cities,
Past bleak land, past Russian land,
Past our land, land of our fathers.

I remembered the burning towns,
And the hot wind blowing ashes,
And girls on the district committee doors
Crucified by biblical nails.

And the crows circled unafraid
And kites feasted as we watched.
A wiggling spidery sign marked
The executions and the butchery.

In my grief — as if from ancient songs —
I leafed through villages like chronicles.
I saw Yaroslavna in each old woman,
Every stream was the Nepryadva.[1]

My blood is loyal to our holy
Things. To it I mourned with the old words:
Russia, mother! My endless world!
What vengeance must avenge you!

Bob Perelman & Shirley Rihner

1 References to the heroic epic "Lay of the Host of Igor."

VLADIMIR SOLOUKHIN   b. 1924

THE WIND

The wind
Flies above the sea.
Not long ago it was no wind but
Still, warm air suspended over the ground.
It
Enveloped the daisies,
Smelt of the green summer
(Over the field of rye, the yellow, transparent heat).
Then,
Stirring the grains of sand,
Bending the grass a little,
It began to move. The air grew into a wind.
And now
Above the sea
It flies, it has gathered great speed,
It has acquired great strength. And it has spread great wings.
The waves of the sea
Are rising.
The wind rips the foam from their tops.
The foam flies in the wind, scudding above the waters.
The bright,
Bounding wind
Smells not of honey but iodine,
Smells disturbingly of salt, smells vaguely of distress.

(My arms, they are like wings. My heart is wide open.
The wind plunges into me. It talks to me):

"I slept
In the peaceful meadow.
I slept above the daisy in its field.
Golden bees pierced me through and through.
But I became
A winged wind,
I fly over the dark sea,
On the sea roads I break chains, don't joke with me!
I
shall be frank with you:
You must choose what you want.
You must learn to look at things straight.
Whether to be
A gentle
Daisy, to smell of honey,
Or to fly above the world, shattering time with your wings?"
What am I
To answer?
"Our paths are similar,
But wind, I reject
                    your principal line of thought.
If you
Had not been calm
Air suspended over the daisy,
Where could you have begun,
                    wind, where have you made your start?"

Daniel Weissbort

HOW TO DRINK THE SUN

Ignoramuses
Cut the pomegranate with the knife
Before eating it.
Pomegranate juice flows over the knife,
A little red pool collects on the plate.
We

200   Vladimir Soloukhin

Don't waste pomegranate juice.
The huge
Sunlike fruit
In its yellow skin
Revolves slowly in the hands.
You study it from all sides,
To see if the skin is intact throughout.
And your fingers already sense the seeds
Through the skin,
Large and tender.
You probe gently
(A crimson shadow appears),
Three seeds have loosed their blood
(But there's little room in there to spurt —
They burst silently and succulently).
Now we number the seeds off
Carefully, row after row.
The spurting juices collide under the skin,
Flow, mingle.
The hard pomegranate grows soft
And spongy.
The hands proceed more and more gently, more and more delicately.
One must take care that the fruit does not burst —
For that can happen with pomegranates.
Patience and tenderness above all!
The surface seeds are easy!
One must know
How to reach the seeds
Deep inside,
Thoroughly to crush those at the center . . .
And to bite through the skin,
And then
To suck in mouthfuls,
Raising the precious fruit to the sky
And
Throwing back the head!

Daniel Weissbort

Vladimir Soloukhin   201

FOR THE TREE TO SING . . .

What has to happen for a tree to sing?
You can take it from me — a lot has to happen,
Even if the wood's like copper, red, and resonant.

Let's suppose
A sapling has pushed its way through the heavy, loamy soil,
A cow comes along and simply flattens it with its tongue,
A man comes along and treads it under heel,
Because a sapling, growing close by flowers,
Is frail and slender as a blade of grass.

Just as the future Paganini
Or the future Mozart were like
Those born in the same year as they —
Future shop keepers, monks, sailors —
So it is like the nearby couch grass,
It is feebler than the nearby blade of grass,
And no one would believe that the shadow of its branches
Will cover thousands of blades of grass, spreading far over
                                                    the slope.

It is dangerous
To live level with the grass,
Which mowers
May cut.
But it is far more dangerous
To rise two yards above the grass.
A peasant might hack it down to make a shaft for his spade,
Or boys to knock their rubber ball about with.
One blow of the axe and that's an end to rainfall, thrush
                                        or morning dews.
Or dawn.
And an axe blow is the simplest of things.

But meanwhile the tree is gaining strength.
Like hoops, rings are added.
The wood darkens,
Saturated by the resin that grows golden with the years.

202 Vladimir Soloukhin

The needles now are rough and sharp.
The thick, hard bark is covered with moist scars.
The mossy branches, dark and aged, do not tremble,
For the fir is no chattering aspen tree.

What has to happen for a tree to sing?
It needs a history. No doubt of that at all!
And to remember its first,
Gentlest of showers,
And the drawnout anguish
Of a smarting wound,
And cruel summer, torturing it with thirst,
And iron January, savagely freezing it,
And the poorness of that soil in which its roots
                    search stubbornly for nourishment.

Now the fir would do fine as a golden log,
To be turned into timber,
A cart, a wardrobe
Pliant, resilient plywood.
It could be cut up for firewood.
A coffin could be made of it.
The wood is good for many uses — it is fragrant, well-seasoned —
The wood is good for many uses,
But still not good enough for a violin.

To hell with it!
What has to happen for a tree to sing?
A history? It has one.
The master craftsman's hands. Here they are.
Strike it with an axe: How the solid, resinous body rings out!
Split it and examine it, fiber by fiber.
Temper and draw the golden string,
So that the seasoned body, answering, might start to sing.

What a disappointment!
Either the wood is muffled, like cotton wool,
Or too shrill, like glass.
Where is the copper, where is the honey?

Vladimir Soloukhin   203

Where is the winds' voice and the smile of the morning sun?
But now the dealer enters:
"Signor Stradivarius, once again, as always, you're in luck —
I have found it.
A fir burnt by lightning. It will make an enchanting violin!"

Yes, that is what the tree needs if it is to sing!
An uncommon fate.
Celestial fire to descend.
The storm to course along the taut fibers to the very roots,
Singeing, steeling the wood,
Like a soldier's heart in battle.

The blue flash and the voice of lightning and thunder.

I have matured. I am ready. I stand out boldly.
I shall sing as no man has ever heard.

Let the heavens strike me!

Daniel Weissbort

THE APPLE

I am convinced that finally
Isaac Newton ate
The apple that taught him
The law of gravity.

The apple, born of Earth and Sun,
Came into being,
Sprang from the seed,
Ripened
(And before this bees flew to it,
Rain fell and a warm wind blew),
Not so much that it might drop
And by its direct motion demonstrate
That gravity exists,

But to become
                    heavy and sweet,
Beautiful, juicy,
To be admired and picked,
Its scent enjoyed —
And with its sweetness
To delight a Man.

Daniel Weissbort

KONSTANTIN VANSHENKIN   b. 1925

WE CAME BACK LATE FROM VISITING

We came back late from visiting.
The entrance gaped.
The dawnlight poured into the streets
And stayed.

From my balcony I gazed into
Dawn's depths below
As from a bridge. It seemed to me
This was not Moscow.

It seemed to me from all the yards
A bellowing herd
Was flowing past the garden, down
Towards the river.

Dawn's chilly current stung
Me to the quick.
Somewhere a horn rang out, the crack
Of a herdman's whip.

Don't think I had not drunk enough —
Why should I care! —
I heard you taking off your dress
Inside, back there.

The new day was as yet unlived.
The dew lay thick.
There was an hour left for sleep,
Or maybe less.

Beneath the fading moon
For a brief space,
The earth revealed to me
Its other face.

Daniel Weissbort

RAIN

For E. Vinokurov

It rattles dully on the roof,
Noiselessly streams down the pane,
Mutters in the tub in the corner,
Seethes in the concrete drain.

In the dark of night it sighs above
The field, rustles over leaves . . .

Were I happy with myself,
How well I would sleep!

Daniel Weissbort

THE FOREST IN WINTER! . . .

The forest in winter! From edge to edge
A frozen, resinous wall,
Making the restless heart beat fast
At the unlikely silence of it all.

It oppresses me with its grandeur,
Its renunciation of all things,

Konstantin Vanshenkin   207

And its bland indifference
To life beyond its boundaries.

As though the gay lights of the distant
Towns did not exist. As though
There were neither joy nor suffering.
As though the earth did not rotate.

Only, sometimes, a raven rising steeply,
Disturbs a splendid fir,
And, for one whole minute, gently
Rages a storm in miniature.

Daniel Weissbort

THE GIRL DREAMS OF HER LOVER . . .

The girl dreams of her lover at night,
And he of her.
He dreams of her full lips,
Her long eyelashes.

The elderly poet dreams
Of splendid lines.
Never did life call forth from him
Poems so fine.

Of sums and calculations the schoolboy dreams,
Of inkwells.
The happy woman dreams her man's
Unfaithful.

And all these folk have different,
Incongruous dreams.

While, like children, pilots dream
Simply of flying.

Daniel Weissbort

THE PATH

Though the walkers walk alone
And their clothes be dusty and soiled,
Yet their bare feet have worn
A pathway through the world.

What then has been achieved, you ask?
Nothing superfluous!
A complicated task
Faultlessly carried out.

Keeping duly within bounds,
It pursues its course.
No engineer would find
It simple to project.

In the stooping willow's shade,
Over the exposed rock bed,
All its windings logical,
Each turn justified.

Daniel Weissbort

THE SUNSET FADES, . . .

The sunset fades, and from the little hill
Light passes, while in a cloud of dust
The herd moves on. And there's no patch
Of living earth to tread, with this asphalt crust.

I am tired. Farewell, great city,
Where there is only concrete, metal, glass.
The need to earth myself cries out in me,
So that this tension too might pass.

It's not yet night, but on the hour
The habitual star has taken to the sky.
I do not know its name, although
I must have seen it countless times.

Konstantin Vanshenkin   209

Far off a whisp of smoke comes from a bonfire.
Already the plain is bathed in moonlight.
But you must learn to tell between
Your true path and mere vanity.

On this long journey having encountered much,
I gaze upon these peaceful fields and see
The land of my fathers, of my grandfathers,
And of my children and my children's children.

It is no accident I dwell here too.
I hear the dread music of the spheres.
And now you write me that in his speech
Georgy Markov failed to mention me![1]

Daniel Weissbort

[1] Secretary of the board of Writer's Union.

210   Konstantin Vanshenkin

YEVGENY VINOKUROV b. 1925

WHEN THE PARACHUTE DOES NOT OPEN

When you tug at the rip cord
And the parachute does not open,
And there beneath you lie endless forests,
And it is plain that you will not be saved,

And there is no longer anything to cling to,
No longer anyone to be met on the way,
Spread your arms softly, like a bird,
And enfolding space, fly.

There is no way back, no time to go balmy,
And only one solution — the simplest:
For the first time to compose yourself, and to fall
With the universal void in your embrace.

Daniel Weissbort

I DON'T REMEMBER HIM

I don't remember him.
I never saw him
In his Moscow flat,
Trying to catch hold of his braces
From behind, to fasten them

Onto his trousers at the back.
I don't remember him in the quarantine station either,
As he stood naked in line,
Waiting for the handful of liquid coal-tar soap.
I don't remember him even
In that moment of shame,
When he forgot the word "sling swivel,"
And stared dumbly at the ground,
Under the frosty gaze of the sergeant.
I don't even remember
His terrible screaming . . .
All I remember are his two eyes,
Looking out from under half-closed lids,
When I cradled
The stumps of his legs,
To stop them banging against the boards
Inside the jolting truck.

Daniel Weissbort

EYES

Exploded. To the ground. On his back. Arms apart. He
Raised himself to his knees, and bit his lips.
Across his face were smeared not tears
But eyes shot out.

Awful, awful. Bent double, I heaved
Him to the side. He was all
Covered with clay. I could hardly
Drag him across to the village.

In the field-hospital he cried
To the nurse: Oh it hurts! When you change
The bandage it's hell! And I gave, as one does,
The man something to smoke as he lay dying.

212 Yevgeny Vinokurov

And when (taking him away) the wheels began
To whimper sharply, over all the voices
I suddenly remembered, for the first time:
My friend had pale-blue eyes.

Anthony Rudolf

OBJECTS

From the cycle "History"

I am deeply convinced that objects
Are more eloquent than words . . .

Here is the bell that summoned the weavers,
Furriers and tinsmiths to the *veche*.[1]

Here is the bugle the Jacobins sounded
To herald the ending of the age of evil.

And here is the poker with which
They stirred the white ash in Auschwitz.

Daniel Weissbort

I DO NOT LIKE THE CIRCUS

I do not like the circus:
                          over there
Some of the folk are chewing, and the others
Are sitting in their coats,
                          while straining every
Nerve the girl turns perfect somersaults
In the heights, among the lamps, half naked.

1 Town assembly in certain cities of northern Russia between the tenth and fifteenth
centuries.

Yevgeny Vinokurov 213

I cannot bear the beach:
                              this man makes jokes;
That one sprawls under canvas, looks out yawning
As a woman goes into the chilly sea,
Her golden edges glittering with blue.

I get cross at the movies.
                              This chap's drunk
And that one sleeps. The people chatter, giggle
Fearfully. And a woman fills the whole
Screen with her unclothed sacred body.

  Anthony Rudolf

ADAM

On the first day, gazing idly about him,
He trampled the grass down and stretched himself
In the shade of the fig tree.
                              And placing
His hands behind his head,
                              he dozed.

Sweetly he slept, his sleep was untroubled,
In Eden's quiet, beneath the pale blue sky.
And in his dreams he saw the ovens of Auschwitz
And ditches filled with corpses.

He saw his own children!
                              In the bliss

Of paradise, his face lit up.
He slept, understanding nothing,
Not knowing good and evil yet.

  Daniel Weissbort

214   Yevgeny Vinokurov

HAS THE TIME COME . . .

Has the time come to draw up the accounts?

. . . The sick man starts to think about
His savings, or about his god.
How petty are these nocturnal fears!
Life rises up in all its grandeur
Still promising something good!

. . . And the desire to live is strong as always.
"What's the weather like outside?" he says.
Frowning, he gazes out the window . . .
And this thirst for life is simple as
The crows flocking upon the branches,
Cawing, cawing without end.

Daniel Weissbort

ALL GROWS OLD

All grows old. And what has aged
Has the mystery of age.
Sarmatian arrow from the crossbow
Or the mossy stone of the fortress wall.
The years impart grandeur to the plane tree.

The wheel of the century turns, —
An ordinary man,
                   One day I'll become
Distant and mysterious . . .
                        Like everything

Daniel Weissbort

BULAT OKUDZHAVA   b. 1924

FRANÇOIS VILLON

While the earth is still turning, while there is still
    bright light,
give Thou, Lord, to each
    what he has not:
To the wise give a head, a horse to the cowardly,
give money to the happy . . .
    and don't forget Yours truly.

While the earth is still turning — Lord,
    Your mighty power!
Let those straining for power
    rule each other all they want,
give respite to the generous,
even to the fall of day,
to Cain offer repentance . . .
    and don't forget Yours truly.

I know: You can do all,
    I believe in Your wisdom
as the soldier looking at death believes
    he is going to Heaven,
as every ear believes Your quiet
    speech,
as we ourselves, the consciousless, believe
    what we create!

216

Lord, my God, my holy green-eyed
                                        One!
While the earth is still turning, and this even to her
                                        is strange,
While there is still time enough, and fire,
give thou to each a little at a time . . .
            and don't forget Yours truly.

Denis Johnson, Shirley Rihner, & Alexander Petrov

I NEVER SOARED, . . .

I never soared, never did I soar
Among the clouds through which I never soared,
And never did I see, I never saw
Metropolises that I never saw.
And never molded, and never did I mold
Any pottery I did not mold,
And never loved, and never did I love
The women whom I did not chance to love.
So what do I dare?
                        And what then can be done?
Really only that which I can not do?
And really will I ever come to run
Toward a house toward which I don't run?
And truly, will I ever come to love
Those women whom I do not come to love?
And really, will I ever come to cleave
The Gordian knot I never chance to cleave,
The Gordian knot that I shall not unloose,
In the word to which I never shall give voice,
Within the song I never shall compose,
In the undertaking I shall not propose,
In the bullet that I don't properly deserve.

Denis Johnson, Shirley Rihner, & Alexander Petrov

ONCE THERE WAS A SOLDIER BOY

Once there was a soldier boy,
None handsomer or bolder.
And he was nothing but a toy —
He was a paper soldier.

He wanted to remake the world,
So all in it were joyful.
But he hung upon a string and twirled —
He was a paper soldier.

He would have charged through fire and smoke,
To die for you twice over.
But all you did was laugh and mock —
He was a paper soldier.

You showed no trust in him at all,
You were a great withholder.
Why was it? Well, it was because
He was a paper soldier.

He cursed his unadventurous lot,
Excitement was what he spoiled for.
"Fire! Fire!" he shouted. He forgot
He was a paper soldier.

Into the fire? Forward march!
I've told you none was bolder.
He perished — he had not gained much —
He was a paper soldier.

Daniel Weissbort

SAVE US, THE POETS, SAVE US, . . .

Save us, the poets, save us, we have but
A century, a half, a year, a week,
An hour, three minutes, two, no time at all . . .
Save us, but remember — save us all.

218   Bulat Okudzhava

Save us with our sins, our gladness, or without . . .
Somewhere fine, young Dantes wander out.
No time to let the past damnation fade
Before the call to take his gun and load.

Somewhere our Martynov weeps, recalling blood,
Already he has killed, he wants no more,
But this is fate, the bullet will be cast.
And thus the twentieth century calls to him.

Save us while you still possibly can,
But not so that we can lie down as bones.
And not as huntsmen preserve their hounds,
And not as the tsar preserves his huntsmen.

Rescue us from the hands of idiots,
From ludicrous pronouncements, blind amours;
Poetry through all time will sing your praises
If you will only save us, the poets, save us.

Denis Johnson, Shirley Rihner, & Alexander Petrov

BELLA AKHMADULINA b. 1937

A CHILL

Maybe I'm sick, I've been shivering
For three days, like a horse waiting for a race.
My snotty neighbor, who lives on this floor,
Even he cried:
"Bella, you're really shaking!

But please come to your senses! Your strange illness
Shakes the walls and penetrates through everything,
It inflames the spirit of my children
And it even rattles my dishes, in the night."

I answered him:
"I'm shivering
More and more, but I'm not practicing witchcraft.
Listen though, tell everyone on this floor
That I'll be leaving the building this evening."

But this tremor was shaking me so much
That it inserted mistakes into what I said,
Danced within my legs, and prevented
My lips from coming together into a smile.

My neighbor, leaning over into the stairwell,
Watched me squeamishly, but genuinely curious.
I encouraged him:
"You've seen
The opening act: what do you think will happen next?"

The plot of my illness didn't get boring!
With an aura of sadness, I saw within myself
Strange wild creatures, glimmering
As in a water droplet under a microscope.

More and more severely the shivering
Lashed me, drove sharp, small nails into my skin.
It was like a hard rain pelting
An aspen and scourging all its leaves.

I thought: how quickly I am left behind!
My muscles rush away and have their own good time,
And my body, breaking my discipline,
Is behaving itself freely and easily.

It's going farther and farther away. And will
It disappear as suddenly and dangerously
As a ball of yarn rolls from a child's
Hand and unwinds a thread from his finger?

I didn't like all this.
I told
The doctor, although I am shy in front of him:
"I have my pride, you know, and in the future
I will not endure my body's disobedience."

The doctor explained:
"Your illness is simple.
Normally, it would be absolutely harmless,
But the frequency of your vibrations
Prevents me from examining you — you can't be seen.

You see, when an object is vibrating
And the frequency of its oscillations is
Great, then it is reduced visually
To almost nothing — it looks like a faint haze."

Then the doctor hooked up his gold
Instrument to my indistinct features
And a quick wave of piercing cold
Electricity shot through me, a green fire

And both the needle and the scale were
Horrified! The mercury began to seethe
For its leap! A deathly splash of glass followed
And its splinters carved blood from my fingers.

Get worried, my good doctor, look around!
But he, not seeming to be concerned at all,
Made his announcement:
"Your poor body
Now appears to be functioning normally."

I was sad. I myself knew
Of my involvement in the higher frequency.
Its excessive number, not fitting
In the narrow mind, floated above me.

And my nervous system was taught
By a many-digited number of ordeals.
Like springs in an old mattress, it broke
Through, tore my skin and the air around me hummed.

Disfiguring my hand, the huge pulse
Always beat, always wanted to be free.
Finally I figured: what the hell!
Let me choke on it like Petersburg on the Neva!

And at night the brain sharpens, waits.
My hearing is so open, so excited by
The stillness — a book falls or a door squeaks
And — boom! it's all over! that's the end of me!

Yes, I did not dare tame the beasts
Living inside me, sucking my blood from my flesh.
Always from the door in front of me
A draft! Always a candle, suddenly blazing, went out!

In my pupils, hanging over the edge,
The eternal bulk of a tear glowed brightly. I spoiled
Everything with myself! I would corrupt
Paradise with the lousy discomforts of hell.

The doctor wrote the prescription out in proper
Latin, and, with the wisdom flowering in man,
The lady in the drugstore read it
As easily as you read a piece of music.

And now the whole apartment house is softened
By the medicinal kiss of valerian.
For a long time the medicine
Licked my wounds with its mint tongue.

My neighbor is quite pleased. For the third time,
Through his children, he congratulated me
On my recovery, and, they say,
He praised me to the management, personally.

I returned visits and social obligations,
Answered letters. By myself, I take walks,
Beneficially going around
In circles. I don't allow myself wine.

Around me, not a sound, not a soul.
And my table died and has been buried under
Dust. There the pencils sit and stare
Into the darkness with their blunt, illiterate mugs.

And now, like an over-worked horse,
Every step I take is tentative and halting.
Everything's fine! But in the dark
A dangerous foreboding is bothering me.

Still my doctor hasn't found me out.
It's meaningless for me to puzzle him. Even
With all his attention and his treatments,
Instantaneously I shall burn or freeze.

Like a snail in a bone coffin,
I'm going to escape by blindness and by silence.
But tickling my forehead, sickening,
The tips of my antennae are waving above me.

O falling stars of dots and dashes
I call on you, crumble! Let
Me vanish, shuddering in pure silver
Of mermaids shivering, burning along my back.

Strike me like a tambourine, don't
Spare me, chill, I am all yours! We can't live
Without each other! I'm the ballerina
Of your music, the shivering puppy of your frost.

For the present I no longer tremble, o no,
No, now there can be no thought of that.
But already my far-sighted neighbor
Has grown quite cool with me when we meet.

Bob Perelman & Kathy Lewis

FIFTEEN BOYS, OR PERHAPS EVEN MORE

Fifteen boys, or perhaps even more,
or perhaps even fewer than fifteen,
said to me
in frightened voices:
"Let's go to the movies or the Museum of Fine Arts."
I answered them more or less as follows:
"I'm busy."
Fifteen boys presented me with snowdrops.
Fifteen boys said to me
in broken voices:
"I'll never stop loving you."
I answered them more or less as follows:
"We'll see."

Fifteen boys are now living a quiet life.
They have done their heavy stint
of snowdrops, despair, letters.
They love girls —
some more beautiful than I,

224   Bella Akhmadulina

others less beautiful.
Fifteen boys with false bravado and sometimes gloatingly
greet me when we meet,
greet in me when we meet
their deliverance, their normal sleep and meals.

You will come in vain, last boy.
I shall put your snowdrops in a glass
and silvery bubbles
will overgrow their stocky stems.
But you'll see, you too will stop loving me,
and mastering yourself you'll address me arrogantly
as though you had mastered me,
and I shall walk on down the street, down the street . . .

Daniel Weissbort

LUNATICS

The rising moon revenges herself
for the pain of her remote and haughty station.
Lunatics stretch out their arms
and track her with their doomed vision.

Shrugging off the cares of flesh,
on the wings of consciousness they rise
effortlessly, these transparent beings,
negotiate the moon's glancing light.

Glimmering as sparely and as coldly
and promising nothing in return,
my distant art draws me to it
and makes me swear to obey.

Will I be able to withstand
its torments, its display of signs,
and make something you can touch
and handle out of the moon's shine?

Daniel Weissbort

THE SNOW MAIDEN

What pull did that leaping flame
exert over the Snow Maiden?
Rather a death by drowning,
or under horses' hooves.

Yet in a blue swirl of skirts,
a flash of legs, up she soared
and was no more — converted
instantly into so much thawed water.

How often has her life
merged thus with air and ended.
It is our fool's fancy to play with fire,
it is our age-old sport.

The vivid color draws us to it,
gives us so little space to pass,
and the body once it has surrendered
ceases to be a body, melts.

And yet we are always lighting fires,
playing this dangerous game,
and risking our very lives
in the bonfire's flame.

Our fate is still unresolved, obscure,
still hidden in the bunching smoke,
whether we bring our skins out whole
or melt into the flames for ever.

Daniel Weissbort

A QUEEN

There goes a queen!
Slow sway of pendant.
Admirers gaze with reverence
after her dainty foot!

Silk rustle of her dress.
Moist depths of her eyes.
Momentarily those lashes
take us all by surprise!

How noble her bearing!
Holding her tray aloft,
this cafe waitress walks
under a blue roof.

One customer or another
seeks council of her,
and snowy serviettes spire
into peaks under her hands.

While over her short cut hair
floats a starched crown,
haughty and severe
and cold as a pearl.

Daniel Weissbort

I WAS SO BUOYANT

I was so buoyant
in that month of May, that month of me.
The weather was meant
for flying. I was so free,

so free and generous
in my joy, on the point of song —
and light-hearted as a finch
I dipped my feathers in the air.

But thank god my vision grew
sharper and more exact,
and each sigh, each flight now
takes an increasing toll.

And I am privy to the secrets
of the day, its forms
and presences. I look around me with
the smile of an old Jew.

I see the rooks clattering
high above the dark snow,
and bored women hunched
over their knitting.

And somewhere, blowing a tin whistle,
heedless of the flower-beds and borders,
a strange child runs about
violating their established order.

Daniel Weissbort

YEVGENY YEVTUSHENKO   b. 1933

DWARF BIRCHES

We are the dwarfed birches
wedging like splinters
under the fingernails of the frost.
And the kingdom of the everlasting frost
uses varied and disgusting means
to crush us further.
Does that sound odd to you, horse-chestnuts of Paris?

Palm-groves of pride, does it pain you
how terribly low we are?
Fashion-watchers, does it embitter you
we are Quasimodos?

In that hot place our citizen boldness
gives you some pleasure,
sadly and self-importantly you send
moral support.

Colleagues, you decide
as trees we are not your equals:
but that a kind of green however ugly
is progressive where frost is permanent.

Thank you; we shall somehow endure
ourselves, under the heavens
and brutally contorted by the wind
without moral support.

You are more free
but we are stronger rooted,
and we are not Parisians of course
but in the tundra we have our value.

We are the dwarfed birches,
we have cunningly invented postures,
but these are not meant too seriously:
our compression is our recalcitrance.

The bent and the mutilated, we believe
that everlasting frost is impermanent,
that the nastiness will shift in the end,
and that we shall find the right to proportioned shape.

And when the climate alters
what if we then discover
branches incapable of shapely growth,
since we have got used to deformity?

This tortures us, it tortures us,
and the cold contorts, it contorts.
We are as deeply planted as splinters —
dwarfed birches.

Peter Levi & Robin Milner-Gulland

A HUNDRED MILES FROM THE
CAPITAL CITY OF HOPE

A hundred miles from the Capital City of Hope,
and the Hotel Ukraine and the Hotel Budapest,
and the cafes of the young
and the sturdy auxiliary police
and the big cars of the ambassadors
and the hard currency shops
and the gravity of the ministries
and the levity and charm of layabouts

230 Yevgeny Yevtushenko

and the crosswords in the newspapers
and the quiet security checkings
and the roar Kill the ref!
and the peace congresses
and touring musicals on ice,
as still as stillness like a paradise
runs the river Ugra,
(it cooks itself pancakes)
— there the whole world runs to its own time.

A hundred miles from the Capital City of Hope
is a village without bridegrooms or brides,
with three cottages falling to pieces,
and three old women in three cottages,
and one old man boasting and talking on:
like one samovar for three women.

The three old women fish and mow grass,
they say, Be careful you don't ever die,
we shall bring water and mow grass,
just keep talking, you damned old man,
from the heart and as well as you can.
The old man says, I've ploughed my piece.
The old man says, I've talked enough.
Moscow and war took my children,
the grass is sprouting on my roof,
I am confused in my mind:
and what gossip can I talk, old women?

He stares at the ceiling,
he is no gossip,
he lies like a prophet.
And the roof which is heavy with goosefoot
totters above the jut of his beard.

The Sunday fisherman from the Capital City of Hope
has finished visiting the natural world:
It's wonderful our Russian hay-making!
He pushes the sweat off his forehead:

'Well ladies, where's your old tsar?'
'Our tsar doesn't reap these days my dear,
he has turned his old eyes away from us,
he lies down on a bench, he wants to die;
but what I think of is this my dear,
I was dying once, but then it passed.'

The scythes whistle. They cut easily,
after one wave of grass, another wave.
'And where were you dying? When was that?'
'It was in the captivity my dear.'
Moving in joy, moving in pain,
moving maybe in both at that moment.

'What captivity? You mean the Germans?'
'Oh no, in ours, my dear son, in ours.'
The Sunday fisherman from the Capital City of Hope
moved awkwardly, stumbled to one side.
'I hope that the old man recovers.'
'God grant he does,' behind him tranquilly.

In confusion the Sunday fisherman
from the Capital City of Hope starts his car.
Better give your soul an airing on asphalt.
Better to buy fish in the fish-shop.
Better live happy among the unknowing
who don't comprehend the price of hope.

Flying overhead, God help them,
went big planes, Russian born,
fastidiously lifting their undercarriages
over the weeds on shaggy roofs, in heaven.

Peter Levi & Robin Milner-Gulland

ANDREY VOZNESENSKY   b. 1933

MAYAKOVSKY IN PARIS
To a street artist

Lili Brik, stretched on a bridge,
Ironed flat by automobiles,
Under leather, under rubber,
Like a coin her eyeball gleams.

People passing drop some change
And, like an open wound,
Mayakovsky, at aching dawn,
Framed like a playing card,
Is daubed upon the bridge.

How goes it, poet with your love?
It has to be so, to recall your fate —
That your face
Should be printed on the road
              like something in Hiroshima.

Hurrying across your breast are crowds.
The Seine laps away at your back.
And the little bus rushes past,
Like a tickling, comic ladybug.

Genius. Prodigal. Carrot-bearing futurist.
He, the world's rep, has clung to the bridge.
Did no one come
          to your exhibition,
                    Mayakovsky?

233

We would have come.
You would have read us something.
We miss you badly.

You, Mayakovsky, match the bridge.
Spanning time,
                            like a gymnast,
You touch ROSTA[1] with your boots,
And with your palms —

                                          us

Your square is like the bridge.
Like the cars below the bridge,
Below the feet of Mayakovsky
Is Mayakovsky's Moscow.

The thousands in stadiums yell.
What do you think of it?
                            How does it smell to you?
Mayakovsky, Comrade Bridge?

Bridge. Paris. We await the stars . . .

The setting sun conceals itself.
The firmament is slashed across
With the red
                    track
                            of a plane,
Like a razor across a face.

Daniel Weissbort

---

1 Initials of the Russian Telegraph Agency, for which Mayakovsky designed posters
with versified captions. In 1935 it became TASS.

THE BEATNIK'S MONOLOGUE

Flee — into yourself, into the Churches, to the lavatories, to the
                                        Egypts, to Haiti —
Beat it!

The dark machines
Have enslaved us like Baty Khan.

In trials, their brazen minions,
Blowing gasoline out of glasses,
Calculate: Who was it in England
That led the uprising against machines?
Let's beat it.

And getting over its shyness at night
The cybernetic robot
Says to its maker:

"Give up your wife!
I've got a weakness for brunettes," it says. "I love
At thirty revs a minute. Better give in like a good fellow . . ."

O raping creations of our age!
Upon the soul a veto's laid.
We go off into the hills and into beards,
We dive into the water, bare.

But the rivers grow shallow, or
In the seas the fish die . . .

My soul, my young beastling
Among city side-scenes,
Like a puppy with a scrap of twine
You rush about and whine!

And time whistles beautifully
Over fiery Tennessee,
Enigmatic as the woman-breasted
Bird with a duralumin chassis.

Daniel Weissbort

STRIPTEASE

The burlesque dancer
                              gestures and strips . . .
Am I bellowing? . . .
Or do my eyes ache from the stage lights?

She plucks off a foulard, a stoll, the tinsel,
Just like you strip an orange of its peel.

And her eyes contain that tedium of the birds.
They call this dance "striptease."

The dance horrifies. At the bar, baldheads and whistling,
The drinkers' eyes have filled up
                              like leeches.
One, red-haired, as with egg bespattered,
Stumps like a pneumatic hammer!
Another, like a bedbug,
                              is apoplectic and terrible.
The saxophone blows in apocalyptic gusts.

I curse the scale of you, O Universe,
Martian radiance on the bridges.
Worshiping and wondering,
                              I curse.
The woman ripples in the jazz dance.

"Are you America?" I ask, like an idiot.
She sits, rolls a cigarette.

"What a funny accent you've got, kid.
Make mine a Martini on the rocks."

Daniel Weissbort

A NEW YEAR'S LETTER IN WARSAW

To A. L.

When, towards morning, faces
shine, pale as magnesium, in the mirror,
and, like toilet paper, powder
lies transparent upon cheeks —
how old these mugs have grown!

How predatory are their red hands,
lying on the napkin, side by side,
like crabs on a plate!

You wander among these monster dishes.
You cool your brow against tall wine glasses.
You tear off your shawl. You burn.
"It's stifling in Warsaw," you say.

But my windows are thrown wide open
on the tall city like a garden,
and the snow smells of winter apples,
and flakes hang in the air,
they do not move, do not fall,
they wait,
        stock still,
                light,
intent,
      like icon lamps,
or tobacco plants in summer.

They rock a little
when touched by a slender foot
in a Polish boot.

The light snow smells of apples.

   Daniel Weissbort

FROM THE WINDOW OF A PLANE

In the world of friends, in the world of long-distance travel,
What are you doing down there where it's raining?
With whom are you sharing pieces of tangerine?
What exams are you taking again?

Once more brilliantly failing,
Furiously, furiously,
You run a cymbal stick over
Pilaster and railing!

My little vocalist, is it another game?
Or do you leave your bed, shivering,
And roam about barefoot, and hesitate
To pick up this dumbbell of a receiver?

You are married. All's forgotten and healed.
Why, fresh-faced, bright-eyed, are you freezing,
As above the streaming landscapes
Freezes
       this static
           wing?

Daniel Weissbort

YUNNA MORITS   b. 1937

MEMORANDUM

To Sergo Lominadze

Syvatoslav had no use for comfort,
Slept rough, ate in the field.
The Pechenegs fell upon him
And cut him down where he stood.

The Pecheneg prince was a lover of art,
A crafty warrior, a trapper.
The shape of the human head
Thrilled him in an obscure manner!

Fame lay heavy on the prince's soul.
He was suspicious and envious.
He ordered Svyatoslav's skull
To be preserved and made into a cup.

So wine in the new cup was brought
To his tent with its cordon of slaves.
Merrily it reflected
The yellow skull stripped by death.

All that was left of the scent of battle,
Fatigue after victory, lust for a slave girl,
And the other passions, the prowess, the courage,
Was the yellow flicker of bones.

But in the pink heart of the wine,
In the cup of his mortal remains,
The heavens as always stood high
And life was having its fling!

Daniel Weissbort

THE LEADER

In his narrow, gleaming eyes
The flame of arrogance hissed,
A prisoner of his own dull instincts,
And so a bear, not a horse.

Not long ago, this timorous fellow
Had jumped at a charred log,
And with his white paw battered
A young walrus over the head.

When did he grow so large and strong?
Anyway, slow as a beetle,
He crept onto the white shore,
And disposed of the old leader.

Lying in his own bright blood,
Not knowing the reason why,
With his dead eyes the leader
Congratulated his successor.

And the head turned gradually to stone.
A blanket of snow covered all,
And wretchedly his widow stood,
Like a downy little fool.

Meanwhile the newcomer dryly
Patted her flanks with his paws
And his hot breath shot
Straight into her pink ear.

240   Yunna Morits

Then the animal's contours melted
Into the mists of drifting snow,
The long muzzle of his profile,
The arrogant coat of youth.

I could not grasp immediately
That the snow would hide the blood,
That the animal's memory
Would be untroubled by this death.

In his gleaming coat how briskly
Did he flick the snow away.
And his track reminded me
Of something seen before.

Daniel Weissbort

THE FISHERMAN

The weary sun
Sinks over the cape.
In the deep jug
There is cool kumys.[1]
The tough overalls
With their body smell
Hang on his hot
Sweating shoulders,
And a blue drop
Trembles on his brow,
And a white fish
Lies on the sand.
I see the fish
Rapidly flapping,
Greedily flapping
Its transparent gills.

1 Fermented mare's milk.

Yunna Morits 241

And its moist eye
Turns up towards me.
And the fisherman
Strokes the fish's back.
His fingers, stained
With the sun's ochre,
Fondle a moist,
Pinkish fin,
As they would a woman,
Lovingly, hungrily,
As he presses an unshaven
Cheek to her dress.
A man's memory,
Ignoring the trivial,
Will retain till death
The rustle of silk,
The rustle of sand
And of gleaming scales,
The noise of the minutes
Flying above!

Daniel Weissbort

ALEKSANDR KUSHNER b. 1936

A PICTURE

Not reigns of kings now vanished,
Nor any single ruler,
Assyria! All I can
Recall is a certain picture.

There, the wicked Assyrians,
Armed to the teeth, with shield and spear,
Sail the country end to end
In ox bladders.

How odd to sail without boats,
Making not a bit of spray!
The flat Assyrian beards
Sweep the waves.

It's fun to bob up and down
In company on the water.
"Hey soldier in the pointed helmet,
Aren't you afraid of war?

Hey soldier in the pointed helmet,
You'll end up on the bottom!"
But the soldier in the pointed helmet
Doesn't answer me.

243

I shall forget all about them
and only god knows when
I'll go burrowing in the lumber room
and find that book again

With its cover of cardboard.
Then I'll hear the splashing inside.
"Are you still afloat?" I'll shout.
"We still are!" they'll reply.

Daniel Weissbort

DON'T BOTHER ABOUT THE NEWS!

Don't bother about the news!
It floods in every day
From provinces and towns
And villages tucked away.

It scarcely finds room
In the newspaper sheets.
And it ends up in Moscow
Where everything meets.

There's charm in a little country
Where in cheese they excell
And the short-distance traveler
Looks out and sees a windmill:

Half an hour of shrubbery
And a town slipping by.
A crowd and sails suddenly,
And that's the whole country.

It's like slides flashed on a screen
With the lights turned out,
When all the news is drink and rain
And the postman and a boat.

244 Aleksandr Kushner

But how could we ever bear,
In our wide open spaces,
Where night and day are near,
Such enchanting constancies!

When the snowstorm rushes
Over rail and over heath,
It's the size of our news
And breathes with its breath.

Daniel Weissbort

THE AIRMAN

Why was the airman taking such pains?
Perhaps, such was his passion for it,
He was trying out his hand —
The uprights and the slants.

Resembling neither bird nor angel
He was like a button when
He flew, risking a fall,
Underneath the dome of heaven.

Only the forest witnessed these
Lines, these loops, these turns,
In all their beauty —
Everything else slept.

Night started awake in terror
To see at his controls this man,
Flickering like mother-of-pearl
On its night-shirt.

The airman believed in perfection.
Trifles did not get him down.
It was sheer bliss
To hug the clouds.

Aleksandr Kushner 245

In his radiant airplane,
High above the dawn-lit earth,
He is sewn — do not pull him off —
To the sky with a loop.

Daniel Weissbort

THE OAK

I gaze at the lonely oak . . .
    (A. S. Pushkin)

This lonely oak,
with its tattered foliage,
its mildewed bark,
rustles dully overhead.

How dismal, how bewildered
it is, how uncertain
it's going to outlast me.
All this makes our relationship

an odd one. I leave
the road every time for it,
embrace and console it,
when really it should be consoling me.

Daniel Weissbort

THE STAR BURNS OUT OVER THE TREE TOPS

The star burns out over the tree tops,
all but falling short.

And the wind blows . . . but not so hard,
firs crash into the gully.

The rain lashes the forest,
slackens, however, with brightening skies.

Who so keeps the world in check
that the fledgeling may sleep in its nest?

Daniel Weissbort

TO B. P.

In the middle of the day,
Gray-haired, you stand,
The porch, the terrace,
The doorframe behind.

What is it — a parting
That casts its shadow, or
Leaves rustling? Your arms hang,
Your big hands are clasped together.

In a tie, formal,
Is it, you're waiting for something?
Day after day you stand alone.
You do not bother with fashions.

Is it the snow, the thin rain,
Or the heavens in their glory?
You stand, guilelessly
Squinting up at the sky.

Not murmuring, not complaining,
Not searching for words,
You ask nothing
Of this bounteous world —

Neither cloud, nor a blade of grass,
Neither tears, nor oblivion,
Nor to gaze at photographs
As I am gazing now.

Aleksandr Kushner   247

Tossing back a lock of hair,
Tight-lipped, you look
Through a chink in the air,
Invisible to all but you.

There is light there, so much light,
It's hard to control yourself —
But that is why
You must keep silent.

Daniel Weissbort

ROBERT ROZHDESTVENSKY　b. 1932

THE WINTER OF THIRTY-EIGHT

The winter of thirty-eight.
December,
Bitter cold weather . . .
Father,
        back home
from work
later than ever.
Now he's looking for
the large dish of jellied meat on the windowsill.
Now he's saying,
"Smells good!"

But suddenly,
           for some reason,
                     father's
legs gave way under him, like cotton wool.
And collapsing
          heavily
               onto the bed,
he cried out:
"Not guilty-ee!
Not one
        of them
is guilty!"

What's he saying,
                        Mama?
What's the matter,
                        Mama?
Is he crying? Father?!
Why?
He's
        strong.
He's so huge.
He's
        stronger
                        than anyone!
And mother is wailing,
"Not so loud . . . !"
And she says, again and again,
"My god . . .
What if someone hears . . . !"
Hears?
Hear's what?!

I was
        in my seventh
                        year.
I don't remember
anything else.
The traces
                have all been wiped out . . .
I didn't understand that cry
of my father's
for a long time.
Not for twenty
                        years.

Daniel Weissbort

THEY KILLED THE LAD

They killed the lad,
                    for nothing,
just for its own sake.
Calmly.
As though it were a game . . .
And this didn't happen
                    five hundred miles
away.
But right here.
In the yard.
The windows were still alight . . .

Meanwhile,
pressing his hand to his breast,
                    he cried out,
as though he wanted
his cry to carry
beyond the long silence
                    lying ahead of him . . .
The cry
        had a separate existence!
It grew like a wall.
It climbed high,
tumbled down from the roofs.
A lacerated,
            desperate,
                    sick
inhumanly tremendous
cry!
It flowed along the pipes,
                    crawled along corridors,
filled basements
            and attics.
Crazed,
it pushed
bellknobs!

Robert Rozhdestvensky   251

Forced doors

        and screeched in locks! . . .

And the air was almost set on fire.

And cigarettes

        jiggled in the mouth:

"If only it wasn't at night.

If only it was in the daytime . . .

If only it was at the front,

        then I'd . . ." —

That's all.

Just a flash of lightning.

That's all.

The age

        did not come to a standstill.

What a marvel

is man!

What

    an

        abomination

Is man.

Daniel Weissbort

NOSTALGIA

Nostalgia

        is in my house.

In the mountains,

the hydros,

the rivers.

The deserts,

        the sun-bleached rocks,

the impossibly crystalline

birches.

The steppes

with their heavy blizzards . . .

Nostalgia,
nostalgia
for you.
I miss you —
              each little sigh.
I miss you —
              each little moan.
I miss you
              reluctantly waking.
Your eyes, your shoulders
                        so naked.
Each moment when
you are with me.
the hot nights
              without sleep.
The tears,
the heedless words.
The smiles
and even the fights!
Your lips that are
              dry from the frost . . .

I've made up my mind
                    to resist.
I leave!
I storm the platforms . . .
But somehow
I'm yelling
down lines!
When I reach you
from Vladivostok
on the telephone,
I am ecstatic!
Crazed by the screaching
                    of wheels,
I write you
interminable letters.
I beg you:

Robert Rozhdestvensky   253

        "Please come to my rescue!
I'm choked with nostalgia."
You are silent.
You are
in no hurry
           to save me . . .

If I'm cured
you'll know
right away!

   Daniel Weissbort

MAYA BORISOVA

THE DRY BIRCH TREE STOOD

The dry birch tree stood,
Not knowing it was firewood.
But a man cut it down,
                                    struck a match,
Warmed himself, and made some thick soup,
But then
                    was too lazy to trample out the fire,
And living trees perished.

The silent snow fell, not knowing
That tracks would stay on it.
But by these tracks
                            one man found his loved one
And was happy,
While another
                    hunted his enemy down
And killed him.

Lightning coursed across the sky,
Not knowing that it was electricity.
But man caught it
                        like a fish,
On a long iron rod,
And forced it to illuminate a house,

And set it to work in machines,
And led it
                  to the dim terminals
Which are locked to the electric chair.
And the world looked at man
And wondered at his wisdom and his many talents.
But to be on the safe side,
                              it hid uranic ores,
As mothers hide matches from their children
In the deepest drawer
                    of the kitchen table.

Daniel Weissbort

IT'S NOT WHEN THEY LEAVE . . .

It's not when they leave
                        that they really leave.
It happens
          quite differently.
One day,
        a Sunday or a weekday,
He'll put on his slippers as usual,
And clean his teeth with his hard brush,
And mend the broken
                    switch.
After breakfast he'll read the paper,
Check
      the football results,
And suddenly he'll notice
                          a strange woman
Holding a plate:
                "Would you like some more?"
And everything
              will be
                      the same as always.

256   Maya Borisova

The breakfast table won't burst into flames,
And the soap
          in the bathroom won't turn to stone —
It's got "Family" written all over it —
But the years begin to vanish
               out of sight.
Peace gathers, flowering in the house,
Yet the woman will begin to feel
            a chill,
Not knowing herself the reason for it.
Her husband is a sober
          and substantial man,
And yet
      it's like a presentiment of rain.
And then one day he leaves.
           One day he leaves
And doesn't bang the door
        behind him.

Daniel Weissbort

VIKTOR SOSNORA   b. 1936

DO YOU ENVY, MY COMRĀDES-
IN-ARMS, . . .

Do you envy, my comrades-in-arms,
this imagined home of mine? It is large,
a phantasmal temple to my mind,
a storehouse of illusions — books.

Come up to my house and you will see
how laughable is this comfort prized by man,
there birds (oh, celestial melancholy!)
sing half-forgotten words.

My house, alas, is rich, and simple too:
rich as a dandelion, simple as death.
But instead of a fair maiden and heavenly roses,
a six-winged beast lies on the nuptial bed.

So, do not envy. In this house there is
neither laurel wreath, nor crown of thorns.
Only on the hook for your utensils
hang my hearts, like a string of onions.

  Daniel Weissbort

258

WHERE ARE OUR HORSES, OUR BLACK HORSES?

Where are our horses,
                        our black horses?
Where are our lances,
                        our burnished lances?
The horses are spent,
the lances have sped.

In the sad, silent grove, fatefully
a strange raven quivers on the branches,
quivers and sighs,
                        on its immense face,
its feathered face, a sorrowful look.

We don't need anything:
                        neither foreign lands,
nor horses, nor lances . . . In autumn's vastness
luck is with us:
white garments,
a sad pine wood
                and a raven,
                        a burnished raven.

Daniel Weissbort

THE OWL AND THE MOUSE

Once upon a time there was a roof covered with tin.
Due to corrosion
this tin was scruffy, like a puppy's fur.
Once upon a time there was a chimney-pipe on this roof.
It was terrible and black
as the inkwells of the police.
The pipe stood up at attention,
like a coward before the generalissimo.
Already many years before in apartments

steam-heating had taken root.
So the pipe, it turns out,
stood useless —
an obscure architectural excess.
As the stoves were never lighted
no smoke ever flew from this chimney.
In order somehow to make up for this dereliction,
precisely at midnight,
just as the clock was striking twelve
(though the clock never struck,
as in this house
many centuries before
the ancient chiming clock had broken down
and now there were only alarm clocks,
so the clock didn't strike,
however . . .
just as adults read books not aloud, but to themselves,
it seemed to the children
that the clock gave out at midnight
its magical twelve strokes,
not aloud, perhaps, but to itself,
or so it seemed to the children,
though at twelve midnight they were already deep in sleep,
having been put to bed much earlier
than the adults,
the majority of whom, in the evenings,
turn to reflect on the questions of the universe,
concluding these and similar reflections
long after midnight),
thus:
at that moment, as the clock was striking twelve,
out of the pipe flew a cat.
It flew out like smoke, or instead of smoke,
and just like smoke it was light blue.
It flew out and dispersed into the starry night.

And exactly at that moment along the roof a mouse ran.
This mouse was enormous — as big as the sheepdogs on any continent.

260   Viktor Sosnora

The mouse was shaggy, like the aforementioned sheepdogs,
and was shaking itself like a sheepdog after a bath.
In place of a tail, a black tooth protruded from the mouse,
and instead of teeth from its mouth
protruded 32 tails, long and bare.
The tails were the same length as a human hand
but thicker, some with fingers, some without.
The tails rose and fell, curling like snakes.

And on the pipe sat an owl.
It was tiny, like a little brooch.

"Hello!"
                    the huge mouse blabbed obsequiously at the tiny
owl.

"Greetings . . . ," muttered the owl.
"It's midnight already," offered the mouse.
"How keen-witted of you to say so," the owl displayed amazement.
"It would never have occurred to me that its already midnight!"
This sarcasm was lost on the mouse.
It explained to the owl why it was now midnight, and no earlier,
obsequiously jingling
the chain of its own logic.
"Your reasoning is awfully complex
beside my own perceptions of the world," yawned the owl.
"Let's talk about food,"
and the owl inspected the huge mouse hungrily.
For we all know well
that rodents make up the basic diet of owls.
"No, no," the mouse shifted nervously.
It glanced cautiously at the owl
wagging the 32 tails that protruded from its mouth.
"No, no, we'd be better off talking
about the international situation."
"Nonsense," yawned the owl.
"Food also occurs among nations."
"Let's talk about cinematography!"
The mouse began fidgeting.

How do you like the amazing Latest Film?
"Nonsense! The Latest Film is senseless as a pea!"
The owl began to grow angry
and thinking of a pea, licked his lips.
"Where do you think the word 'mouse' came from?" blurted the mouse.
"Where?" The owl evidenced a vague interest.
"From 'musing.'"
"Nonsense!" The owl laughed negatively
                                        "the word 'mouse'
derives from 'mouthful' — 'mouse-full!'"

It began to grow light.
The yardkeeper woke up. The yardkeeper was a woman.
She, like many, had a Tartar face.
She lit her pipe.
Sparks flew from the pipe like lightning.
A broom or mop shone and was lost somewhere.
At that moment the clock had struck six.
And when the clock had struck that number of times,
the owl's dimensions began to increase rapidly
while the mouse shrank.
In a few seconds the owl was the size of a frigate
and the mouse had shrunk to the size of the little finger.
The owl exulted:
now he would devour the mouse without further discussion.
On the owl's face the feathers bristled.
But the owl had grown so large by now
that it couldn't see the mouse anywhere.
The owl sat,
rolling its eyes in hunger and anger
so they seemed like two bike wheels revolving with blazing spokes.
Not one of the building's inhabitants imagined
that every night on their remarkable roof
the scene described by me took place.
An absurd scene!
Why, when the mouse is as large as a sheepdog,
doesn't it think of devouring the owl?

262   Viktor Sosnora

Why doesn't the cat ever notice the mouse?
These things only the children in my country can fathom.

When the clock struck six,
the cat that had dispersed into the starry night
collected its body in droplets, like a stormcloud,
condensed,
and, blue, flew back into the pipe.

and several million radio receivers
positioned in the bowels of the building
uttered in a single affirmative voice:
"Good morning, comrades!"

Denis Johnson & Kathy Lewis

THE FOOTSTEPS OF AN OWL AND
   HIS LAMENT

One-two! One-two!
Along the sidewalks strides an owl.
    In a rectangular cardboard cloak,
    A brass trident clanks on his shoulder,
    Past courtyards — wooden caves —
    The owl walks and laughs.

One-two-One-two!
Along the sidewalks slinks an owl.
    Millionaire and pauper! — don't gape!
    Poet spewing hymn words!
    The owl will string everyone on the trident
    Like macaronis on a fork!

One! Two! One! Two!
On the sidewalks rejoices an owl!
    You'll slip away? Two late! You're dead!
    He pecks the liver, splits collarbones,
    Sucking the wounds, he gouges
    With his beak like a syringe, like a syringe.

One . . . Two . . . One . . . Two . . .
On the sidewalks sobs an owl.
    In quiet and dark sobbing — it's pitchblack.
    Big tears well up on his toes.
    Now his big toe
(Like a candle, he lights . . .)

  Kathy Lewis

NOVELLA MATVEYEVA   b. 1934

I'M NO FIGHTING MAN, HE SAYS

I'm no fighting man, he says.
I'm a split-in-two man,
I'm a triply split man,
I'm quartered,
Crucified!
You're no fighting man, I say,
You're a split-in-two man,
You're a triply split man,
But you're no blunderhead.
Puffing at your pipe,
Taking yourself apart,
Like a mincing machine,
You may well be right.
But do you know, tonight
Enemies will come.
I see them plain as daylight,
I hear their footsteps drum . . .
You hear them?
You don't hear them?
They're hurrying already . . .
Like mice, they make a raid on
Your spiritual store.

And swiftly, in the dark,
In the silence, they will filch
The chopped-off, splintered parts
Of your infirm spirit.
— And what will they be doing
To my spirit, when they find it?
And what will be doing
To this broken thing but grand?
— The second part they'll paint,
The third, rule with a ruler,
The fourth they will ferment,
And the fifth they will inflate,
The sixth they'll set on fire
And themselves run away.
The man was no fighter,
The man was split in two,
The man had pieces missing —
And was kidding all the time.
For, learning of disaster,
He started blinking faster,
And raked these parts together —
And collected them alright!

Daniel Weissbort

THE GINGER-HAIRED GIRL

To I. Zemskaya

A ginger-haired girl in a blue sailor's jacket
Sits on some bleached planks.
She'd like the sea to wash away
This slow
Downpour of slope . . .

Slithery and wet, like a bar of soap in its dish,
The mollusk slumbers in its opalescent shell.

266 Novella Matveyeva

Silt
Cloys to the heap.
I fall asleep
And cover
My tracks with sand.
Wholesome dreams
I dream:
Magnificent groves,
Enchanting, palm-filled
Gardens cut from felt.

Come on, admit it!
You're laughing at me!
I'll not forgive you!
I won't!

But the sun too is laughing at me.
It serves me right.
If the sun stops laughing,
I'll mope.

Jelly fish don their flared skirts
And breeches of light
And drift off to the festival of phosphorescence,
Holding up mirrors
To themselves . . .
Sparks fall out of the current,
Scorching the rock bed with blue flame.

What's that?
A shop window,
Or
A sail?
I can no longer tell
What's land, what's sea . . .

Like luminous posters
The fish sail across the sky,
Moving

Novella Matveyeva   267

Their fins of flame
Slowly . . .

Come on, admit it!
You're laughing at me!
I'll not forgive you!
I won't!

But the sun too is laughing at me.
It serves me right.
If the sun stops laughing,
I'll mope.

Daniel Weissbort

THE EGGPLANTS HAVE PINS AND NEEDLES

The eggplants have pins and needles.
Long dreams have plagued their sleep.
By the redbrick garden wall
Cucumbers droop like whips.
The poppylamps blow out in the wind.
Petals flock the air and settle
Like colored reflections.
The sun, like sea-drowned amber, peers
Through a dense silt of cloud.
But nettles go on being nettles
And roosters go on being roosters.
Listen! A stubborn beating of wings!
One bird, well-advanced in years,
Feeling the winter coming on,
Plucks up his courage and lets forth,
But has clean forgotten the song,
The words, and the rasping sound
Sticks in his gullet.
The rooster stiffens,
Clenches his pale yellow foot.

Fatigue and rheumatic pain overwhelm him,
As winter wags its blanched finger.
His plumage flutters somberly,
Like a fire behind bars.
His comb glows like elderberry.
His feathers gleam,
Rheumatically mossed,
And the rooster's faint shadow
Smells distinctly of the cold.

Daniel Weissbort

RE-CONVERSION

"I have made silken verses
from stone,"
the great Rudaki once said.
Aye, but he did not know
the translator would
re-convert them.

Nigel Stott

VYACHESLAV KUPRIYANOV   b. 1939

FOR A LONG TIME HE TRIED TO SURVIVE

For a long time he tried to survive
her one and only kiss,
before coming to die,
pressing to his lips snow, wormwood,
he touched the white bark of the birch,
he wandered by night until he found lakes
steeped in the young roots of wandering stars,
he wrapped himself in mist,
tried to cure himself with long journeys,
with a dream in which she resembled many;
for a long time he was nursed by other hands,
bewitched by other lips,
the sound of surf, the clatter of crockery were prescribed to him,
and for a very long time he tried to survive,
and yet all the same, after about forty years, he died,
without even the time to sense before his death
whether now, at last, they would be together,
or whether only now had they parted for ever.

Pamela Davidson

A LESSON IN NATURAL HISTORY

You say, I love
the woods,
fields,
nature . . .
But sometimes our thoughts
are like a dark forest.
Living one's life isn't like
crossing a field. Nature
can't abide
emptiness.
So try to find out
if they love you:
the woods, fields, nature.
Don't be in such a hurry
to speak of love.
Think about
reciprocity.

Pamela Davidson

EVERYTHING GETS FORGOTTEN

Everything gets forgotten.

The moon was forgotten
in an old cupboard.
The mice ate it up.

Since then, baby mice
have shone
from birth.

The cats didn't eat them,
they were scared,
the cats died, the cats
were forgotten.

Pamela Davidson

IV
POST-WORLD WAR II ÉMIGRÉ POETRY

NINA BERBEROVA   b. 1901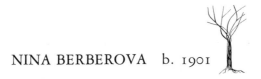

TO SHAKESPEARE

Oh, genius of Stratford, return!
Return to your foggy Avon
Where men still are men of grandeur,
Of wisdom — severe and gray.
Return, unexpected as before.
Stride into the world in Brabantine lace,
In an old camisole and high boots
That have been patched on every stage.
You were the beloved of kings,
The fool and god of lordly savages.
Three witches whisper, whisper, spin;
Borne by you, they would bring you back
At this terrible hour
When Birnam Wood moves on Dunsinane,
When the swamps of Polessia quiver,
When a rainbow hangs over the Volga,
And somewhere between the Ilmen and the Don
An emperor peers into the eyes of fate.

Millions, legions-strong, they fell,
Mingling with tartar bones,
Lithuanian bones, French bones —
On a field once known as Kulikovo,

On the broad plain of Poltava,
Over the Neva, where the first emperor
Had flashed his eyes at Europe.
They have fallen and will not rise again.
They sleep sweetly in Polovtsy arms,
Embraced by Gedimin's regiments, Napoleon's guard.
And soon, soon the Russian grain
Will rustle over them . . .

                                    But he who has shaken the age
Cannot end his days without you.
Oh, genius of Stratford, descend upon him.
Lead him into thy throng of horrid fates,
Teach him . . . his last calling!

Three witches whisper, whisper, spin
Their thread is thin, their whisper garbled.
The Forest of Kursk heaves above a tyrant,
Bending oaks while a thread runs on.
There is no sleep in an Empire palace
Built under Alexander.
Here in medals and mustaches a barbarian lived;
Here in '18 was a place of torture,
Here in '31 they built a hospital,
Here the parquet grows green with moss
And portraits of beauties with Asian eyes
Stare from damask walls.
The forest heaves.

                        And now he ventures forth
To listen to the Russian storm.
What is the will, what portends the whisper
Of these old women? Will he wield the knife?
Or will another? Whisked into exile?
Or hauled animal-like in a cage
To degenerate Paris? A thread runs from darkness
Into darkness, and we do not understand
The twentieth century.
The wind of tragedy shakes no heart,
And poetry — like a dead eagle —

274   Nina Berberova

Lies in the dust. Music is silent,
Love does not burn and thought shrivels away.
Only blood still flows. There is
Blood. We are all in blood,
Water in blood, land in blood, air
In blood. He who has not eaten dead flesh
Throughout his life — as we —
He too stands chest-deep in blood.
Oh, genius of Stratford, powerful spirit!
You loved blood. Help us
To end this path of gore!

1942

John Glad

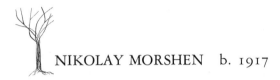

NIKOLAY MORSHEN   b. 1917

IN SUPERSTITIOUS PANIC

In superstitious panic
I stared at walls surrounding me:
What space encloses me —
Four-dimensional or four-walled?

I opened the door. It was twilight.
Objects gradually disappeared behind each other
And the air rustled lightly like foam —
Palpable, yet elusive.

The tide of dark air
Rose to my knees, to my chest
And I had only to cross the threshhold
To swim and swim, choking on stars.

John Glad

A STORM

You awoke at midnight. Beyond the window
The sky thundered and flamed
Just as on that day when all around
Was the shudder and shrieking thunder
Of exploding metal.

Do you remember how storms used to be
In the poems of Tyutchev and Fet? —
A wet orchard and puddles on a path.
And now? Even at eighty
Your first thought, poet,
Will be of ack-ack fire and bombs.

John Glad

AT THE LIGHTHOUSE

Here birds fly south,
Skirting occasional squalls.
Here hurtling waves shatter
Into bitter dust on the rocks.

Here surf shakes a mane
Like a sweated white horse
And here in the foaming blackness
A light lights in the lighthouse.

But migrant birds
Are used to unpopulated darkness,
And with their breasts
They thud, ignorant, against the lighthouse.

And that which was winged becomes lead,
Disappearing into the sea dust.

.   .   .   .

In the distance
Ships bellow gratefully in response.

John Glad

THE ANDREYEVSKY CHURCH

Bright, all white and blue
Elevated by a hill into the blue sky,
She almost flies above the dark spring river.

Erect and sheer she stands — smiling,
Musing on distant tender things
While all around squat-browed houses
Squint at her with black windows.

A plodding crowd, they have gathered here
To glare with dark and ancient envy
At this hurtling, upward flight,
At this lightness of bold lines.

John Glad

GEORGY IVANOV 1894–1958

THE OLD MAN SHUFFLES TO THE FISH MARKET

The old man shuffles to the fish market
To buy half a pound of perch.
A mimosa glitters with drops of rain,
The river's smooth surface gleams.

O, these provincial lodgings.
Local voices. The barking of dogs.
Life here consists of food and drink.
A bed. A roof. Tobacco.

Vistas. Clouds. One's like an angel,
Another's like a Newfoundland dog,
And a third is the image of Wrangel,[1]
With a monocle screwed in his eye.

But Wrangel — that was in Petrograd,
Poetry, champagne and snow . . .
O, pity him, with his thickening blood,
For God's sake — his legs ache so!

No one will take pity on him.
And why pity him — why?
The creaking old man is dying, dying,
As all men have to die.

1 Baron Pyotr Nikolayevich (1878–1928), general, leader of the anti-Bolshevik forces
during the Civil War.

What's left, I ask, all the same,
For me still to relish?
Gardens verdant after springtime rain,
The mistral, half a pound of fish.

  Daniel Weissbort

OH, HOW FASTIDIOUS YOU ONCE WERE

You were given an incomprehensible name,
You are oblivion.
Or, more accurately, potassium cyanide
Is your name.
  Georgy Adamovich

Oh, how fastidious you once were,
My friends.
You did not drink vodka, could not abide it,
You preferred Nuit St. Georges.

Now our daily bread is potassium cyanide,
Mercuric chloride, our drink.
No matter. We got used to it, we grew accustomed,
And did not go out of our minds.

Quite the contrary even — we resist evil
In this senselessly wicked world.
In a sepulchral waltz, the tenderly couples
Whirl at the émigré ball.

  Daniel Weissbort

A QUARTER CENTURY OF EXILE
HAS PASSED

In Petersburg we shall meet again
As if we had buried the sun there.
   O. Mandelshtam

A quarter century of exile has passed
And it has become absurd to hope
The radiant sky over Nice
Has become our native sky for ever.

The peaceful, abundant South,
The murmur of waves, the golden wine . . .

But the Petersburg blizzard sings
In my window shrouded by snow,
That the prophecy of my dead friend
Must in the end come true.

   Daniel Weissbort

SHOULD I TELL OF ALL THE ABSOLUTE FOOLS

Should I tell of all the absolute fools,
Who hold the fate of mankind in their hands?

Should I tell of all the scoundrels who
Depart into history crowned with wreaths?

Should I — hell!
            Under the bridges of Paris it's quiet
And why should I care how things turn out.

   Daniel Weissbort

UNHARNESSED, THE WHITE HORSE AMBLES ALONG

Unharnessed, the white horse ambles along.
Where are you going, white horse?
The sun shines, an early spring breeze
Rumples the shirts and handkerchiefs in the garden.

I who one day took my leave of Russia
(On a night preceeding an arctic dawn)
Did not turn round, nor cross myself,
Nor notice how suddenly I came to be
In this obscure European hole.

If only I were bored . . . . But I am not bored.
Life was lost, but I cherish my peace.
I receive letters from dead friends
And, reading them, burn with relief
In the blue late winter snow.

Daniel Weissbort

ON THE BOUNDARY OF SNOW AND MELTING

On the boundary of snow and melting,
Of movement and repose,
Of light-mindedness and of despair —
Is palpitation, virtigo.

Blue night of solitude —
Life smashes itself to bits,
First name and patronymic vanish
And the surname runs like ink . . .

Like stars, the prophecies rise
And fall away . . . . They are not fulfilled!

Daniel Weissbort

NOT SO LONG AGO, THE WORLD WAS COMPLETE —

To T. G. Terentevaya

Not so long ago, the world was complete —
Linden trees and paths in the ancient parks.
There Turgenev brooded . . .

               The world was complete,
White columns, a study, a living room . . .
There Turgenev brooded . . .

               And life seemed to be
A poem, music, a pastel drawing,
Where worldly fame shone, but without warming,
Where the snowstorm was yet a far-off thing,
And the golden autumn of serfdom held firm.

Daniel Weissbort

YURY ODARCHENKO 1890–1960(?)

ONLY FOR YOU MY TEA ROSES

Only for you my tea roses,
Only of you my random dreams,

You with your hovering smile,
You with arms rounding like swans.

Your hair is silk spinning,
Your voice a sleighbell all silver,

And the eyes in your talking face
Are two green tsetse flies.

Theodore Weiss

THE PATH I'M FOLLOWING

The path I'm following
Is a surefire road to hell.

But from there, by a velvet ladder,
Warbling blithesome ditties,
I'll return to earth
Tucked out as a tomcat on a roof.

And I'll live with a little girl
In her little pink, prim bedroom,
And I'll be purring softly again
But about what nobody'll know.

Theodore Weiss

284

CLAUDIA PETROVNA

Claudia Petrovna,
Prepare the samovar.
Glistening like a copper star
That's spouting smoke,
It quakes with fiery love . . .

Tea at twelve sharp!

Shiny candies in crystal bowls,
Fresh napkins on the table,
Your napkins neatly monogrammed,
All your children at the table,

Claudia Petrovna!

Poppa, pacing his room,
Didn't sleep all night
And is late for tea.
But he himself ordered:

Tea at twelve sharp!

She went to the door. There
She turned. A mortal fear
In the clouded mirrors.
She fell to the parquet floor. Ah,

Claudia Petrovna . . .

Theodore Weiss

Yury Odarchenko   285

YURY IVASK   b. 1907

SHALL WE FORGET THE SHIVER

Shall we forget the shiver
Of the cold aspen's
Rounded leaves —
Of an insult
Eternally alive?

Up there it's quiet,
Empty, blue —
The sky yawns
And life is forgotten —
As are aspens
      and insults.

   John Glad

EMILY DICKINSON

The mad old maid of Amherst —
a face like the moon, eyes on fire,
her quill pen scraping.
       On the left
a window. Another on the right.
And from beyond the wild roses,
the hawthorn and the maple (the glistening
garden) — flowers for Thee, Bright Absentee . . . .

To Him! Staccato down the road
roaring with a thousand wheels —
the mysterious, generous
                        spendthrift
of a galloping soul. With axle squeaking . . .
Into the churchyard — an open grave.
But death is smashed. Not she — triumphant
maiden spinning off, away.
                        Oh, Bliss.

Emily's July! The joy of the garden.
On Globe Roses: the bee. Psalteries
of Summer. Chirruping.
                        And she
needs nothing else, her honeyed horizon
outside of time. Let's fill the empty heavens.
It is already done! And she, she
has become his Noon:
                        and dying flows

with summer's paradise . . . .

William Tjalsma

ODE FOR THE DANCING KHLYSTY

Stamp, roar like our Russian poets, like Derzhavin,
like Petrov, like Bobrov — crash like thunder,
like Igor's great Poem,
like all Time to come.

My sea-horn bellows,
open like the lips of a cannon.
Singing descendants of descendants of descendants?
No: my horn sings Freedom, not Fate.

Iambs howled, rambled, roared,
laughing and crying: hey! hey!

Yury Ivask   287

Like a rose-warm dawn
I'd burst — and then?

Go, go, see the kerchiefs waving,
and scream, and tell the future, and dance
with silver Khlyst doves, dance in
the soul's wide blue meadow.

All of them, dancing, dancing,
camels and mountains and lions and Orpheus
too, knee-bent, stamping,
none of them casting a shadow.

Praise them with waves, with words?
How: I don't know — but
howl with these hearty monsters,
rip out their music on your harp!

Like lightning, like a bull-headed ram,
and me, like a donkey,
and angels sing, shine
and roosters crowing out loud,

And Mexico, a fire-bird, yes,
in bed with Ivan, Prince Ivan,
and Cinderella, my sister, a bluebird
flitting in and out of eternity.

But Fate is sorry, she is, she's cruel and she's
sorry, and she's fooling with heroes,
and ringing, and all wound round
the gold rope of happiness,

Hissing and humming and singing
like summer-lightning from Heaven — tra-la, tra-la,
oh you're off to Hell, down to Hell,
unless you beat time, yes, and promise

salvation, and bliss . . . .

Burton Raffel & Alla Burago

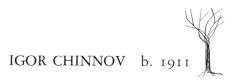

IGOR CHINNOV b. 1911

DO YOU THINK WE MIGHT GO
TO HELL TOO?

Do you think we might go to Hell too?
And a devil green as a cockatoo
Will say: "Do you smoke? Cock-a-doodle-do!
And where are your curriculum vitae? Oohoo!
And, oh yes, your preference please:
Skillet, skewer or stew?"

The frying pan's heated to a beautiful hue
Where we play leap-frog without shoes.
Oh, grasshopper-devil, fiendish kangaroo,
This frying pan just ain't for you.
Thyself go screw. Quid pro Quo.
Shishkabob. Aoooooo!

Oh you simple-minded satans,
Stop whispering of our sins.
In searing steam sits Kikapoo.
But we will escape this devilish stew,
Skim over the sea, sail into the blue,
Pelt each other with snow balls — just us two.

Oh, please. Send snow for her seared fingers!

John Glad

A BLACK BIRD . . .

A black bird on a black and snowy branch —
A hieroglyphic of sorrow.
A black burdock in the snow —
An ideogram of winter.

Shadows, mine and yours, on the white snowdrift —
Graffiti of silence.

The quivering of black branches and trees.
How restless
The Chinese calligraphy of the winter garden,
How fleshless
These abstractions of light and snow.

John Glad

A GUST OF MEMORY . . .

A gust of memory stirs faded letters;
Dry trees rustle on the island of memory.
Old ghosts know no sleep in the night's heavenly hotel.

There a forgotten name falls on the snow like a blue shade,
And shadows of branches cross in riddled inscriptions. I do not know
The language of the nether world. In the British Museum
I saw a black Egyptian bird. It sat silently —
Its yellow eye like a small moon. It was more a bird
Than all the birds of the world.

It was evening in Hawaii and I walked among the branches
Of a petrified forest. I longed in loneliness to hear
The ticking of my watch. But it had stopped
Out of respect for eternity. No, I do not hint
Of the heart; I speak of the silence of insomnia, of faded letters.
Transfiguration awaits them in the fireplace: orange butterflies,

Azure butterflies, blue butterflies, black butterflies,
Shades of a forgotten name, tiny salamanders.

John Glad

IN THE LAND OF SCHLARAFFENLAND

In the land of Schlaraffenland,
Beyond the clouds in the land of Schlaraffenland
A zoologist and tourist named Kannitfershtan
(From Copenhagen) dropped into a café chantant,
But it turned out to be a crematorium.

He was absent-minded and got all burned up,
So he scattered the dust and said: "You can have it."
But right away he got lost in the labyrinth
Of laboratories of world history,
Lost in the night where Leviathan lay on the bottom
And where chameleons scampered around mooing
(Turning red and blue and green in the process).

And thus in a society of centaurs, minotaurs,
Reactors, ministers and mortars
Kannitfershtan sits and drinks his Manhattan
And watches a black acquarium
Where chimeras and monster-roaches
Quack at Gulliver.

John Glad

AN INSTANCE OF FORE-ORDAINED HARMONY

An instance of fore-ordained harmony:
The newly-born became the newly-dead.

An empty cathedral. Don't cough. The service.
Funereal sobbing on marble

Igor Chinnov   291

(The last mute kiss . . .)
Let's take a look at the flowers by the coffin.

Look how that slanted ray strikes its little face.
But in this best of all possible worlds all's for the best . . .
It died without pain — unconscious.

. . . At the cemetery: Wonder if
That dim lightning over there means anything?

. . . Bronze roses on the crucifix,
Reflections on an obelisk. A pietà.
Pity, and sorrow, and apathy.

   John Glad

IVAN ELAGIN b. 1918

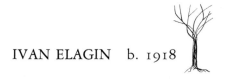

MY MURDERER IS NO THIEF

My murderer is no thief
Lurking in the night.
He won't sneak up from behind
And blow out my brains with stealth.

Instead there'll be a trial
With lots of pious jurors.
And they'll murder me
For the sake of some ideal.

And as I lie in my blood,
Sniffing stones beside the road,
Bliss and justice will ensue,
Righteousness will triumph,

The earth will bear fruit,
And all those good things
Shall come to pass
Which I, alive, resisted.

And my brother in the muses will sigh,
Recalling a folk proverb:
"When you chop down a forest
The chips will fly."

John Glad

AMNESTY

The man is still alive
Who shot my father
In Kiev in the Summer of '38.

Probably, he's pensioned now,
Lives quietly
And has given up his old job.

And if he has died,
Probably that one is still alive
Who just before the shooting
With a stout wire
Bound his arms
Behind his back.

Probably, he too is pensioned off.

And if he is dead,
Then probably
The one who questioned him still lives.
And that one no doubt
Has an extra good pension.

Perhaps the guard
Who took my father to be shot
Is still alive.

If I should want now,
I could return to my native land.
For I have been told
That all these people
Have actually pardoned me.

Bertram D. Wolfe

BORIS NARTSISSOV b. 1906

A MARATED BASTILLED AGE

"One step forward — two back"
   V. Lenin

A Marated Bastilled age
Trumpets the lilies' doom
And raises a defiant standard
Through the red poppies of banners and caps.

The ages sweep past the naive flotsam of your
   dream:
The same striking men, the same mouths
Crying for bread.

The writhing streets mirror your crimson sheen,
While — two hundred million strong —
You brandish a pentagram over Moscow.

But your beloved children are impotent.
Like you, they dwell in,
                              are
                                    simplicity:
"One step forward — two back."

Throughout the ages
Your labor bears the same fruit:
Lavoisier on a scaffold,
Gumilyov in a cell.

   John Glad

295

V
THE NEW WAVE IN RUSSIA

YURY GALANSKOV 1939–72

THE INTELLECTUAL

When they cast our words,
line by line, into the sieve,
we throw off our coats,
tear at our shirts.
You get ready to spring,
pen in fist,
like a knife, only to find your cuffs hanging,
heavy as chains, from your wrist.

Olive Dehn

MURDER

A trial.
Closed doors.
The judge-beast roars,
clenching his paws.
The defendants,
their mouths tied
with gags, sit side by side,
silent.

From their eyes beams of anger dart,
tear the room apart,
pierce the heart
and for the power-drunk
tyrants spin
a noose to hang them in.

The clerk proclaims the sentence in a clear tone.
The end of the conversation.
In the morning the silence whispered
"Quiet!" "Quiet!"
The sun rose higher, higher,
and limply threw away
a single ray.
On a branch a bird whistled:
"They were,
they are no more,
they killed them,
I saw . . ."

At the stroke
of the Kremlin clock, people awoke.
Everyone rose, ate,
drank, had a good stare
at his plate,
wondered about the affair —

and went off to work.

Olive Dehn

I AM IN PAIN

I am in pain.
Take your hands away.
I don't expect you to be kind.
I am not out of my mind.
I know where I'm going — I'm not blind.

Where there is fear — but not the fear of a slave:
where there are passions reaching beyond the
  grave:
where men walk in terror of their lives,
step by step, dancing on knives.
A red-hot lasso is hurled from the sky.
Crack! And the hypocrites writhe as it lands.
There am I
in shreds, like meat,
clapping my iron hands.

  Olive Dehn

THE LAST PLATFORM

From the scaffold,
to the triumphant executioner,
who has sliced my head from my body,
I,
headless,
shall cry:
"Proletarians of all countries uni . . . ."
But your fake happiness,
your slogans,
your banners,
I rip to pieces
and throw into the sunset's furnace.

  Olive Dehn

THE BIRD-CHERRY WAS MY WIFE

The bird-cherry was my wife.
I stroked her, caressed her,
laid bare her heart with a knife,

Yury Galanskov   299

peeled off her bark, undressed her.
With what red lips I burned her skin:
she held me in a witch's spell,
half-smiling as the sweet resin,
drop by drop, from her branches fell.
Blindly I clasped her sap-filled waist,
with my arms I made a ring:
her leaves swept down across my face
like birds fluttering
on to the grass. And there I lay
a long time, empty of thought, as if I'd died,
and watched a rainbow-colored ray
between my eyelids slide.

Olive Dehn

IT SHAMES ONE TO LOOK

It shames one to look.
Having done their stint,
the work over,
stamping the streets with their lifeless faces,
the crowd of idiots placidly walks
in drab hats, black and gray.
Yes, look,
go on, look!
See how
the clammy flesh pours through the gates . . .
As though the factory had gorged itself
and were vomiting everything up.
And tomorrow
the dismal brick walls will again
open their iron implacable jaws,
and the greedy throat of the hungry siren
will tear the town to pieces.
I'll not take any more.

300 Yury Galanskov

Do you
hear?
It's enough.
This very night
my mad head will blaze up
and . . . your composure will be ripped to
shreds.

Daniel Weissbort

VLADIMIR BURICH

PRECEPTS FOR CITY LIVING

When I go out, I switch off the light.
I cross at the crossing.
First I look left, then when I get to the middle —
 right.
I mind the cars.
I mind the falling leaves.
I don't smoke.
I don't leave any litter.
I don't walk on the grass.
I wash my fruit first. I drink my water, boiled.
I drink champagne and natural juices.
After eating, I wash my hands.
Before going to bed, I brush my teeth.
I don't read in the dark, or lying down.
In this way I have reached the age of twenty-six.
And what for?
To keep my money in a savings bank.

 Daniel Weissbort

VSEVOLOD NEKRASOV

AND I SPEAK OF COSMIC
   THINGS

Whether or not I shall fly
To the moon or the stars, who can tell.
But I got the taste of the moon
In my mouth, in Kazan — in forty-one.

The black-out. War.
But the moon was there.
White
Light,
White
Snow,
White
Bread — not a bite,
Not a bit.

It's years since I've been back in Moscow:
I dine almost every night.
But the moon looked a tasty morsel
And the taste of the moon was white.

   Daniel Weissbort

GENRIKH SABGIR

RADIO GIBBERISH

He lies groaning on his bed.
There's no one in the room.
Just a black loudspeaker on the wall,
Vibrating to a folk choir.
He reaches out, tugs the wire!
The plug's here, the socket's there.
He can't believe his ears:
A sound,
A crackle,
A metallic rumble,
The radio starts to mumble:
"Here is the news,
A special report!
. . . At the scene
Of the crime.
. . . By a majority of votes.
. . . Below
Zero.
. . . The threat of
Nuclear attack.

Epidemics . . .
War . . .

The quota has been exceeded."
The choir again. Against the background of
The choir, an airplane solo.
The roar
Of jet aircraft,
An explosion
Of applause!
The patient stares glassy-eyed.
His hand
Convulsively grips
The blanket.
Someone appears
In the door, far away.
— Doctor!
— My bolts
Need tightening.
Announcer:
"The Moonlight Sonata
Will be played on the balalaika."

Daniel Weissbort

IGOR KHOMIN

THEY DRANK. THEY ATE. THEY SMOKED

They drank. They ate. They smoked.
They sang. They yelled. They danced.
Sorokin tried surreptitiously to kiss Julia,
Sakharov fell asleep in his chair,
They vomited on Sidorov.

Daniel Weissbort

THEY MET AT THE TAGANSKY SUBWAY STATION

They met at the Tagansky subway station,
He spent the night at her place.
He's an accountant at the undertaker's,
She's a nurse at the maternity home.

Daniel Weissbort

A DIKE, A FLOWER BED, A BARE
LINDEN TREE

A dike, a flower bed, a bare linden tree.
A barrack-type building.
A passage. Eighteen apartments.
On the wall a slogan: "Peace to the world."
In the yárd Ivanov
Is exterminating bugs.
He's a bookkeeper at the State Loan Society.
The Makarovs are having a binge.
The Baranovs are having a fight.

Daniel Weissbort

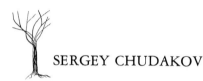

SERGEY CHUDAKOV

SUICIDE IS A DUEL WITH YOURSELF

Suicide is a duel with yourself.
You looked for a woman with winged feet,
Now she's loaded into a revolver,
Smelling of gunfire and rifle grease.
The inflation of leaves is like a run on the stock
    exchange.
The streets are asphalt rinks of rain.
Your angel of death has turned into a vegetarian,
Mislaying serviettes and kerchiefs.
It's intolerable as an old man's wandering mind,
And a little sick, mentally.
But autumn sends pale phantoms
Of mail trains out into infinity.
When breathing's no longer a game,
Exhale at the end of the line.
The butchers will cut up hatred,
Like a liver, with their clanking knives.

Daniel Weissbort

308

WHEN THE CRY GOES UP: "MAN OVERBOARD!"

When the cry goes up:

         "Man overboard!"

The ocean liner, huge as a house,

Comes to a shuddering stop.

Lines are lowered

        and a man's hauled up.

But when

      a man's soul goes overboard,

When he's choking

        with fear

        and despair,

Then even his own house

Doesn't stop for him

        but continues on its way.

Daniel Weissbort

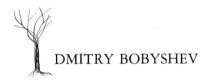

DMITRY BOBYSHEV

INDIFFERENCE

Indifference —
A house stuffed with ice,
Filled with snow.
 Indifference —
A house not for living
But for freezing in.
The cellar. A plush vault.
Indifference. A house.
Dusty bread and boxes.
Crusts, dead birds, combings, leftovers.
Look, there are even people here,
Two-humped freaks!
And dying of boredom.
People!
People — they're camels!
And girls — tarts.
Look.
But just try dropping in —
Just you try!
I'll turn into a quasi-doctor.
Pluck out an eye, knock some teeth out,
But return them!

Indifference.
A grave. Carrion.
Ants and mouse droppings on the floor.
Carrion.
A dead house. Birds' feathers. Smashed crabs' claws.
Indifference. A house. Indifference.

Daniel Weissbort

SERGEY MOROZOV

POEM ABOUT THE BLUE HORSE

To Vl. Batshev

The roundabout winds wearily down,
and the crowd gushes through the park gates,
and the Blue Horse sets about
searching the whole world for a mate.
Through temples, palaces, its course
takes it, through humble two-room flats,
troubling the world's lyre with its quartet
of legs, finding its creator in his court at last.
Peacefully he sleeps on an old trestle-bed,
and where the hair is, where the shavings are,
cannot be told. Cares, chilled by the hard frost
of night and moon freeze on his brow.
"Joiner! Joiner! Make a steed,
as blue and Russian as I am,
with the green of his eyes just a little bit sad,
that we might understand each other."
But the joiner sleeps on an old trestle-bed,
and where the hair is, where the shavings are,
cannot be told. Cares, chilled by the hard frost
of a winter's night, grow faint on his brow.

Daniel Weissbort

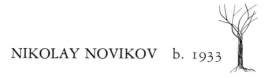

NIKOLAY NOVIKOV b. 1933

WHITE ON WHITE'S A FLATNESS

white on white's a flatness
snow on snow
on the pole a tablecloth
muteness on paper

white from white's a paradox
a white fever from innocence

red on green's power
a throne in the meadows
madness in a thicket
a ruby on a toad

green from red's faith
the ovary of a flower from flame

yellow on violet is a spot
gaiety in the twilight
a judaic star on a soutane

violet from yellow is hope
a violet from a decayed skull

orange on blue is lightning
god's beard in the ancient ocean
a burning bird in the sky

blue from orange is woman
lakes of eyes from the sunrise

black on black's an abyss
night with night
grief on velvet
mourning on a murderer

from black black's a decline
feeble-mindedness out of melancholia

when green violet blue
leave the world
it will become hollow —
a void in a mask
of red yellow orange

then history hovers above us
captivating and already ours no longer

but white and black
guard the entrances and exits

as usual

9 May 1974

Daniel Weissbort

FROM THE CYCLE *STONE AND SKY*

To Ernst Nyeizvestny

in our world it's unusual
                    the cry
— no weeping in the dark
no message
                 dispatched into the blue distances
no plea to judges
no appeal
this cry
        is not a cry from the heart
and it's not words sounds
— it is shreds of flesh and objects

314   Nikolay Novikov

fingers nails teeth that have left the skull lips that have
                        separated from the face
and stones —
                    innocence grief anger joy turned into stones —
the body throws them out
the mind hawks them up
                        against the dumb
                                        wall
and the bones rumble
a chain of kidneys heart lungs rattles
the temples of the head wrap their brazen roar round the ears
silently the tongue penetrates the larynx
                                    — the cry resounds in our
                                                world
                            inaudible perhaps
                                        but a cry
    I
the point
is the place where passions meet
meet —
            that is:
                    they converge come together alienate each other
                                    finally unite
the passions are
                bodies:
                        oblong circular wedge-shaped crack-like
                                plain apertures
when apertures unite
                    there arises a peak
                                    a highest point
    2
sometimes in place of the point
                            occurs a wound —
        here the passions assembled acute
                                toxic
                                burning
not to fill
            the wound

with tears as well as other things
                                the wound
                                            is a point
                in infinity   become infinity
    3
the line
            is skin stretched tight
                        cut open
                                by the hand of a master
                the body gives at the seams
                                    twisting towards the sky
                                            —the line
is flesh opened wide —
                    a drawn line
                        it is —
                                    no coincidence
                                    an opening itself
                when a point enters a line
                it is conception
    4
the skeleton
holds the body firmly
in a cage-like grip
so it should not scatter
should remain itself
and the parts of the body
are suspended on it
look out
at the world
                there
the sun flirts with freedom
the skeleton
                is the morality of the body
in the same way as
                    prison
is the morality of our world

   Daniel Weissbort

MIKHAIL YERYOMIN   b. 1936

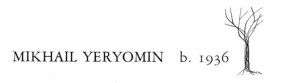

FACETED GRAINS OF WISDOM

Faceted grains of wisdom,
Primordial shape of space.
Russian holiness and vagaries
And the swamp's stork-like spiceyness —
These are the slimy tracks I seek
In an autumn manuscript
Where sheets are like the dresses of an onion
Hiding tears in their folds.

John Glad

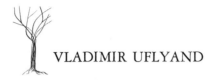

VLADIMIR UFLYAND

IT HAS FOR AGES BEEN OBSERVED

It has for ages been observed
how ugly is the diver in his suit.

But doubtless
there's a woman in this world
who'd give herself even to such as he.

Perchance
he'll issue from the watery depths,
wrapped around with streaming ends of algae,
and there'll be a night in store for him tonight
filled with all manner of delights
(and if not this time,
then another just like it).

To many that woman has denied her favors.
You —
rubbery,
steely,
leaden-legged —
are what she absolutely wants, O diver.

*   *   *

And now,
although not rubbery,

you stand,
another slimy fellow and
quite repulsive,
especially when nude.

But since this is precisely what she wants,
there is a woman waiting just
for you.

Daniel Weissbort

THE PEASANT

The peasant
is sturdy of bone.

Principled, plain, no fuss.

I would like to become a peasant,
to join
a kolkhoz,
if I must.

His lot is an ancient one —
to scatter seed on the ground,
to reap,
and from time to time,
now and then,
from German, Varangian, Greek,
to deliver his Russian home.

The cold weather comes to his aid.

I too shall grow sturdy of bone,
a principled man
and plain.

Daniel Weissbort

THE WORKING WEEK COMES TO AN END

The working week comes to an end.

Some can't believe it.
Others make such a hubbub.

Only I get a hold of myself,
board a bus
and go home to my suburb.

There, I place myself under a tree,
gape, pretend I'm a birdhouse, but see —
though by this I am somewhat misshapen
to make up for it, I merge with nature.

And in multifold melodies dressed,
parodies flow from my breast,
though I swear
I am not their creator:

then a starling awoke, simulator.

The course of my week's
not in question —
I work in my government section.
If in me there's a spark of divinity,
one day I'll become a minister.

Daniel Weissbort

NOW, AT LAST, EVEN NIKIFOR'S A SUITOR

Now, at last, even Nikifor's a suitor.

Holding in one hand a rose,
he speaks:
>"Close is that much desired future,
>when there will be a wife to press my hose.

An hour ago, I'd still no notion
that I had reached my moment of destiny.
Sitting in a tea-room, leaving — I know
they're gnats, but still they seem spirits divine to me,
circling around their axis, a circus,
entertainment for me and my fellow workers.

I realized that what this said
was the whole Republic ordered me to wed."

But the spirits broke into quadrilles
and (what is much less conceivable)
seemed to be dumbly saying, as it were:
"Was this not why our fathers stormed the Winter
Palace — so that the village worker might
find a helpmate and a friend for life?"

(I know women, in appearance womanly;
yet all the other signs proclaim them heavenly.)

Thus
did I understand the spirits.

*　　*　　*

To what end?
Here I am, holding a flower in one hand.
Although it has not been my way at all
to clasp in my arms the blooms of camomile.

The district sleeps.
                    A phantom orchestra, symbolic,
echoes within me, really quite symphonic.

Daniel Weissbort

VI
THE NEWEST ÉMIGRÉ WAVE

JOSEPH BRODSKY   b. 1940

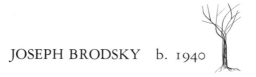

LAGOON

For Strobe Talbott

I

In the lobby, three old women, in deep armchairs, sit
chatting about the Cross, as they knit;
    the Academia Pension along with the whole
of the universe sails towards Christmas to the hum
of a TV: with the ledger shoved under his arm,
    the desk clerk spins the wheel.

2

And a guest climbs on board, he mounts the ladder
to his room, in his pocket a bottle of grappa,
    a nobody in a raincoat, owned by nobody,
who has lost his memory, his country, his son;
if there's any to spare a thought for him
    it's the aspen that longs to break his bones.

3

Venetian churches like tea cups chime
in this box, from under the casual lives.
    The bronze octopus of the chandelier,
in the three-leaved mirror clogged with weed,
licks the damp mattress swollen with
    dirty dreams, caresses, tears.

323

4

By night the Adriatic with its Easterly wind
fills the canal, like a bath, to the brim,
        rocking the boats, like cradles; at night
a fish not an ox at the bedhead keeps
vigil, while in the window, as you sleep,
        the rays of a star out at sea stir the blinds.

5

So, let it be like this — dousing the wet
flame of the grappa with the glassy, dead,
        decanter water, hacking up bream
and not goosegirl, so that Your chordate ancestor,
O Saviour, might satisfy our hunger
        on a winter's night in a damp country.

6

A snowless, treeless Christmas, not a trace
of balloons, by a sea that is map-constrained;
        letting the shell-half sink to the bed,
displaying its back, though it hides its face,
seductively Time rises out of the waves
        changing the tower clock's hands — only them.

7

The drowning town, where hard-baked reason
is transformed at once into moist vision,
        where the Northern sphinx's brother from the South
the wayward and literate lion
shutting its book with a bang, will not cry
        "Help!" — glad to choke in the lapping of mirrors.

8

The knock of gondola against rotting wood —
the sound rejects itself, words
        and hearing; and also that power
with arms outstretched like a forest of pines
before a small but greedy demon
        — where the spit freezes in your mouth.

9
Drawing our claws in, let us fold
the left arm over the breast and hold
    the right one firmly wedged in the crook
of the elbow: in a gesture resembling
the hammer and sickle — and bravely we'll let
    the age, in the shape of a nasty dream, look on.

    10
The raincoated body inhabits a place
where Hope, Faith, Love and Wisdom
    have no tomorrow, but there is always
today, however bitter to tongue
are the kisses of Goy and Jew, and the towns
    where footsteps leave no trace,

    11
like a boat that glides on the waterways
and covers a distance that equates
    to zero, if numbers are used,
leaves no deep tracks on the squares that seem
wide as "goodbye," or in the streets
    narrow as "I love you!"

    12
Spires, columns and carvings,
bridges and palaces; if
    you look up, you'll see the lion's smile
on a tower wrapped in wind,
indestructible, like grass beyond
    the fields, girdled not by a ditch but by time.

    13
Night in San Marco. The passerby
with a crumpled face might be compared
    in the dark to a ring removed from a finger,
biting his nails, bathed in peace,
he peers into a "nowhere" where
    thought, but not the eye, may linger.

Joseph Brodsky   325

14
And beyond this nowhere, beyond its borders
— black, colorless, or, maybe, white —
    there is some thing, some object.
Maybe a body. In the age of friction
light speed is the speed of sight, even
    when no light exists.

Daniel Weissbort

FROM *SONNETS ON THE STATUE OF MARY,
QUEEN OF SCOTS, IN THE LUXEMBOURG
GARDENS, PARIS*

I

Mary, the Scots are sots in any case:
What sept of the tartan clan had foreseen
That you would abandon the movie-screen
And as a statue give these gardens grace?
The Gardens of the Palais Luxembourg no less.
I wandered over from a restaurant
To gaze at the Park's new gates and pond
With an old ram's stare; and there of course
Was where we met. Because of that meeting and since
"What's past revives in a care-worn heart,"
I take a charge of the Classics' powder
And ram it up this worn-out breech
And waste what's left of my Russian speech
On your features and your pitted shoulders.

8

In my declining years, in a land beyond the ocean
Discovered, I believe, when you were still alive,
Dividing my crumpled iconostasis and devotion
Between the stove and well-worn divan,
I think that if we'd come together,
We'd have scarcely needed any words.

326 Joseph Brodsky

You'd have simply called me your Iván
And I'd have just replied: "Alas!"

We would have made of Scotland our matrass,
And I'd have shown you my Slavonic pride
And argosies slipping up to Glasgow on the tide
Would import sweetmeats, borsch and silk.
We'd be condemned together but execution might be stayed,
And the execution axe would have a wooden blade.

9

A part of the field. Trumpets sound and two men enter;
Alarums and the clash of battle. "Who be ye?"
"Tell me who ye be yerself." "Who, me?"
"I am Catholic." "And I, a true defender
Of the Reformation." "Aye? Take that, ye craven!"
And then remains are spattered everywhere.
The endless cawing of the ravens.
A winter scene ensues, with sleighs and frosty air.
Mary trying silken shawls. "Where is Damascus?"
"Where the peacock is more gorgeous than his hen."
"But even there, can't he be crowned? What then?"
(The scene: A game of draughts — respite from love's toils).
                              "Don't ask us."

Night in a Hollywood-Gothic castle. Then the field again
Where two men fight with vicious howls,
                              till both are slain.

17

That which ripped an amazed scream
From out the English mouth, which makes
My own mouth curse in its greed for lipstick,
Which forced King Philip to turn his face
A moment from his portrait
To fit out an Armada was — but I cannot complete
My ranting speech — anyhow, your wig
Falling from your falling head (Eternity
Is a fool), I hope this, the only bow you ever made,

Joseph Brodsky   327

Didn't rouse the watching crowds
To fisticuffs but was the kind
To bring your enemies to their feet.

18

Will a mouth that's muttered its goodbyes
To you and no one else still care
What tasteless muck it feeds upon
When it's left you far behind?
Maybe you're not one to sing in tune:
Don't be angry if this isn't true.
A tongue is like a rat, grubbing litter through
And always stumbling on things that it can use.

Forgive me, dumb and charming idol.
Yes, lips are still not fools at parting.
Although they often seem to leave a hole.
Eternity lies between us and an ocean too;
The censorship in Russia is a real gulf in fact,
And there they didn't need to use the axe.

20

With a simple, truly unrebellious pen
I've sung of an encounter in some distant garden
With that queen who, in nineteen forty-eight,
Taught me tender feelings from the movie-screen.
I submit to your judgment, for condemnation or pardon
Whether (i) he was a serious student, on reflection
Or (ii) for the Russian public it was something new,
Or (iii) it was his weakness for case-endings and for flexion.

The capital of Nepal is Kathmandu.

When it's inevitable, the accidental or the casual
Renders useful any work at all.

With the lifestyle that is my way,
I'm grateful to all those once-white sheets
Of paper I've crumpled up and thrown away.

Bernard Meares

MIKHAIL GROBMAN

IN MASS GRAVES THE BODIES OF PLANTS

In mass graves the bodies of plants
still retain their living death,
the odor of their many decays
clinging to the skin of the earth.

Above the edge of desert and sky,
beneath the hard savanna of anguish,
blades, leaves and petals
sigh like hollow memories.

Their mouldering breath burns —
imperceptibly, and warm is
the sacred sway of their souls,
the limpid glass of their thoughts.

Through the unslaked transparency of the nights,
their body longs for resurrection
and a return to flesh.

Thus again and again
these native shades visit, torment us,
and, overcoming the chain of forgettings,
they speak of a past world.

And in a sudden ecstasy of recognition,
of pain and of disaster,
in our own slow-motion consciousness
we see the footsteps of God.

John Glad

ANDREY AMALRIK   b. 1938

LAKE BASKUNCHAK

There is no road here — not even a path —
Just clear pools within the green salt water.

You cannot tear your eyes from it,
Not rip your fate from its emerald spell.

It is ice slashed with wrinkles —
Like the faces of Kazakh women.

It's a blue sky, white salt,
A myriad of Van Gogh's suns.

It's a burned shore, the contour of a mountain
From a different, distant time.

Like an overgrown puppy,
A cold sun sits tamely at your feet,

Baking your forehead,
Making sand from salt water.

And on a scratched sheet of tin
Patterns seem suddenly fixed in space

As if someone's sudden vengeance
Held them captive.

John Glad

NATALYA GORBANEVSKAYA b. 1936

SQUARE OF THE HOLY PASSION, . . .

Square of the Holy Passion, gaze on the demonstrators.
Oh, let not the bells of the monastery sound.
Amid the impassive crowd, the ground wind
covers even these futile traces.

And this other, in his cloak, his chains, tilting his curly head,
can he still be thinking of his "cruel age."

Daniel Weissbort

A CURSE! JOY! WRITING!

A curse! Joy! Writing!
Words move like mountains!
While I, like a butterfly,
flutter among the lines.

Only yesterday, skirting
unbelief and sadness,
did I not dumbly squirm
like a stranded fish.

331

And now each little stream
chatters like a goldfinch.
The river flows — its speech,
a warble at my cheek.

And in my weak, woman's throat
(Goldfinch! Cuckoo! Starling!)
The breeze of the universe
wanders among the lines.

Daniel Weissbort

THE SAVAGE COLD OF RUSSIAN WINTERS

The savage cold of Russian winters,
My devastated pedestal!
Twisted with the pain of the pose,
I am seeking warmth, a piece of southern stone.

Pygmalion has no love for Galatea.
Someone's easy laughter holds him in sway.
In impotent silence, I rage,
bleeding from the nose, breathing the frozen air.

Daniel Weissbort

HOLD OUT A HANDFUL OF SNOW . . .

Hold out a handful of snow,
I kiss your hand,
tell no one of these days,
I do not weep, do not sorrow.

Bullfinches on the snowdrifts,
how warm are your eyelashes,
give me a handful of snow,
tomtits in the aspens.

In the light autumnal snow,
pricked by short blades of grass —
I shall scald myself
with a handful of snow.

Daniel Weissbort

HURRY, TAKE PLEASURE IN THE OBLIQUE CARESS OF RAIN . . .

Hurry, take pleasure in the oblique caress of rain while the sun shines,
while the earth is unparched, the sky not yet dried up,
while the Neva and Onega run deep in their banks
and the damp powder has not yet fallen from the musket.

Daniel Weissbort

DROUGHT, MALEVOLENT STEPMOTHER . . .

Drought, malevolent step-mother
of the fading petal,
scent of the east in dandelion seeds,
flat waves of sand.

Before nightfall, read out what is writ
upon the tablet suspended from above . . .
Virtuous mother, three-handed one, defender,
wipe the dried blood from the temple.

Daniel Weissbort

Natalya Gorbanevskaya   333

THAT TIME I DID NOT SAVE WARSAW, . . .

That time I did not save Warsaw, nor Prague later,
not I, not I, and there's no atoning for this guilt.
Let my house be tightly shut and let it be cursed,
house of evil, of sin, of treachery and of crime.

And chained by an eternal, invisible chain to this terrible house,
I shall find pleasure in it and I shall find comfort where lives
in a dark, dirty corner, drunkenly, wretchedly,
my people, guiltless and godless.

Daniel Weissbort

IT IS TIME TO THINK

It is time to think
not of the pleasures of the flesh
and to scorn also the delights of the spirit.

It is time, grain by grain, to count through
your hoard of bitterness
and make an amulet of it . . .

Time, my friend, it is time . . .

Daniel Weissbort

YURY IOFE

A THING OR TWO ABOUT CHILDHOOD

To Nadezhda Shatunovskaya, My wife

The aroma of fresh bread
And haylofts
Mingles through childhood.
Right.
No!
My childhood smelled differently:
Of gasoline fumes
And asphalt vats,
Of acrid printer's ink,
Black and tacky
On a Soviet newspaper.

The gas light wavers:
Life's depths hidden
By a light ripple.
The Moscow River area, small shops,
Debris of the twentieth century,
The twenties.
In the sky,
Sirius and Vega gleamed blue.
Here on Earth —

           like a burn —

The red stars of the Kremlin.
Where is childhood?
It rustled past, evaporated —
    like the rain.
I'm almost fifty,
                I have a grown daughter.
But there's nowhere to go.
There's nowhere to hide
From the geography of childhood.
And I wander about Varvarka on Razin Street.
The sultry day is hot
            and ugly.

As in a delirium,
The cathedral's quarter decks
Sparkle through the fog.
Razin's street is served up
For idiot tourists:
Resprinkled with tinsel.
Le style russe.
It's all a lie, black and tacky
           like printer's ink.
It's all been betrayed.
There's nothing left.
May it be damned —
Childhood. And youth.
              And old age.

    John Glad

THE OLSANSKI CEMETERY

The Russian cemetery is too shabby for dawdlers;
In smoky Prague nightingales don't sing
In the old orthography
To Orthodox archpriests and yesterday's colonels.

The fates of a confused and anguished Empire
Have been crushed between the smoky glass of those years,
And in the émigré cathedral of the Assumption
A local deacon sobs for an unknown Moscow.

The wounded Empire died under the knife,
Its grave heaped with dusty thorns instead of live flowers.
There's nothing left but dead colonels
And broken markers in an alien town.

Stern colonels, where are they today?
Perhaps in the netherworld they're recalling the free Don
And at a Divine ball they kiss the fingers
Of rosy-cheeked ghosts, dead prima donnas . . .

The Russian deacon sobs softly, trustingly
In the cathedral's quiet. What can I do with this old man?
Outside the Sun laughs over Averchenko's grave
As if it were reading his Satyrikon.[1]

John Glad

1 Averchenko was a Russian writer who edited a humorous magazine before the revolution.
He emigrated and died in 1925 in Prague.

NAUM KORZHAVIN   b. 1925

WE CAN STRING WORDS . . .

We can string words on a line
Like beads on a string,
But no one will call us
To rebellion on Senate Square.

There'll be no crowns for us,
No real women will follow us
In carriages through the snow,
And our December will never come.[1]

John Glad

1 A reference to the Decembrist Uprising of 1825.

ALEKSANDR GALICH   b. 1918

HOSPITAL GYPSY SONG

It was booze made my boss talk of Stalin's days,
And he wouldn't stop grabbing the wheel,
So that later the ambulance men carted us
Where the notice says 'Accidents here.'
Took my pants and my old army coat away,
And they stuffed all my things in a sack,
Then along came Marusya the orderly
With a pill to put me on my back.

   I told them that I wasn't hurt,
   But if I was, and all that stuff,
   Then in this best of possible worlds
   I'm sick and tired, I've had enough,
   I've had enough, I've long been tired
   Of everything.

There was I on my cot like a mental case,
With the angel of death hovering nigh,
But my boss, he belongs to a better race,
Gets a ward to himself, nice as pie.
It's got curtains a nurse puts up specially,
He gets personal service, the swine,
He gets seen by a Jewish professor too,
And has parcels sent in from his wife.

With caviar and even wine.
And cheese, and all that sort of stuff,
But me, I get the hospital shit,
Though I don't care, I've had enough,
Though I resign, I've long been tired
Of everything.

From the jelly they give me at dinner time
I save some for the ward sister's kid,
Though I know that I'm in for a thin old time,
I'm not getting the same as his nibs!
And I've driven that sod of a boss of mine
In his limousine all over town,
You're fine fellers, the best bosses possible,
Pride and joy of this country of ours!

He might be a number one or two,
Etcetera, all that sort of stuff,
But I'm no worse than all his crew,
And I think rank's a load of guff,
'I'm higher than you' — it makes me spew
Like everything.

I put on my pijamas next morning time,
And I'm off for a smoke on the sly,
Who comes by? — It's Marusya the orderly,
'Hello, love! Where've you been all my life?
Be so kind as to tell me what's going on'
— It near knocked me down, her reply:
'I'm afraid your old boss is a goner, love,
Had a heart attack during the night.'

And things went on in all the wards,
And noise, and all that sort of stuff,
But I just stood there lost for words,
I felt as if I'd had enough,
All sudden I was sick and tired
Of everything.

Fair enough, never mind, Missus Orderly,
But I'll tell you that in the front line
That old coat of mine covered my boss and me,
And not only on just the odd night,
We've supped vodka together from used tin cans,
We've been roasted by enemy fire,
No my lads, you can bet that I've little chance
Of replacing the boss who's just died!

Me crying? No, it's just those drops,
And all the blessed sort of stuff,
I've had my lot, I've had my lot,
I've really had more than enough.
I've had my lot, I've had my lot
Of everything!

Gerry Smith

THE GOLDMINERS' WALTZ

We've called ourselves adults for ages now,
We don't try to pretend we're still young,
We've given up digging for treasure trove
Far away in the storybook sun.
We don't make for Equator or polar frost,
Or get the hell off out of sight!
It's silence, not treasure, that's gold for us,
And that's what we dig for, all right.

Hold your tongue, and you'll make a bomb,
Hold your tongue, hold your tongue, hold your tongue!

For years we hardened our minds and hearts,
It was wiser to keep your eyes low,
Many times, many ways we played silent parts,
But that silence meant yes, and not no!
The loudmouths and moaners who caused a fuss,
Not one of them's lived to grow old . . .

It's the say-nothings now who rule over us,
Because, you know, silence is gold.

Hold your tongue, you'll make number one!
Hold your tongue, hold your tongue, hold your tongue!

And now we've survived to see better things,
Everybody keeps talking a lot,
But behind the bright jewels of rhetoric
That old dumbness spreads out like a blot.
Someone else can lament about violence,
About hunger and insults untold!
We know there's more profit in silence,
Yes, *we* know that silence is gold!

It's so easy, making a bomb,
It's so easy to make number one,
Or to have someone shot for a song:
Hold your tongue, hold your tongue, hold your tongue!

   Gerry Smith

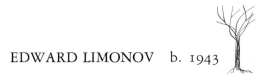

EDWARD LIMONOV b. 1943

AS IF A QUIET BRANCH DREW A LINE . . .

As if a quiet branch drew a line
so in memory the southern Alpine meadow
with a tree growing in it tenderly inclines
like the footsteps of a beloved person
on water

The little old house
built on the whim of fortune

Scattered sunlight
The lacy blouse hangs on one shoulder

The cheerfully inclined meadow
moves aside to show the lower view

of the polished peaks. mountain terrors
and severe clouds
make the hair stand on end

The effect intensifies with the growl of wild animals
and freedom-loving tigers

Leather-footed hunters humming roughly
set out after meat
The girl sits near the window filled with expectation
the soft parts of her body tremble

Far up ahead the frog-beast
sings his cool song
and here in a carriage the guest drives up

The guest is full of good feelings and infelicitous plans
he's lightwinged and his roughnecks accompany him
The guest stands out against the background of one of them
and turns out to be the forgotten relation
He and one fellow settle in the house
they walk to the small waterfall for water
Their leather armchairs rarely see them
rather, the bright flowers do, often
Sometimes the guest is mysteriously quiet
and then the girl invents her hopes
So in July both of them
put on a performance

Shaggy music, shaggy flowers
The deaf gardner — monument to times' past
In the heart all time is trouble. The occasional rain
intensifies everything. Her dresses are characterized
by unchecked fantasy. She tears them wiggling through
the bushes.

What could be more mysterious and beautiful
than July shifting into August

When you walk toward the old trees and
the liquid vineyard plasters your eyes shut
suffering you will remember
the grief of God. the divine shame

that's how it was. how it will be again. Who dares
say she didn't tear her dresses. It was
a pretty face that tore them often
laughed out loud laughed laughed . . . and left . . .

Mary Jane White

344   Edward Limonov

FROM *SECRET NOTEBOOK*

It is good in May, in marvelous wet May, to be the chairman of the All-Russian Extraordinary Committee in the city of Odessa, to stand in a leather jacket on a balcony overlooking the sea, to straighten your pince-nez and breathe in the stupefying smells.

And then to return to the depths of the room — coughing, to light a cigarette and start the interrogation of Princess N, who is deeply impli-cated in the counterrevolutionary plot and universally known for her great beauty, this twenty-two year old Princess.

*   *   *

. . . and it's the summer civil war
in the city as hot as a dream
and the leader of the uprising the half-Latin, half-Russian Victor, and Rita, a woman with straight hair, and the bluish-haired faggot Kendall — all came to my room and stood by the door, and Victor threatened me with his sub-machine gun because I had betrayed the cause of the world revolution for the sake of the thin, spiderish hands of the 15 years old daughter of president Alberti — Celestina, for the sake of her pink dresses and sea smiles, for the sake of her little, child-like peeper and her ever pinched earlobes, for the sake of hedgehogs in the garden of her papa, the hedgehogs and the snails on the fence . . . . All that has brought me to this morning, and my closest comrade and former lover Victor is speaking terrible words in a subdued voice; Kendall, in a thin coat, hysterical as usual, isn't looking at me. And, Rita's tense face . . . .

And little Celestina cried in her bed for hours, her naked child's breasts quivering, and her father — the honorable President has already gone into the capital with a tank unit, and the betrayed west suburbs have been shaken, and comrades have been shot in the courtyards.

*   *   *

Edward Limonov   345

The Japanese restaurant is good in autumn — in dank weather — the hot napkins, the warm sake. When a north-easterner is blowing. And it is especially good before an attempt on the Prime Minister's life, with the last of the money, in whistling November.

* * *

For whisper and orchestra

I kiss my Russian Revolution
On her sweaty, boyish light brown locks
Which spill out from under a sailor's hat
or a soldier's sheepskin headpiece.

I kiss her white, Russian hands covered with scratches
I cry and I say:
"My white, white one! My red, red one!
My gay and my beautiful, forgive me!

I've accepted the Georgian general's service cap for you,
All those, military and civilian
Who grew up on your grave,
All those fat and disgusting worms of the grave,
Those whom I am against. And who are against me and my verse!"

I weep for you in New York. In a city of damp Atlantic winds.
Where the infection grows endlessly. Where people are slaves in service of lords, who at the same time are slaves, too.

And at night. Me in my dirty hotel. Lonely Russian, dumb. I dream of you, I dream of you all the time. Of you. Who died young and innocent, beautiful, smiling, still alive. With scarlet lips — white neck — tender being. Scratched hands on the strap of a rifle, speaking Russian — my Revolution, my love.

* * *

346 Edward Limonov

Fantastic! The pygmies have taken the city of Muchacha! Four feet in height — the radio reports laconically. I was ecstatic. It is pleasant to know that the pygmies have taken the city of Muchacha. Did they think to rape all those big women? And to turn the town?

William Tjalsma

LEV MAK   b. 1939

BEHIND THE SLAUGHTERHOUSE, EVENING

1

We exhausted the earth and the sky. Where human desire
Is cramped, there is room for the birds;
Bonds of faith
Install the Creator at the web's center.
Each one catches himself in a shameful, importunate gesture.
On each rooftop
We contemplate Him contemplating,
Unable to stop Him, to force Him
To intervene and to save us from ruin, once again sending us,
If not his Son, then his Daughter; for surely
God must have a Daughter, a sister to the universally known
    brother? . . .

2

To live in the present is almost impossible. In the throat
Of the hour glass, between NOT YET and ALREADY, in the
    narrow neck
Of Pantagruel's Grael, in the capillary,
In the swelling blood clot, on the edge
Of the crystal of fire, in the kiss, the agony, the gesture
That invokes metamorphoses —

                        and, certainly,

More in poetry than in prose.

For the future, like an eye that has been put out,
Becomes the past for us, in a cry of pain.

3

Again the prophet of optimism is needed.

Now the question
Of UTILIZATION is resolved: a new type of rat
Has been bred, a devourer of plastic, of deodorants.
Games of love, no more smelling of fish,
Have made life more pleasant . . . The development
Of a range of electronic devices advances the coming of the age
Of handmade nature.

Once again the biblical parable
Of expulsion from paradise is timely. A messiah is needed,
Who will teach us to believe scientifically, a teacher
Of life technology in the concrete expanses of the world of the
     future.

The ancient guilt complex has been eliminated: man
Now has the option of blaming it all on machine.

4

The biologist studies filaments, the stomatologist — cavities.
What does the locust not devour?

To destroy a man
Is much easier than to cure a toothache. It is simpler
To stifle our souls than to know them.

The devil again
Makes a clock out of a mincing-machine, cuts
A new banner out of cloth impregnated with poison;
We kiss it, swearing an oath . . .

At midnight,
His study windows are ominously alight.

The pure breeze
Enters impure lungs and leaves them impure;
The souls
Of our children, forged by us out of the resonant,
Shining copper of good intentions,
Are recast as soldiers' buckles, rocket cases, radar antennae.

5

What can we say about love, if the meaning of life escapes
    us? . . .
Pattering quietly onto
The Kremlin parquet in kid booties,
The shoemaker's son knew what to cut
From the shagreen leather skin, broken on the rack of Russian
    freedom,
Henceforth and forever,
The death of mankind is within the General Secretary's
    capability —

                                            To call him
Impotent now is, unquestionably, hard.
                              For each second
Of life we're indebted to his equanimity;
                                    in concert, the press
Calls him PEACE-MAKER.
                          It may be
From the Creator of the World he differs only
In his love for meat patties.
                        Meat patties aren't easy to eat,
And the nations and countries are frozen in fear.
But, luckily, in the pouch of the holster,
Which like a deadly thermometer is tucked in his "tester's"
    armpit,
Apart from the weapon, is kept a packet of sodium
    bicarbonate . . .

    6

Freedom is the invisible ceremony
Of the abrogation of time, taking place
Simply, without formality, in complete silence,
And with an unconcealed contempt for space.

In the system of unities, the pain of freedom
Is isometric with love. The distance
Of one from the other is equal to the sum
Of chasms. Hell and Paradise are metaphors of freedom . . .

350   Lev Mak

But in our poor metaphysics
Space is a deity, while time, time
Is not money but the devil.

Die, die! cries the night bird.
But by day we are killed on someone's orders.

7

That's how the ordinary person feels,
Afraid of illness, shadowing, denunciations,
A microphone in his bedroom the bellowing voice
Of propaganda. Fearing oblivion,
Going gray in games of terror,
With collections of secret hiding places,
This is what we do and how we speak.
Irony is our pathos. Fallen into a trap
Set by the wise, man-eating giant,
We vanquish death, merging with the flock
Of his endlessly bleating sheep.
We bleat in a chorus.
                        Here bleating is the password,
Acknowledging submission, surrender
Of the privilege of freedom,
Commutation of the death sentence to the slow,
Lifelong torture of betrayal.

8

This sin lets fate loose, and the angel
Can no longer protect your head,
With his curved blade he severs the tough,
Invulnerable, celestial catgut,
By which the soul is tied to the sinciput.

Encountering the sun over the shoulder of the murderer,
Who does not hurry overmuch with the execution,
Glancing round quickly at the flowers, the wings
Of soaring birds, feeling the earth,
Baring the throat to any hope,
We see not Eden, not the Lord's

Primordial garden, lost through
A foolish calumny, but PRIMAL HORROR!

9

Are the peacocks, drinking from the vessel twined around
With a steeply rising, predatory vine,
Both equally immortal? Or is the one on the right,
The mirror image of the lefthand one,
More immortal than his companion? What is higher —
Bread broken by God, or wine
Poured by his hand into goblets? . . .

Answer, oh guardian angel, painted
In reddish ochre on crumbling plaster! . . .
Again the ideals of death move life,
And one must know how He lives Who
Stands invisible behind the mirrors
And reflects hatred in love.

10

Flying through time, oh unseen,
Preposterous observer, help me
To make ends meet, to slap cause in the face
With a handful of effects, to divide
The fruits in the gardens of Semiramis,
Inhabitant once of the Tower of Babel,
Among the captives and slaves, mixing the clay
For bricks throughout all her estates.

The quotient obtained we must
Multiply on the authority
Of Twentieth Century science —
                                        Angel of Death,
We will list the emotions, and sum them up.
You are pain, I am Joy, we will trace
The curve of fear's dependence on hope,
Love on falsehood, to get as a result
A trillion orgasms and a million death throes! . . .

11

What am I prattling on about? . . . — don't trouble,
Most loved, to drive me from the church:
Truly, I'm no agnostic. Blasphemy,
In our arrogant age, primed for disaster,
Has long ceased to be a sin; it is a sign of curiosity
(Cynical, true) about the permanence
Of the symbolism of life interpretations . . .

The heart is inverse to the cosmos, hope
Is like an hallucination . . . in the glimmer
Of a crumpled tinfoil chocolate wrapping,
You may easily see night on a southern beach,
The moon's pupil, and hear the hoarse murmur of the sea.

In hypnosis, there is a problem of analogy.
Metaphor de-bags myth.

12

The snake recalls a sausage.
The bill of rights, freedom.
The crematorium is like a stoke-hole,
    the stench in the outdoor privy
Promises rain and a change
In the prevailing winds.
                        The appearance
Of Arab chairs in Russian shops
Will set the world on its heels, à la chinoise.

13

History, a picture with a long perspective
Of wars, births, marriages,
Insignia and national claims,
Is a chorus of expanses and destinies,
Merging like voice and flute . . .
                        On the crowded stage
Caligula and Stalin meet
At the whim of the sinister prompter,
Attila conquers Troy,

Lev Mak   353

Plucks Helen like ambrosia, she
No longer wishes to be Jacqueline Onassis.
The minotaur leads blinded Theseus
Into the Lyubyanka yard for a little exercise . . .

The world, born blind, wails between the plump, red
Knees of war —
                when and with whom did she fornicate?
Who is your father, foundling? . . .
There is no answer.

Good and evil, two heavenly twins
Joined at the thigh, with knife and truncheon,
With bandages and Goulard water,
Lame in their common leg,
Hurry to the client, to beat and comfort him,
And, drying his tears, to leave him in bitter
Perplexed fear in the face of life.

    Daniel Weissbort

FAREWELL TO RUSSIA

The apartment is empty. My wife's slip hangs weightlessly, twisted over a
    chair.
The rag-doll sprawls, loosely embracing a potty. Sadly
The teddy bear sits on my trunk. Soon
I shall leave my house, never again to return.

THE CHILDREN HAVE GONE TO THE ZOO TO LOOK AT THE ZEBRA

It's bad being a zebra in Odessa. Slightly better
To be a Jew in Russia and, understanding your times,
To accept each day, each second, your chastisement —
Dissolving in the heat, to await the rattle and howl of the hunt,
Throat on fire, to drink the putrid liquid that trickles
From the rusty faucet in your place of refuge! Scorn, scorn! Scorn!

THE HUNTING DOG HATES THE QUARRY, THE HUNTSMAN MAKES MERRY,
AND ONLY THE BEATER IS AFRAID.

They're recruiting them now in the Jewish quarters. Worldly wisdom,
Fear, and Darwin, all studied in school,
Have made the choice easy for them. In the evening paper
There's a picture of a wolf, gnawing the hide
Of the ill-fated sheep he'd sprung from that morning . . .

SUITCASES LINE THE WALL. THE CHILDREN, MOTHER AND WIFE
REMAIN. PERHAPS FOR EVER.

What makes us good, what makes us evil?
Wise? Base? Blessed? Is it that force which molds
The clouds and the hills, which folds back the bristling red sabres
Of grasshoppers, to permit them to leap,
Which has given to man his omnivorous stomach and delicate soul,
And allowed him to live, filling the one and the other . . .

YOU GET USED TO ANGUISH, LIKE THE SMELL OF FISH THE NEIGHBORS
ARE FRYING.

No, I cannot, I do not want
To know what the chief thanatologist on the Kremlin's military staff will
grunt
As he smacks the map of the Mediterranean down on the dissection table,
Disembowelling Palestine, like Poland before, so the Jews might be
Salted and dead, like their pitiful dead sea,
To become the chosen of fate, the personal, intimate friend of Nemesis,
To confirm sentences, and by making them perfect myself be confirmed,
To know who will be separated from his beloved, and when,
What the bullets will twitter and chirp encountering each other,
Who will roll in the grass with a goalkeeper's cry on his lips,
Gripping an invisible ball in his palms,
Whose eyes will shut tight forever, who will cry . . .
To become the betrayer of brothers who languish, hermetically sealed, in
foul-smelling barracks,
Fated to feed on the leavings of camp-kitchen harpies.
To make rags out of pinebark, and live from letter to letter! . . .

Lev Mak   355

Farewell, Russia. Forgive me my tearful goodbye.
Do not weep over me — behind you, even now,
Lurks the spy with the barbed tartar noose —
Both eunuch, and husband, and impotent violator is he! . . .

Lousy Jew! — he cries through your lips.
In a whisper, I answer — Farewell, Mother!

Daniel Weissbort